HOME VISITING

To all home visitors, especially those with whom we have worked.

HOME VISITING

Procedures for Helping Families

Barbara Hanna Wasik
Donna M. Bryant◆Claudia M. Lyons

Foreword by
Richard N. Roberts

SAGE PUBLICATIONS
The International Professional Publishers
Newbury Park London New Delhi

For information address:

SAGE Publications, Inc.
2455 Teller Road
Newbury Park, California 91320

SAGE Publications Ltd.
6 Bonhill Street
London EC2A 4PU
United Kingdom

SAGE Publications India Pvt. Ltd.
M-32 Market
Greater Kailash I
New Delhi 110 048 India

Printed in the United States of America

Library of Congress Cataloging-in-Publication Data

Wasik, Barbara Hanna.
    Home visiting: procedures for helping families / by
  Barbara Hanna Wasik, Donna M. Bryant, Claudia M. Lyons.
        p. cm.
    Includes bibliographical references (p.).
    ISBN 0-8039-3541-2. — ISBN 0-8039-3452-0 (pbk.)
    1. Home-based family services—United States.   I. Bryant,
  Donna M., 1951-   .   II. Lyons, Claudia M.   III. Title.
HV697.W37   1990
362.82'83—dc20   89-28041
                                                                 CIP

92 93 94   15 14 13 12 11 10 9 8 7 6 5 4 3

Sage Production Editor: Diane S. Foster

Contents

	Foreword	7
	Preface	9
1.	A Historical Overview	13
2.	Philosophy of Home Visiting	45
3.	Illustrative Home Visiting Programs	69
4.	Personnel Issues Related to Home Visiting	91
5.	Helping Skills and Techniques	121
6.	Managing and Maintaining Home Visits	147
7.	Visiting Families in Stressful Situations	173
8.	Professional Issues Facing Home Visitors	201
9.	Assessment and Documentation in Home Visiting	219
10.	Future Directions in Home Visiting	249
	References	265
	Appendix: Home Visit Report Forms Used in the Infant Health and Development Program	283
	Author Index	289
	Subject Index	295
	About the Authors	303

Foreword

Home Visiting: Procedures for Helping Families represents one of the first modern attempts to present comprehensive information about procedures and issues related to home visiting with families. It defines models of best practice for the use of home visiting and raises a number of serious issues which home visitors, trainers, program directors, and policymakers will find important as they operate the thousands of home visiting programs that are in existence across the United States. Though home visiting has been used as a service delivery procedure for several centuries, until recently it has not been a particularly visible strategy for family support. With the expansion in social programs in the last three decades, however, the number of home visiting programs has also increased. This growth has underscored a need for standards of practice in training, supervision, and services to families. This book provides needed information in these areas and serves as a valuable resource for home visiting programs, which often work in isolation and without guideposts to mark the way.

This book is particularly timely because individual states are beginning to plan and implement programs for children and families under Public Law 99-457. National interest is focused on developing new models to support families with young children who have a handicapping condition, are medically fragile, or are at risk for developmental delay.

Home visiting is one component of a larger service network that must be developed to support families with special needs children and to provide a base for appropriate primary prevention efforts in this country. Surgeon General C. E. Koop's (1987) call for care for children with special needs, which is both community-based and family-centered, highlights the necessity for programs that place a strong value on family involvement and are solidly based in the community. Home visiting is a natural component of such an approach. Health, social service, and educational interventions can all be provided through home visiting.

Home visitors across the country are actively providing needed services to families through programs ranging from small community-based efforts to large state or county systems of care. This book is written for these front line workers and their supervisors. In this book, home visitors will have an opportunity to trace the historical development of services in the home over several centuries. Issues faced daily by every home visitor are discussed in sufficient detail to provide insights for both the new home visitor who is struggling with the development of her professional role and the more seasoned home visitor who may be interested in how other programs have solved difficult issues. Models are also presented to help programs organize important components of training and supervision, taking into account the diverse needs of home visiting programs.

Complex and formidable issues sometimes stand in the way of any comprehensive network of services. At the national level, the lack of a coordinated social policy regarding family support has often resulted in a patchwork of services. Nevertheless, there are encouraging signs that the nation is moving toward a more systematic effort to provide family services, and home visiting should be an important part of this effort.

Though home visiting is both an old institution and a new initiative, until now little has been written specifically for home visitors. This book, through its comprehensive presentation of relevant issues and procedures, provides a firmer foundation for the field to move forward.

Richard N. Roberts

Preface

We wrote this book for home visitors to provide them with a sense of the history and philosophy of home visiting and to give them specific information on many of the skills essential for home visiting. It is written for home visitors from many different backgrounds, including health, social service, psychology, and education as well as those without professional training. This book is also directly relevant for trainers and supervisors of home visitors, and for directors of home visiting programs to provide them with a guide for their supervision and administrative responsibilities. Local, state, and federal administrators responsible for establishing and funding such programs should also find it useful.

We saw a need for a book such as this from our collective experiences in the field of home visiting. Each of us has been involved in home visiting since the 1970s, as home visitors, as trainers of home visitors, as developers of home visiting programs, or as consultants. Much of our work in home visiting has been in two early intervention programs, Project CARE and the Infant Health and Development Program (IHDP). Project CARE, initiated in 1978, was designed as a longitudinal comparison of two early intervention programs for children at risk for school failure. The Infant Health and Development Program was a national collaborative study conducted between 1984 and 1988 that focused on low birthweight infants. In both programs we trained home visitors and their supervisors and developed the curriculum materials. In this work we discovered that very little information had been written specifically for the training of home visitors. Consequently, we planned this book to provide both beginning and experienced home visitors practical information on day-by-day home visiting procedures. It includes information on essential clinical skills, professional issues, managing visits, and guidelines for helping families under stressful circumstances.

During the preparation of the book, we had advice from many wonderful people, including the home visitor supervisors in the IHDP: Joanne Crooms, Rebecca Fewell, Mimi Graham, Marcia Hartley, Katy Lutzius, Sandy Malmquist, Beverly Mulvihill, Joan Rorex, and Randi Shapiro. They influenced our thinking about home visiting throughout the duration of the IHDP, and also through their feedback on this book.

Our knowledge about home visiting has also been increased by those home visitors with whom we have worked. They have often taught us as much as we presumed to teach them. Three home visitors gave us real-world feedback on sections of the book: Carrie Bynum, who worked in Project CARE both as a home visitor and as a supervisor, and Pamela Evans and Margie Vinton, both of whom worked in the IHDP.

During the writing of the book, we also benefited from interactions with two individuals from the United States General Accounting Office, Washington, DC. The General Accounting Office has been active in documenting the effectiveness of home visiting programs for the Congress of the United States. We especially want to thank Lois-ellin Datta for reviewing our writings on the history and philosophy of home visiting and David Bellis for generously sharing information on home visiting programs in the United States and Europe.

On our own University of North Carolina campus, a number of individuals provided information on home visiting, especially information on the history of home visiting in the fields of social work, nursing and medicine. We thank Jean Chapman of the School of Public Health, Margaret Miles of the School of Nursing, and Constance Renz of the School of Social Work.

Our major experiences with home visiting have taken place within the context of early intervention programs for at-risk children. In these efforts we have collaborated closely with three colleagues at the Frank Porter Graham Child Development Center of the University of North Carolina over an extended and productive period of time; namely, Craig Ramey, Joseph Sparling, and Isabelle Lewis. To each of them, we are deeply grateful for their supportive and intellectually challenging interactions.

We also owe a special debt to two other colleagues. One is Richard Roberts of Utah State University whose efforts in the field have helped shape our thinking and kept us sensitive to national issues. Another is Donald Meichenbaum of the University of Waterloo who served as a consultant to the Infant Health and Development Program and encouraged us to write this book.

Several people helped in the preparation of the manuscript, including Marie Butts, Karen Thigpen, Jane Trexler, and Kelly Maxwell. To each we say thanks, especially to Marie, who was often the glue that held it all together. We also appreciate the support of the Frank Porter Graham Child Development Center and the School of Education at the University of North Carolina. We extend our thanks to our publishers and to Terry Hendrix, in particular, who believed in the importance of this book and encouraged our efforts.

Each of us discovered in the process of writing this book just how time-consuming and demanding such a project can be and we especially appreciate the encouragement and patience of our friends and family. To each of you, we say thank you, especially John, Gregory, Mark, Jeffrey, Shannon, Rebecca, and Leah.

Barbara H. Wasik
Donna M. Bryant
Claudia M. Lyons

A Historical Overview

Friendly visitor, district visitor, homemaker, visiting teacher, visiting nurse, family social worker, home visitor, family physician—all have provided care and support to families through visits in the home. Professional and lay workers, paid and volunteer, they have brought to families child care information, emotional support, health care, knowledge of community resources, help in learning to cope with everyday problems and, at times, direct homemaker services. Though such services currently address a variety of family needs, traditionally most home visit programs were prompted by conditions of poverty, illness, or infant and child needs.

In this book, home visiting is defined as the process by which a professional or paraprofessional provides help to a family in its own home. Such help typically focuses on social, emotional, cognitive, or health needs and takes place over a sustained period of time. Though home visiting can be used to provide services for any individual in the home, ranging from infants to chronically ill adults, our book focuses on home visiting services for families with children, including services that begin prenatally.

Among professional groups in our society, nurses, social workers, and teachers are the major primary providers of home services, although other professionals (including physicians, psychologists, counselors, physical therapists, and speech therapists) also provide services in the home. Many paraprofessionals or lay workers throughout the country provide family support in the home. These individuals often share common experiences with the families they visit. Parents, for example, may be recruited to visit other parents, or people from particular ethnic or economic backgrounds may visit those from similar backgrounds. We will use the term *home visitor* when referring to any of these individuals who provide help in the home.

Home visiting may be initiated for a variety of reasons. It may be offered as a universal service to families in a designated group; for example, a local health center may provide home visiting by nurses to all first-time parents of newborns within its geographic area. Such services could include support and encouragement to the new parents as well as information on nutrition and infant care. Home visiting may be offered as a prevention or intervention procedure prompted by the special needs of children. As a prevention effort, home visiting services may be offered to families whose children are at risk for school failure. As an intervention effort, educational agencies may provide home visiting by teachers to parents of each developmentally delayed child within a school district. In both cases (intervention and prevention), home visitors could help parents learn ways to enhance their child's social and cognitive development. In other instances, families may request services, as might occur with a family caring for a physically handicapped or chronically ill person. The judicial system may also require home visits, for example, in child neglect or abuse cases or in disputes involving child custody.

Home visiting has been encouraged and promoted over time because it offers unique advantages for working with families. It often reduces barriers to available services, such as lack of transportation or child care, poor physical health, or low motivation. As a result, needed services reach many families who otherwise might not receive help. Home visiting can reduce the need for hospitalization by providing the support necessary for individuals to stay with their families. Home visiting is also influenced by the increased interest in self-care, the lower costs of home care compared to institutionalization, and the increased willingness of insurance providers to cover the costs of home care (Berg & Helgeson, 1984). Home visiting provides a unique opportunity to obtain relevant information about the family's environment, resources, and needs, and enhances a service provider's ability to individualize services.

Structural changes in the family, including a high divorce rate and large numbers of teenage parents and single-parent families, have created an increased number of women and children living in poverty (Zigler & Black, 1989). As a result, there has been an increased societal focus on poverty and its associated problems: high rates of infant mortality, and premature births, child abuse and neglect, drug abuse, and high school dropouts (Bronfenbrenner, 1987; Halpern, 1987; Moynihan, 1986). Social, educational, and health agencies provide many programs aimed at preventing these problems or reducing their incidence. Based on the advantages of home-based services, many agencies are emphasizing home visiting as an extremely valuable procedure for addressing these pervasive social concerns.

The practice of visiting families in the home is based upon several assumptions. The first is that parents are usually the most consistent and caring people in the lives of their young children, and the home is the most important setting for the child. For the majority of parents, interaction begins with their children in infancy and continues throughout childhood, adolescence, and beyond.

A second assumption is that parents can learn positive, effective ways of responding to their children if they are provided with support, knowledge, and skills. Some parents have less access to parenting role models and knowledge about children than do other parents. Helping such parents acquire knowledge and skills can have a very positive influence on their child's development.

A third assumption about home visiting is that for parents to respond effectively and positively to their children, their own needs must be met. Parents who are out of work, worried about housing or food, or experiencing emotional problems from events such as divorce or other family stress often find it difficult to care for others. Thus, even when the goal of home visiting is to help parents learn more effective ways of enhancing their child's development, attention must be focused on helping parents address problems in their own lives that make it difficult for them to be responsive to their children.

These assumptions about the practice of home visiting are validated by the preeminent role accorded the family by current political and social policy. For example, a 1987 executive order signed by President Reagan required that all federal policies be judged in terms of their influence on families, evaluating whether they strengthen the authority and rights of parents and the stability of the family (Datta & Wasik, 1988).

To put into perspective current home visiting practice and learn from and build on the work of the early leaders in this field, we will trace the history of home visiting from its early beginnings to the present in this chapter. This history has not been chronicled by many writers, and the accounts that do exist generally focus on the historical events within particular professions such as social work, education, or medicine. Levine and Levine (1970) presented a historical account of visiting teachers and social workers; Buhler-Wilkerson (1985) described the history of public health nursing; Holbrook (1983) described the social worker role in home visiting; and Datta and Wasik (1988) discussed historical and current social, economic, and political events that have influenced home visiting.

In this chapter we will present chronological historical developments across different professions and with diverse populations in order to provide the reader with an understanding of the rich heritage shared by those who visit in the home. Though other societies have provided services to families through home visiting, we have focused our review on events in Europe and the United States. A time-line depicting these major events is seen in Figure 1.1. From a review of these events, it will become clear that, over time, societies have debated the merits of where to best serve children and families in need, shifting back and forth between emphasizing institutional care and emphasizing home care.

History of Home Visiting

It is difficult to date the beginning of the home visit movement because caring for those in need has traditionally been a responsibility assumed by relatives, friends, and neighbors, with societal efforts developing gradually when informal support could not adequately provide for family needs. Since the middle of the nineteenth century, a number of circumstances have contributed to organized formal efforts to help those in need. In the late 1900s,

ENGLAND

1500	1800	1850	1900	1950	1970
Outdoor Relief	Almshouses	District Visiting / Visiting Nurses	Maternal and Child Care	Children's Act of 1948	Warnock Report (1978)

UNITED STATES

1500	1800	1850	1900	1950	1970
Outdoor Relief	Almshouses	Friendly Visitors	Visiting Teachers / Visiting Nurses / Visiting Social Workers / Public Health Nurses	Social Security Act of 1935 / Homemaker Services	Home Care for Handicapped Children / Initial Research Studies on Preschoolers / Federal Initiatives Home Start CFRP PL 99-457 / State Initiatives Local Initiatives Expanded Research Focus

Figure 1.1. Time Line for Major Events in England and the United States in the History of Home Visiting

17

an increasing number of poor people living in urban settings, especially those who were sick, could not afford institutional care, and needed support in the home. At the turn of the twentieth century, when immigration was combined with continuing urbanization, further increases occurred in the number of urban poor and a corresponding increase occurred in the social conditions associated with poverty (Levine & Levine, 1970).

Formal home care dates at least as far back as Elizabethan England when services were provided to paupers in their homes (Fink, Wilson, & Conover, 1963). These services were known as outdoor relief, because they were provided outside, rather than inside, institutions. This practice of providing care at home was adopted by colonial America as the dominant method of public care for poor children and their families, and was a shift away from institutional care. By the nineteenth century, however, another shift in philosophy occurred, and institutional care came to be considered superior to home care for poor children. Children were taken from their own homes and placed in almshouses when families could not provide for them, neglected them, or left them orphaned (Fink et al., 1963).

In England, widows were not provided support in their homes, but their children were sent to almshouses, where hundreds of children often resided. The state of New York built almshouses in every county to house and educate poor children. By the mid-nineteenth century, almshouses had been established in all major seaboard cities (Moroney, 1987). Such efforts were not without strong critics, who described the negative effects of these arrangements in breaking up families rather than keeping them together (Bremner, 1971). As a result, some states continued home care during the nineteenth century, and the state of New York began to shift its emphasis to home care.

While these shifts in philosophy were occurring, the foundation was being laid for the provision of home care by trained home visitors. Through her efforts on the part of the sick poor, Florence Nightingale was one of the most important pioneers in this field. Her first public comments on home visiting appeared in a letter to William Rothbone in November 1861 (Monteiro, 1985). Rothbone, a member of the District Provident Society in Liverpool, had employed a nurse to care for the sick in his geographic district. This procedure of district nursing was similar to district visiting, in which the district assigned each visitor to certain geographical boundaries (Richmond, 1917). When Rothbone tried to expand these services to other districts, he could not find trained nurses, so he turned to Nightingale for support. She recommended that nurses be specifically trained for his project and proposed a plan for the training and employment of women in hospital, district, and private nursing. Following her advice, Rothbone opened a training school in Liverpool the following year.

Nightingale's concern with the sick, especially the sick poor, continued throughout her life. She linked the importance of home care with nursing care. In 1867, she wrote, "never think that you have done anything effectual in nursing in London till you nurse, not only the sick poor in workhouses, but those at home" (Monteiro, 1985, p. 181). Though one of the major themes of her writings was the need for the adequate training of nurses, she also called for rural health missioners, or non-nurse health visitors, to provide hygiene instruction to mothers living in rural towns and villages (Nightingale, 1894). Her final reports on district nursing and home care overlapped with an era of major social and cultural changes in America: the 1890s to World War I. During this same period, many advances were being made in home visiting in the United States.

The Emergence of Home Visiting in America

At the turn of the century, demographic changes in the United States influenced the development of the visiting nurse, visiting teacher, public health nurse, and social worker. Many new child and family services were developed to address the conditions associated with urbanization and immigration, especially poverty, contagious diseases, unhealthy living conditions, high infant mortality, school dropouts, and delinquency. During this time period, the helping professions were all strongly influenced by the philosophical view that environmental conditions were major contributors to personal problems and illness. Consequently, intensive efforts were directed at changing poor social conditions, particularly those contributing to illness, accidents, infant mortality, and school problems.

The role of the visiting nurse continued to expand, and two additional roles for service were developed: visiting teachers and social workers. Both professions have strong roots in the settlement house movement in New York, Boston, Philadelphia, and Chicago. Settlement houses were established in communities with high levels of poverty. Their workers, typically well-educated upper-class women, served to improve social conditions and provide support for individual families (Addams, 1935).

The visiting teacher developed as a liaison between the school and the home, as workers in the settlement house saw the need to improve educational conditions for the child by working with the child's teacher. Being in the community, the visiting teacher came to know the family and child and could use her relationships with the schools to help the family and school work together. Classroom teachers also benefited from the input of the visiting teachers, for they often received information about the child's family that made it easier to understand the child's behavior and to provide attention for special needs. As a result of these positive home-school experiences, "a resident in each of the settlement houses took on the special assignment of calling on the families of children who presented special problems of an educational, social or medical nature" (Levine & Levine, 1970, p. 128).

Home visits by teachers began in New York City with a former school teacher as the first visiting teacher. In 1913, visiting teacher services within the city system were allocated funds by the New York City Board of Education. Visiting teachers began work in other urban cities in a similar manner. These visiting teachers, forerunners of the school social worker, worked on "deficit scholarship, truancy, incorrigibility, adverse home conditions and neglect" (Levine & Levine, 1970, p. 44). When the visiting teacher began her work, she used an ecological approach, becoming familiar with the neighborhood, the attitudes of the people toward education, the settings in which people worked and lived, recreational opportunities, school programs, and services of public and private agencies.

The sociocultural events that influenced the development of home services by teachers also strongly influenced the initiation of the field of social work. In addition, Richmond (1899) acknowledged in the preface to her classic book, *Friendly Visiting Among the Poor*, the influence of the Associated Charities that had organized Boston's friendly visitors 19 years earlier. Jane Addams's work at Hull House in Chicago was also a significant event in the development of social services (Addams, 1935). Though social work history and tradition have been intricately woven with home visiting, home visiting has been ignored by most social work historians (Holbrook, 1983).

In writing about the emergence of social work and its joint positions of treating individuals and reforming society's institutions, Holbrook (1983) noted that social work developed during the Progressive era as a reaction to the survival-of-the-fittest advocates and the social Darwinism philosophy of the late nineteenth century. Rather than promote those philosophies, social work tried to protect individuals from social and natural deprivations (Hollis & Wood, 1981). The child-saving movement was born during this time to "save the children" of the working and dependent classes from the social conditions of poverty, urban industrialization, and slum life.

Social workers served as a bridge between medicine and the home and between law and the home (Holbrook, 1983). They were described as concerned with "the positive measures of hygiene, such as the better housing of the patient, better nutrition, better provision for sunlight and fresh air, and above all, instructions to the patient as to the nature of his disease and the methods to be pursued in combating it" (Cabot, 1919, p. XV). Because of their familiarity with families and their homes, social workers often assisted the legal profession by obtaining case-work information that was important in legal decision-making.

Visiting nurses were also adding preventive care to their efforts. By 1910, most large urban visiting nurse associations "had initiated preventive programs for school children, infants, mothers, and patients with tuberculosis" (Buhler-Wilkerson, 1985, p. 1157). Voluntary and publicly funded agencies, however, regarded public health or prevention as their domains and objected to the visiting nurses' involvement in prevention. Buhler-Wilkerson reported that the nursing leadership was "outraged by such assertions. Visiting nurses, they insisted, had always been teachers of prevention and hygiene and had, in fact, 'blazed the trail' for all of the health departments' new preventive programs" (1985, p. 1159). Though debates over the roles of visiting nurses and public health nurses in treatment and prevention have continued to the present, in practice, both groups of nurses have been actively involved in home care throughout this century. Today's community health nurses provide services to the entire community (Leahy, Cobb, & Jones, 1982).

During the same time period in which child and family services underwent a rapid development in America, the progressive education movement also rapidly developed. Philosophers, educators, and psychologists, such as John Dewey (Dewey & Dewey, 1915), William James (1899), and Lightner Witmer (1897; 1915 cited in Levine & Levine, 1970), argued strongly for their views of education, its role in society, and the relationship of psychology to education. Within this atmosphere, Witmer developed the first psychological clinic in 1896 and focused on educational processes, community services, and prevention. He engaged teachers, parents, nurses, and housemothers in the therapeutic process with children, recognizing the importance of the adults in a child's natural environments in childrearing (Levine & Levine).

By the 1920s, the social reform movement, prevalent since the turn of the century, began to lose momentum. In the social work field, professional training became heavily influenced by psychiatric and psychoanalytic thinking, and Freudian psychology came to be accepted by social workers as the most useful basis for understanding personality (Hollis & Wood, 1981). This major shift paralleled developments in psychology in which the dominant mode of therapy from the 1920s to the 1950s was based on psychoanalytic theory that emphasized individual traits in personality in contrast to environmental or situational effects on personality. Social case work itself became formalized and social workers began to focus less on environmental or social conditions and more on the psychological problems of individuals, resulting in a decrease in services in the home.

However, even as the reform or preventive aspect of home visiting was changing in the United States, homemaker services were initiated by several casework agencies in Baltimore, Chicago, and Philadelphia in the 1920s (Fink, et al., 1963). Though these services were initially provided to families with young children, they were expanded over time to include care for the chronically ill, handicapped, and aging. These home visitors seemed more motivated by the practical concerns of making it possible for individuals to remain in their own homes rather than motivated by the social reform concerns of earlier workers.

Thus, over a relatively brief period of time, home visiting developed as a service delivery process within all three major areas of human services: health, education, and social services. Though there were early precursors to these services, home visiting did not become an organized, prevailing component of public agencies until the beginning of the twentieth century. In the following section, significant political events of the twentieth century that influenced home visiting are described.

Public Support for Home Visiting

The beginning of the twentieth century saw a major public commitment to assist dependent and needy children in their homes rather than in institutions. The First White House Conference on children was convened in 1909 by President Theodore Roosevelt. Noting that "home life is the finest and highest product of civilization," Roosevelt called for keeping children with their parents, "such aid being given as may be necessary to maintain suitable homes for the rearing of children" (Bremner, 1971, pp. 375-376).

The adoption of widows' pension laws in 1911 was one of three major advances in services for children to come from this conference. These laws were based on a belief that it was appropriate to use public money to help mothers care for their children in their own homes (Fink, et al., 1963). The White House Conference also led to the establishment of the U.S. Children's Bureau and the organization of the Child Welfare League of America. These efforts all sanctioned the use of public funds for the daily support of families in their homes, thus encouraging and supporting the practice of home visiting.

Home visiting was also influenced by the Great Depression and its aftermath, when many communities did not have the financial resources to meet their needs or were not conceptually prepared to address the complexities of the problems in their own communities (Roberts & Heinrich, 1985). As a result, federal relief was initiated, with a major effort developed under the Civil Works Administration, in which over 10,000 nurses were employed to work in local health agencies, with home visiting an important part of their work.

The nation's involvement in World War II also significantly influenced home nursing. Because medical and nursing staffs in hospitals were greatly depleted, many patients who would normally have been cared for in hospitals were treated at home.

> Families, already stressed, were expected to care for critically ill members, help with home births, or care for mothers and infants discharged early from the hospital. These family caretakers needed much instruction, support, and assistance with direct nursing care and looked to the public health nurse for this help. The American Red Cross organized courses in home nursing and training programs for nurse's aides. By the end of 1942, over 500,000 women had completed the American Red Cross home nursing course, and nearly 17,000 nurse's aides had been certified. (Roberts & Heinrich, 1985, p. 1165)

Much of the work of nurse's aides was accomplished in homes. Federal financial assistance for the care of children in their own homes was strengthened by the passage of the Social Security Act of 1935. This act not only provided for social insurance and public assistance, but it also signified the beginning of a serious effort to provide maternal and child health services, services for crippled children, and child welfare services. The wording of the Social Security Act has changed over time, typically increasing its appropriateness for children. The Public Welfare Amendment of 1962 specifically described, as a child welfare service, the option of strengthening children's own families when possible, an option that home visiting is particularly well suited to help accomplish.

Home Visiting in Europe in the Twentieth Century

Both historically and currently, European models of home visiting have influenced practice in the United States. In particular, the widespread acceptance of home visiting for prenatal and postnatal care throughout Europe is being viewed seriously in this country as a model for practice (Miller, 1987). For this reason, it is helpful to review events in Europe throughout this century prior to reviewing more recent efforts in the United States.

Possibly the most comprehensive home visiting program of any country was initiated in Denmark in 1937. This family and child care system has been an exemplary model of successful service delivery. For these reasons, its home visiting services will be described in more detail than those of other European countries. Denmark's highly developed system dates back to the end of the last century when worldwide concern was expressed about the practice of placing children of unwed mothers and abandoned or orphaned children with private families, where the children were often mistreated (Wagner & Wagner, 1976). A strong impetus for Denmark's program was a 6-year pilot study conducted in four geographic areas prior to 1937 that demonstrated substantial effects of home visiting on the reduction of infant mortality and morbidity during the first year of life.

The Danish response to the concerns of children's placement and the results of the pilot study was to set up a nationwide network of local lay citizens to serve as advocates for children in individual communities. These local citizen groups came to be called the Child and Youth Committees (CYC), and the CYC became a standing committee of every district or township, including elected officials and lay volunteers. The roles of the CYC have been protection, promotion, and prevention.

The CYCs have been staffed by social workers, family helpers, or both. The use of family helpers as ancillary workers became necessary because of an insufficient number of social workers to provide the necessary services. In some localities, the social worker supervised the work of 10 to 20 family helpers. Depending upon the family's needs, a family helper was assigned to visit the family on a daily, weekly, or monthly basis. Priority was placed upon trying to resolve problems within the context of the family. Problems that were addressed ranged from parental depression to teenage pregnancy (Wagner & Wagner, 1976).

In 1980, 259 of the 277 townships in Denmark had a visiting nurse program, thus assuring that 88% of all Danish infants were being seen regularly by a registered nurse specializing in infant health (Dawson, 1980). In some areas, high-risk infants are followed until they enter school. Fewer than 2% of Danish families refuse this service, and midwives and physicians are legally required to report all births to a home visitor (Dawson, 1980; Wagner & Wagner, 1976). The Danish family helper has no exact equivalent in the United States (Wagner & Wagner, 1976), but the increasing concerns about maternal and child health are leading the United States in the direction of home visiting for young mothers (Weiss, 1989).

Norway also has an organized home helper program. Because of a shortage of domestic help and hospital beds prior to the 1940s, women's organizations in Norway began to address the questions of how to bring help into the homes of women, who, through illness, childbirth, or other emergency, could not carry out household responsibilities (Langholm, 1971). A full expansion of these efforts occurred in 1947 when the Norwegian Parliament voted the first state allowance for home helpers. A State Home Help Council was appointed in 1949, and the activities of home helpers were officially described by the Ministry of Social Affairs. In 1956, the Ministry of Family and Consumer Affairs was assigned responsibility for coordinating the work of home helpers and home nurses. Specific training for home helpers and home nurses was required unless the helpers were authorized trained nurses or met other specific requirements.

The now-classic work by John Bowlby on the importance of the relationship between maternal care and child health, published by the World Health Organization, significantly influenced the nature of family services (Bowlby, 1952). In England, in particular, Bowlby's work served as a strong stimulus for the country to promote services that would prevent the breakup of the family. Prior to the 1950s, children in situations of crisis, abandonment, incapacity, or illness were placed in the care of others—foster homes or institutions. Skilled help was not available to assist the child's natural family in dealing with the situation. In England, the Children's Act of 1948 called for an emphasis on the natural strength of the family. As a result, casework was no longer focused primarily on removing children from families living in conditions of poverty or overcrowding. Rather, social policies were developed to address these environmental conditions, and the caseworker focused on interpersonal needs rather than social conditions (Heywood, 1959).

In England in 1978, the Warnock Report on children with special education needs strongly advocated a specific person to be identified as a point-of-contact for each parent. Strong support for home visiting of families having a severely disabled child also came from the Resource Worker Project in London, a two-year project designed to evaluate the effectiveness of resource workers. Within this project, very specific roles were played by workers who provided support and services to families with a severely disabled child. A basic component of the project was a commitment to maintain regular contact with families in their homes so as to assist them with problems concerning their disabled child. In addition to providing family support, regular contacts with the family made it possible for the resource workers to monitor the child's development and changes in the families' circumstances on an ongoing basis without having to depend upon the parent to write or telephone for services (Glendinning, 1986).

The breadth of involvement with the family was judged one of the most successful features of the Resource Worker Project. Glendinning (1986) noted that "the resource workers' involvement encompassed a very broad range of medical, social, educational, practical, financial, recreational, and emotional issues" (pp. 201-202). Even though the workers thought of themselves as social workers and were seen by the families as such, they became "involved in the whole spectrum of problems experienced by families looking after a disabled child" (p. 202). The breadth of help that was provided was seen as a central element in the role of the resource worker.

The most current and comprehensive review of home visiting in Europe is a report by Miller (1987) focusing on pre- and postnatal care. He reviewed programs of 10 European countries: Belgium, Denmark, France, the Federal Republic of Germany, Ireland, the Netherlands, Norway, Spain, Switzerland, and the United Kingdom. For almost all of these countries, home visiting is a routine part of maternity care.

Within the United Kingdom, a wide range of services is available related to childbearing and home care (Miller, 1987). In England and Wales, prenatal home visiting services are generally initiated as a check on those who do not attend prenatal clinics. In Scotland, by contrast, a community midwife attends and counsels every pregnant woman at home. Until the thirty-second week of a woman's pregnancy, a community midwife makes monthly visits to women who plan to deliver their infants at home; thereafter until the birth, she visits weekly until delivery. Miller reports a relatively structured postpartum program in all parts of the United Kingdom. The midwife makes a home visit each day for a minimum of 10 days after delivery. Once the midwife's responsibilities end, a health visitor continues the home visits.

In Switzerland, prenatal home visits are made only for medically defined risks or if requested by the pregnant woman for an acceptable reason. After delivery, home visits are routinely made to all families with a new baby by a nurse with training in maternity and infant care. At least one visit is made within the first 14 days after discharge from the hospital, and another is made four months later.

In Belgium, home visiting is a featured part of maternity care, with a nurse visiting the home twice in the prenatal period. At least one home visit occurs during the first two months postpartum, with earlier and more frequent visits for high-risk families. In Denmark, every pregnant woman is visited at least once, usually by a midwife or a home visiting nurse. Within the first week of returning home, the mother and child are visited. In Ireland, home visiting is available free to the entire population, with special emphasis on perinatal care, child health, and elderly care. As evidence of the acceptance of home visiting, the client usage of these services increased 50% from 1975 to 1983 (Miller, 1987).

The Netherlands has an impressive system of postpartum care. Whether delivery is in the home or a hospital, the lying-in period is 10 days. During this time, mothers and their infants are visited routinely by a caretaker for up to eight hours a day for the first 10 days postpartum, with an average of 64 hours of visits for each family. The home visitor helps care for the infant and mother, advises on infant care, and assists with housekeeping.

Home visits in Europe are not only provided by nurses, social workers, and family helpers, but also by teachers. In describing current home visiting by teachers with preschool and school-age children in England, Hannon and Jackson (1987) noted that the idea of home visiting could be traced back to preschool intervention work in the United States that began in the 1960s. In particular, the results of the early intervention programs, especially Gray and Klaus's (1970) Early Training Program and the Ypsilanti Perry Preschool Project (Weikart, Bond, & McNeil, 1978), as well as the writing of Bronfenbrenner (1974), were instrumental in prompting home visiting as an educational intervention. As a result, educational home visiting was initiated in England in a number of settings with preschool children (e.g., Hirst & Hannon, 1989; Raven, 1980; Smith, 1975), and later for handicapped children (Cameron, 1984; Pugh, 1981). Jackson and Hannon (1987) have noted the emphasis in England upon home visiting with families who have preschool or nursery school children, but they also recommend home visiting for families of older children, particularly as a way to increase the involvement of parents in teaching reading to children aged 5-8.

In summary, home visiting in Europe is a widely accepted practice for helping families. It has been viewed as a responsibility of government to help promote family life. Home visits are provided during times of universal need, as in the birth of a child, or for families experiencing stresses beyond their ability to cope. Home visits by physicians are also a common practice in Europe. The European practices for maternal and child care are often described as a model for practice in the United States, while the research on early educational interventions in the United States have influenced the development of similar efforts in England.

Home Visiting in the United States
from the 1950s to the Present

At mid-century, an increase in the need for home care occurred in the United States as the home became recognized as a desirable setting for the care of handicapped children. Until the mid-1950s, parents of a handicapped child were generally advised to place the child in a state or private institution (Bristol & Gallagher, 1982). Not until after this time did professionals begin to view positively the role of parents in the rearing of handicapped children and to provide support to the parents to allow them to do so. Also, the deinstitutionalization movement of the 1960s led to an increase in attention to community and home-based care for other populations.

Several factors influenced the shift in focus away from institutional care and toward home care and support of the family. One factor influencing the perceptions of professionals toward parents was the recognition of a bidirectionality of cause-and-effect relationships between parent and child (Bell, 1971, 1974). By showing that children's behavior can be a determinant of parent behavior, it became acceptable to incorporate parents as active partners in intervention procedures, rather than blame them for their child's maladaptive behavior. This positive view of parents helped to bring about an increase in home care for children because society no longer strongly believed that the child had to be removed from negative parental influences.

The study of the programs' cost-effectiveness also became prevalent in the 1960s, influencing home-based interventions. Federal and state agencies began to reevaluate the potential benefits of home and local community programs versus large institutional programs, in part because of the lower cost of home programs. As an example of this interest in deinstitutionalization, a number of efforts were developed during the 1970s that were aimed at keeping delinquent youths in their own community, typically in a group home. In many of these group homes, located near the youths' families, the treatment program was modeled on family life; a major objective was to help the youths learn behaviors necessary to live with their own families (Phillips, Wolf, Fixsen, & Bailey, 1970).

Home visiting as a service procedure was also influenced by the concern in the United States in the 1960s with the debilitating effects of poverty on the cognitive performance of children (Hess, 1970) and the increased awareness of the potential for intellectual improvement in children (Hunt, 1961). These events contributed to both the federal initiative to establish Head Start in order to provide early intervention for these children (O'Keefe, 1978; Zigler & Freedman, 1987b) as well as to a series of early intervention research studies (e.g., Lazar, Darlington, Murray, Royce, & Snipper, 1982) designed to determine the effects of early intervention on children's cognitive and social growth. Studies that included home visiting as part of their service delivery procedures included Schaefer and Aaronson's verbal stimulation project (1972), Gordon and Guinagh's (1978) Florida Parent Education Program, Gray and Ruttle's family-focused home visiting program (Gray & Ruttle, 1980), Weikart's and his colleagues' work in the Perry Preschool Program (Schweinhart & Weikart, 1980), and Gutelius and her colleagues in the Mobile Unit for Child Health project (Gutelius, Kirsch, MacDonald, Brooks, McErlean, & Newcomb, 1972; Gutelius, Kirsch, MacDonald, Brooks, & McErlean, 1977).

One of the first studies designed to evaluate the effects of home intervention on the intellectual development of very young children from a poverty background was conducted by Schaefer and Aaronson (1977). Home tutors focused on verbal stimulation with children between the ages of 15 and 36 months one hour a day, five days a week. The data suggested a brief, positive change in cognitive scores for children in the intervention program, but no long-term benefits.

Gordon and Guinagh (1978) studied the effects of home visiting programs of 1, 2, or 3 years' duration for children from low-income families. During the preschool years, children in the intervention and control groups did not differ on measures of cognitive development. In looking at the later school performance of these children, however, they found that children in the home visiting intervention groups performed better than children in the control groups. Children in the one-, two-, or three-year intervention groups did not differ significantly from one another.

Gray and Ruttle (1980) conducted a family-focused home intervention program for children from low-income families. Though the intervention program was individualized for each family, language, teaching style, competence, and behavior management were emphasized with all families. The results showed that during preschool, children in the intervention program scored higher on cognitive development measures than did control children.

The Mother-Child Home Program was developed by P. Levenstein to reduce the risk of school failure for children from low-income families and to increase the mothers' parenting skills and self-esteem (Levenstein, 1970, 1977, 1988). Home visitors took toys into the home and demonstrated their use, emphasizing language and interaction. Research on this program has been inconsistent in demonstrating positive outcomes on child intellectual development.

The Mobile Unit for Child Health focused on both medical and cognitive needs through prenatal counseling for teenage, unmarried, low-income mothers, as well as infant stimulation for their children. Children received well baby care during the first three years of life. Significant cognitive gains were seen at ages 2 and 3 for children in the intervention groups (Gutelius, Kirsch, MacDonald, Brooks, & McErlean, 1977).

The results of these early intervention research programs were influential in supporting the potential of early childhood intervention programs. Though the results of these early studies of home visiting on child outcome variables did not unequivocally support the effects of home visiting, there was sufficient support to justify continued interest in its potential for influencing child and family variables.

In the 1970s, increased concerns about maternal and child health sparked additional interest in home visiting. One of the first people to speak out for young mothers and their infants was a pediatrician, Henry Kempe, who was motivated by the failure of society to take responsibility for providing the services during infancy necessary to prevent child abuse and "failure to thrive" infants (1976). Kempe noted that though there had been calls for early screening of infants for specific diseases, the emotional growth and development of the child was often neglected. He called for giving "adequate attention to the whole child, his family, their total health status, including those emotional as well as physical factors that might affect the child's welfare" (p. 946). Kempe strongly recommended the universal provision of home health visitors for families of newborns, stressing that every child is entitled to effective comprehensive health care. When parents do not or cannot provide for it, society must.

Deinstitutionalization of services for the severely disabled child has increased the responsibilities of families and communities. Two major alternatives exist for community services: One is the clinic-based service in which the child is the identified client, while the other is the home-based service in which the parents are more frequently the identified client (Muller & Leviton, 1986). It is essential that family and community agencies engage in collaborative efforts to support families. An example of this collaboration is the Kennedy Institute for Handicapped Children in Baltimore, Maryland, where home visiting is provided for highly disorganized families or families experiencing a time-limited crisis, such as divorce or death. In such situations, the home visitor helps the parent identify priorities and promotes a problem-solving approach to achieving goals. Once parent needs are addressed, there is an increased likelihood that the child's needs can be served in the clinic (Mueller & Leviton, 1986).

Physicians have played an important role in the history of home visiting, not only by providing direct care themselves but also by facilitating the acceptance of services delivered to families in their homes. Yet, over the past three decades, there has been a dramatic decrease in the number of house calls made by physicians. From 1960 to 1975, a 75% drop occurred in physician home visits in the United States (Cauthen, 1981). This decrease had been influenced by advancing technology that required a physician to have access to specific equipment and resources in order to deliver the best medical care, and by a belief that home visits by physicians were not cost effective. At the present time, there is renewed attention to the importance of house calls by physicians, and schools of medicine are incorporating home visits as part of medical training (Cauthen, 1981; Wells, Benson, Hoff, & Stuber, 1987).

Federal, State, and Local Initiatives

In addition to the original Head Start center-based program designed to provide an educational preschool experience, Head Start has sponsored a number of efforts to help children from low-income families. Possibly the largest home visiting program in the United States is sponsored by the Head Start program, initiated as a demonstration program in 1972 for three and a half years to evaluate the feasibility of providing comprehensive Head Start services through a home visitor (Love, Nauta, Coelen, Hewett, & Ruopp, 1976). In the Head Start home-based program, home visitors help parents provide an enriched environment for their children by focusing on health, education, and social services. Presently, communities may select the Head Start home visiting program as an alternative to center-based programs, or they may supplement their center-based programs with visits to families.

Another major effort within Head Start, initiated in 1973, is the Child and Family Resource Program (CFRP), which has been designed to provide family support and services to promote the healthy growth and development of the child. This program serves families from the prenatal stage through the child's third grade in school. Of particular importance has been the CFRP philosophy that when families are facing major issues, such as alcoholism, drug abuse, unemployment, severe illness, or basic needs for shelter or food, they cannot respond in an optimal manner to facilitate the development of their children and, consequently, service providers must respond to such family needs (Zigler & Freedman, 1987b).

Currently, very strong interest in the provision of family services through home visiting exists at the federal level, as evidenced by the promotion of legislation to assure home visiting for medically fragile children, to assure maternal care, and to assure services for handicapped children. A recent major development of the United States Department of Health and Human Services is the Comprehensive Child Development Program initiative, which is focused on low-income families with young children. This program is designed to evaluate a comprehensive approach to community-based services for families, including such strategies as home visiting. Programs will initiate services when a family has a newborn or during the prenatal period, and will continue until the child reaches school age. Another example of increasing interest in home visiting is seen in the 1989 report of the National Commission to Prevent Infant Mortality. This report emphasized home visiting as a strategy for reducing infant mortality and morbidity by making preventive, prenatal, and pediatric care available for children and pregnant women.

In 1986, the Congress of the United States passed Public Law (PL) 99-457, amendments to the Education of the Handicapped Act, the most far-reaching family legislation of the decade. Part B of this legislation built on Public Law 94-142 by mandating increased services to all children ages 3 to 5, with handicapping conditions. Part H established a state grant program that focused on the needs of handicapped infants and toddlers, from birth to age two, and their families. States are required to develop policies to put the major components of Part H into effect by 1991.

One of the most important components of PL 99-457 is the Individualized Family Service Plan (IFSP), which requires coordinated and individualized services within the context of the family for any child with special needs. This requirement is significant in its focus on the needs of families rather than just the needs of the child. Congress also mandated the formation of the Federal Interagency Coordinating Council (FICC) to coordinate services. Agencies currently included under the FICC are the Administration for Children, Youth, and Families; Administration on Developmental Disabilities; Bureau of Maternal and Child Health and Resources Development; Office of Human Development Services; and Office of Special Education and Rehabilitative Services. Following the passage of PL 99-457, the surgeon general of the United States reiterated the commitment to family-centered, community-based coordinated care (Koop, 1987), reflecting the increasing interests in the United States in providing services to the family. Because of its advantages for family-focused intervention and its compatibility with serving the needs of families with young children, home visiting is being received as an important process for providing these needed family services.

States also began to develop home visiting programs in the 1970s, and private foundations have funded special programs. In Hawaii, the Kamehameha Schools provided home visiting services for native Hawaiian families, initiated with the mother and extended family members during the prenatal period and continuing until the children are three years old (Roberts, 1988). This program is particularly notable for its curriculum, which was developed to be culturally sensitive to native Hawaiian families. The Kansas Healthy Start Program and the Colorado Parent-Infant Project were both developed to provide for maternal and child health through home visits. These latter two programs were influenced by Kempe's proposal (1976) calling for health visitors for all children (Chapman, Siegal, & Cross, in press). Missouri has developed the Parents as Teachers program designed for any parent who has a child from birth to age 3 (Missouri Department of Elementary and Secondary Education, 1986). Minnesota has included home visiting as part of a program for children, from birth to age six, that emphasizes the parent as the child's major teacher (Hausman & Weiss, 1987; Weiss, 1989).

In the early 1980s, the Ford Foundation funded a number of home visiting programs to serve the needs of low-income families (Halpren & Larner, 1988). These programs, called "Child Survival/Fair Start Programs," served a variety of cultural and ethnic groups across the country to improve pregnancy outcomes, infant health, and family conditions that are associated with child development. The populations who were served included migrant Mexican American farm workers, young black mothers in the South,

Appalachian families, and Haitian immigrants (Halpern & Larner, 1988; Larner & Halpern, 1987).

The field of home visiting is currently being influenced by what has been called the family support movement (Kagan, Powell, Weissbourd, & Zigler, 1987). Two categories of family support programs have been distinguished; first are grass-roots efforts developing within communities, and second are university-based programs (Zigler & Black, 1989). These programs are viewed as having in common four principles: "1) a focus on prevention and a recognition of the importance of the early years; 2) an ecological approach to service; 3) a developmental view of parents; and 4) the universal value of support" (Weissbourd & Kagan, 1989, p. 21). These principles are also in evidence in the Comprehensive Child Development Program initiative at the federal level described earlier. These principles suggest a trend toward agreement on some of the major parameters of early intervention and family services. In the section that follows, one can see one or more of these principles influencing program goals and procedures in recent research efforts.

Expanded Research Focus

A number of significant research efforts have been developed over the past two decades. These research studies have focused on a variety of child characteristics and program objectives and have employed a variety of services within the framework of home visiting. Many embody the principles presented above for family support programs. Several of these efforts have focused on child cognitive development, while others have focused on maternal and child health issues or on a combination of child and family variables. A number of studies have addressed the advantage of home visiting for low birthweight infants on a range of child and family measures.

Positive effects on child cognitive development through a family-focused home visiting program have recently been obtained in a study of children in Jamaica from low-income families (Powell & Grantham-McGregor, 1989). This effort provided a comparison of different levels of intensity in the frequency of home visiting; the results showed that weekly home visiting might be necessary to bring about significant changes in child cognitive development.

By contrast, in a replication of the Levenstein (1970, 1977) Mother-Child Home Program with children in Bermuda, no significant effects were found for child cognitive development (Scarr & McCartney, 1988).

The authors of this book, with colleagues Craig Ramey and Joseph Sparling, developed and conducted Project CARE (Carolina Approach to Responsive Education), a research program designed to evaluate the effects of a developmental day-care program and family home visiting program for low-income children. From ages 1 to 5, children whose families received family education in the home and who participated in an educational day-care program scored significantly higher on cognitive measures than children whose families received only family education through home visiting or children in the control group. For child cognitive development to be influenced solely through a family-focused home visiting program, the services would likely have to be more intensive than those provided in Project CARE (Ramey, Bryant, Sparling, & Wasik, 1985; Wasik, Ramey, Bryant, & Sparling, 1989).

A program designed for adolescent parents to help them meet the needs of their young children, as well as their own, is the Parent-to-Parent program developed at the High Scope Foundation in Michigan. It includes long-term home visiting by local volunteers and parent group meetings to address the stresses of adolescent parenting (Halpern & Covey, 1983).

In studying the effects of home visiting on several maternal and child variables, Olds and his colleagues have conducted a program in which nurses visit the homes of pregnant women and mothers of infants. They found that mothers who were either teenagers, unmarried, or of low socioeconomic status and received prenatal home visits by nurses had infants who weighed more at birth. They also found that mothers in the program who smoked had a reduction in preterm deliveries (Olds, Henderson, Tatelbaum, & Chamberlin, 1986). Mothers who received continuing visits showed a reduction in child abuse and neglect (Olds, Henderson, Chamberlin & Tatelbaum, 1985).

A number of home visiting intervention programs have been conducted with low birthweight infants. Field and her colleagues reported significant cognitive gains at 4 and 8 months for preterm infants in a home visiting program compared to children whose families were not in the program (Field, Widmayer, Stringer, &

Ignatoff, 1980). In a second study that compared a home visit plus parent training program and a nursery plus parent training program, children in both treatment programs obtained higher scores on measures of mental and motor development than control children who received no intervention (Field, Widmayer, Greenberg, & Stoller, 1982). In another study, low birthweight infants who participated in an intervention program in which home visits were made for two years performed significantly better on mental and physical development measures than did control children (Resnick, Eyler, Nelson, Eitzman, & Buccizrelli, 1987).

An important issue concerning home visiting services has been the timing of the initiation of services. Larson compared two different intervention efforts for low birthweight infants (1980). She found that home visiting was effective in changing the home environment and maternal attitudes only for the group that received intervention prenatally, followed by postnatal visits. No benefits were found on these variables for those who received visits six weeks postpartum or who were in a control group. In-hospital visits with the mothers of low birthweight infants combined with at-home visits for three months resulted in positive maternal and child outcomes (Rauh, Achenbach, Nurcombe, Howell, & Teti, 1988). Mothers in the intervention group made a better initial adjustment to their low birthweight infant, and at 3 and 4 years of age, children who received the intervention scored significantly higher on mental development measures. These results support the importance of involving the parents prenatally or at the time of birth.

The Infant Health and Development Program (IHDP), a recent national collaborative study conducted between 1984 and 1988 and modeled on Project CARE described above, included a major home visiting component. The program goals were to study the effects of home intervention and day care on the cognitive, social, and physical development of low birthweight infants from birth to age three (Ramey, Bryant, Wasik, Sparling, Fendt, & LaVange, 1989). Eight sites in geographically diverse communities in the United States served as the settings for the program. Families were visited in the homes once a week during the child's first year of life. During the next two years, the child attended a developmental day-care program, while home visits continued to be provided. Cognitive, social, and behavioral measures were obtained on all children (IHDP, 1989). Though the effects of home visiting cannot be separated from other program components, the results, to be published in the *Journal of the American Medical Association* (1990), should provide valuable information on the effects of adding a day-care component to an ongoing home visiting program for children at risk for developmental delay.

Summaries of the research on home visiting programs have been prepared by Gray and Wandersman, (1980); Halpern (1984); and Ramey, Bryant, and Suarez (1985). Though these reviewers all support the general conclusions that services offered through home visiting can be effective in bringing about positive gains in families and children, home visiting is a multidimensional process that varies from one program to another in scope, intensity, and populations served. Though some conclusions can be drawn from the existing empirical studies, these conclusions are limited in scope and emphasize the need for further research.

Surveys of Home Visiting

Several surveys of home visiting have been completed during the past decade, both in England and the United States. Poulton (1983) reports on a 1981 survey of over 50 home visiting programs in England that looked at program objectives. In another survey of almost 1,700 primary schools in England, home visiting was reported to be a part of one-fifth of them, with the majority of these visits occurring in nursery schools (Cyster, Clift, & Battle, 1980). In the United States, a nationwide survey was conducted in 1987 and 1988 to obtain information on home visiting for families with children (Roberts & Wasik, 1989; Wasik & Roberts, 1989a, 1989b). The survey focused on home-based family services that were being offered during the prenatal period and to families who had children from infancy to age 18.

The procedures that were necessary to obtain program names and addresses for the survey provide insight into the organizational status of home visiting programs. In the United States, there is no national association on home visiting and no central source of information on home visiting programs. Consequently, it was necessary to establish a list of home visiting programs before the survey could be conducted. This list was developed by writing to the health, education, and social services agencies of all the states,

Table 1.1: Distribution of Family-Focused Home Visiting Programs in the United States: Administrative Agency and Funding Source

Type of Agency	Private %	Funding Source Public %	Total %
Education	8	19	27
Social Service	15	9	24
Health	6	27	33
Head Start	NA	16	16
	29%	71%	100%

SOURCE: Roberts, R. N., & Wasik, B. H., 1989. National home visitor survey: Agency affiliation, family characteristics, purposes, and services provided. Manuscript submitted for publication.

and by contacting other public and private groups at the national, state, and local level for names and addresses of existing programs. A survey was mailed to each of the 4,162 programs identified through these procedures. The survey addressed program goals, populations served, funding sources, and priority services, as well as information on hiring, training, and supervising home visitors. Detailed survey information available from 1,904 programs made it possible to present a relatively comprehensive description of home visiting in this country as currently provided to families with a child from birth to age 18.

In Table 1.1, data from the survey show the distribution of home visiting agency by the type of service (education, social service, health, and Head Start) and by the funding source (private or public). From this table, it is evident that public monies are funding the majority of current family-focused home visiting programs, although it is significant that almost one in three of the home visiting programs is supported by private funds. Education and health home visiting programs are more frequently funded through public sources, while social service home visiting programs are more often funded from private sources.

Of particular interest are the survey results concerning the priority ratings given to different services by the program respondents. Administrators of home visiting programs were asked to identify 19 services as either of primary importance, moderate

A Historical Overview   41

TABLE 1.2: Priority Ratings Assigned by Programs to Each Service

	Primary Importance %	Moderate Importance %	Minor Importance %	Service Not Provided %
Coordination/Management				
Information Delivery	63	29	5	1
Diagnostic Screening	58	20	7	13
Child Advocacy	56	29	7	5
Family Advocacy	48	35	9	6
Coordination of Community Services	47	41	8	2
Case Management	45	32	12	7
Coordination of Medical Services	42	37	14	5
Direct Assistance to Parents				
Transportation	10	23	30	35
Respite Care	5	12	14	64
Homemaker	4	9	15	67
Psychological Support/Counseling				
Enhancement of Parent Coping	72	20	3	2
Emotional Support	64	31	3	1
Family Counseling	28	31	3	1
Stress Management	25	40	20	12
Job Training Counseling	4	11	18	63
Parenting				
Enhancement of Parenting Skills	80	14	3	2
Enhancement of Child Development	77	15	4	5
Physical Care				
Health Care	40	22	8	25
Nutrition	26	31	18	22

SOURCE: Roberts, R. N., & Wasik, B. H., 1989. National home visitor survey: Agency affiliation, family characteristics, purposes, and services provided. Manuscript submitted for publication.

importance, minor importance, or as not provided by their program. Table 1.2 groups these 19 services into five categories: coordination/management; direct assistance to parents; psychological support/counseling; parenting; and physical care. Because these responses were summed across all agencies and populations, they make a strong statement of the philosophy of home visiting as it is currently practiced. The three services that received the highest ratings all address parenting roles, and suggest a perceived universal need regardless of the special child or parent characteristics that may have initiated the service. Because of the understanding most directors have of family needs, these program-identified priorities should be seriously considered in future funding efforts, for they clearly point to the need for broad family support, especially parental support services.

Conferences

As we near the end of this century, we see home visiting re-emerging as a means of supporting families in need of help. A result of this interest has been the organization of two major conferences focused on home visiting. The first, held in 1980, was sponsored by the American Academy of Pediatrics to explore the use of home visitors in improving the delivery of preventive services to mothers with young children (Chamberlin, 1980). The second conference was held in 1988 and was sponsored by the U.S. Department of Health and Human Services, Bureau of Maternal and Child Health. This conference brought together policymakers, practitioners, parents, and researchers to make recommendations for family support in the home (Roberts, 1988a). The first conference noted advantages of serving families through home visiting; by the second conference, the practice was not only more prevalent, but there were a number of important social and political events, as well as empirical findings, that provided a stronger rationale for home visiting.

Summary

In this chapter, we have considered both the development of home visiting over time, as well as the cultural and social events that have influenced the practice of home visiting. From the historical beginnings of home visiting to its current role in society, it is clear that many countries and disciplines have discovered and rediscovered the value of home visiting. It has persisted as a family service for at least two centuries and in many countries, serving both special populations and the general population. Current legislation, combined with current sociocultural concerns and changes, and an increasing set of empirical findings supporting the effects of home visiting, will result in increasing demands for home visitors throughout the next decade. The magnitude of these political and social events makes it particularly timely to consider home visiting in-depth, including the philosophies that have influenced it, the credentials of home visitors, and issues in the practice of home visiting. This information should help assure that our future efforts are rooted in past and current knowledge and practice.

2

Philosophy of Home Visiting

Home visiting programs are based upon one of two fundamental beliefs, namely that delivering services in the home can ameliorate existing difficulties or can prevent problems from developing later. Such services have been prompted by moral, social, and political forces over time. Many churches and other religious and charitable groups have provided direct relief in the form of clothing, food, and housing, especially in times of crisis or emergency. Governments have also provided direct assistance, generally to the most needy.

In writing specifically about home-based early intervention programs, Halpern (1986) noted that these programs embody a number of paradoxes. "Although they have been undertaken for many years, they continue to appear as a fresh solution to meeting pressing social needs" (p. 387). Furthermore, he noted that though home-based early intervention programs lack "an agreed-upon theoretical basis and clear empirical justification," they continue to be recommended as a means of preventing or ameliorating developmental problems (p. 387).

Given Halpern's judgments of the diverse theory and empirical support for home visiting, one has to ask why the practice has persisted. We believe home visiting has persisted because, across time, people have considered the well-being of the family to be important both for family members and for society, and they have been willing to offer support to families in their own homes in times of need.

One of the strongest recommendations for home visiting was proposed by Henry Kempe (1976) in addressing children's rights to protection and health care.

> It should be emphasized that the use of health visitors should be a universal phenomenon. This is not a kind of detection service used to identify child abuse. It is not a service for the poor or the minorities but rather an expected, tax-supported right of every family, along with fire protection, police protection, and clean water—societal services that we all deserve to have and from which no one can be easily excluded. (p. 944)

Other writers, in describing the purposes of home visiting, have focused on the importance of being able to reach clients who are incapacitated, homebound, or unwilling to come to a clinic or other setting for services. Home visits are considered especially useful for clients experiencing a crisis and in acute need of services (Norris-Shortle & Cohen, 1987). Delivering home-based services can allow children to remain in their family setting while needed support is provided to their parents.

Yet, these humanitarian efforts are not without debate. Many aspects of home visiting, such as the rights of government to be involved in family life, the type of service provided, the credentials of the service provider, and the recipient of the services, have been subject to conflicting opinions. Before addressing some of these major components involved in a philosophy of home visiting, we found it instructive to review a much earlier set of guidelines and principles. In 1899, Mary Richmond identified six "relief" principles in her book, *Friendly Visiting Among the Poor*. We were impressed by the appropriateness of these principles over 90 years later, an appropriateness that most likely stems from the commonality of human needs across the decades and the commonality of concerns among those in the helping professions as they contemplate appropriate, effective, and responsive services.

Richmond's principles reveal an impressive set of professional guidelines. Her first principle called attention to the importance of home services, described how services should be delivered in the home, and stated that the "head of the family should be

TABLE 2.1: Richmond's 1899 Principles of Relief

The first relief principle is that relief should be given individually and privately in the home and that the head of the family should be conferred with on all questions of relief.

The second relief principle is that we should seek the most natural and least official sources of relief, bearing in mind the ties of kinship, friendship, and neighborliness, and that we should avoid the multiplication of sources.

The third relief principle is that relief should look not only to the alleviation of present suffering, but to promoting the future welfare of the recipient.

The fourth relief principle is that, instead of trying to give a little to very many, we should help adequately those that we help at all.

The fifth relief principle is that we should help the poor to understand the right relations of things by stating clearly our reasons for giving or withholding relief, and by requiring their hearty cooperation in all efforts for their improvement.

The sixth relief principle is that we must find that form of relief that best fits the particular need.

---

conferred with on all questions of relief" (p. 149). This statement is a forerunner of today's emphasis on engaging families in collaborative efforts to identify their own needs, priorities, and preferences for services.

Richmond's second principle emphasizes the importance of finding the least official source of relief, a principle not unlike the current principles underlying PL 99-457 that states that services should be provided in as normal a fashion and environment as possible (Johnson, McGonigel, & Kaufmann, 1989). Her third principle identified the need to look beyond present suffering to address future needs of families, a principle currently promoted by many professionals (e.g., Dunst & Trivette, 1987) and exemplified in programs that promote enhancing the family's ability to cope effectively with its own problems.

Her fourth principle related to public policy and how resources should be allocated. She called for "helping adequately" those who are helped, rather than providing too little for too many. This issue is one that state and federal agencies continue to address as they consider proposals for universal home visiting versus more intensive services for those most likely to encounter problems or already experiencing hardships.

Richmond's fifth point seems to place decision-making with the service provider, a role that seems authoritarian by today's standards. On the other hand, this point also addressed the need for clear communication and called for active client participation "in all efforts for their improvement" (p. 160). On the latter point, Richmond predated similar current suggestions for the "maximum feasible participation" guideline of Head Start and the emphasis on parent or client involvement in identifying needs and services.

Finally, Richmond recommended that we find the form of relief that will best fit the family's particular need. This guideline is also consistent with today's emphasis upon providing individualized services to families. In summary, Richmond's principles not only embody the enduring qualities in a helper-client relationship, but they still provide direction for today's visitors. With this historical perspective in mind, we will now consider contemporary views on home visiting.

Current Philosophical Views

Three terms are frequently used today to describe the rationale for home visiting: empowerment, enablement, and enhancement. *Empowerment* can be defined as facilitating or maintaining the client's or family's ability to define its own goals and make its own decisions. *Enhancement* incorporates the concept of building upon strengths that already exist, and *enablement* suggests helping families locate resources that can facilitate the family's own actions.

The word "empower" has gained increased acceptance as a term that characterizes the heart and spirit of family-centered services (Johnson et al., 1989). Empowerment has also been viewed as consistent with the activities and goals of preventive psychology—optimal development, reduction of environmental hazards, avoidance of maladaptation, and enhancement of coping skills and abilities (Felner, Jason, Moritsugu, & Farber, 1983).

In looking at services in oppressed communities, especially black communities, Solomon (1976) has described empowerment as a process in which those who belong to "a stigmatized social category throughout their lives can be assisted to develop and increase skills in the exercise of interpersonal influence and the performance of valued social roles" (p. 6). Solomon also sees empowerment as referring to the development of an effective support system for those individuals in oppressed communities.

Dunst and Trivette (1987) have described three characteristics common to definitions of empowerment, all of which describe the client's behavior: "(a) access and control over needed resources, (b) decision-making and problem solving abilities, and (c) acquisition of instrumental behavior needed to interact effectively with others in order to procure resources" (p. 445). Enablement has also been described by Dunst and Trivette as characteristic of the helping process, defining it as the helper creating "opportunities for competencies to be acquired or displayed" (p. 450). The focus is on the helper's role in promoting prosocial self-sustaining adaptive behaviors, not on treatment or even on prevention. Dunst and Trivette describe the client as an active participant who is assumed to be able to deal effectively with his or her own problems. In many ways, the terms empowerment, enablement and enhancement are interchangeable. They all attempt to capture the role of the helper as one who assists clients to become better able to address goals and problems in their lives.

Writers have defined empowerment in ways that capture the philosophy of home-based family support and help give focus to its goals, yet there are some difficulties associated with this term. Empowerment in common usage means "to give power or authority to" or "to authorize." Though Johnson, et al. (1989) have stated that when describing family services, empowerment does not mean "giving or bestowing power on families - the power is theirs by right" (p. 5), we believe some caution is advisable in the use of this term because of its possible negative connotation.

It may be preferable to describe the rationale for home visiting as that of a "helping relationship" between the visitor and the family, a description that captures both the purpose and process of home visiting. Though more than one definition can be given for helping, we have used the one proposed by Carkhuff and Anthony (1979): "the act of promoting constructive behavioral changes in an individual, which enhance the affective dimension of the individual's life and permit a greater degree of personal control over subsequent activities" (p. 3).

We have noted the concern with the idea of "conveying" power, but a more fundamental concern relates to the use of power in the relationship between a helper and a client. In our contemporary society, there is increasing agreement on the importance of promoting a more collaborative, consultative relationship between helper and client, and on helping the client become more self-sufficient. Yet, in a helping relationship, there is an implicit statement of need on one person's part and an offer of help from a second person. This situation is in itself an imbalance of power. Pinker (1973) has discussed this power imbalance, noting that in the social services, there is always an unequal relationship between the giver and the receiver. We believe that it is not the imbalance that is the problem, but how one works within this relationship. The helper can use this imbalance to foster dependence or independence, passivity or action. Service providers can reduce the potentially negative effects of this imbalance of power through sensitive and thoughtful interactions with clients. They can also work continually toward promoting independence in all aspects of interpersonal coping and problem solving.

Ecological Theory of Human Development

In addition to the philosophical orientation implied by the terms empowerment, enhancement, and enablement, as well as by a helping relationship, other theoretical positions have helped provide a framework for the practice of home visiting. The ecological theory of human development as proposed by Bronfenbrenner (1979) has been especially influential. This theory focuses on family, friends, and community as important environmental influences on an individual's life. Bronfenbrenner stresses the importance of taking such variables into account when planning intervention programs. His theory has served as an organizing framework for many programs that have incorporated environmental variables into their service program and has provided guidance for numerous others.

The ecological concept is perhaps best illustrated from the standpoint of the social support that those in the environment can provide to individual family members or to the family as a whole (Moroney, 1987). When social support is lacking or inadequate, there is a higher likelihood of emotional distress, depression, and physical illness. For example, women with low levels of social support are much more likely to develop complications during pregnancy than women with high levels of support (Nuckolls, Cassel, & Kaplan, 1972). Families who report four or more close friendships seem to cope better with rearing their handicapped child than families who report few close friends (Rees, 1983), and women with a network of friends are more likely to complete a behavioral training program than socially isolated women (Wahler, 1980).

We consider the ecological approach as part of a cognitive-behavioral-ecological theory of working with families. The behavioral aspect focuses on those behaviors important for an individual's or a family's overall well-being. In Bronfenbrenner's recent writings, he calls attention to the need to focus on an individual's behavior as much as on his or her environment in order to have a more accurate understanding of a person's total situation (Bronfenbrenner, 1989).

The cognitive component of this cognitive-behavioral-ecological theory addresses how a person thinks about problems, though it has not been addressed as frequently in the family support literature as the behavioral and environmental components. Yet, such cognitive processes as problem solving, setting priorities, and decision-making by clients are often identified as among the program's top priorities, and each of these processes has a strong cognitive component. Any program that focuses on problem resolution needs to give consideration to all three aspects: cognitive, behavioral, and ecological. An understanding of how these components relate to and influence one another can facilitate the development of effective programs (Wasik, 1983).

Family Systems Theory

A second theory that many home visiting programs frequently identify as influencing their goals and procedures is family systems theory. The major tenets of family systems theory are derived from a scientific systems theory applied to physical systems and extended to biological and social systems (e.g., Ramey, Bryant, Sparling, & Wasik, 1984). The application of these systems concepts to the family has been based in part on the writings of Bateson (1972, 1979), Jackson (1957), and Salvador Minuchin (1974).

Patricia Minuchin (1985) has described the basic principles of systems theory as it is used in family therapy. Two of these principles are particularly relevant to home visiting. The first is that "any system is an organized whole, and elements within the system are necessarily interdependent" (p. 289). She notes that this is the core principle of a systems orientation; it challenges older paradigms of science, questioning any paradigm that does not consider the setting or context of its data. A systems orientation would require one to include all aspects of the universe in any comprehensive theory. Since this is neither practical nor necessary to understand most of life's events, it is important to identify socially significant subsystems. Family systems theorists have identified the family as an extremely important subsystem for understanding and changing individual behavior.

The second principle P. Minuchin identified is also relevant for home visiting: "Patterns in a system are circular rather than linear" (p. 290). This principle calls into question earlier views that identified the relationship between parent and child as a unidirectional pattern in which the parent, typically the mother, influenced the child's behavior. A recognition of circularity not only makes it possible to consider the child's influence on the parent, but it also emphasizes the need to consider the interrelationships of all family members.

The concepts and theories discussed above have all influenced the current practice of home visiting. They have served to focus attention on the needs and priorities of families; they have emphasized the importance of the interrelations within families and between families and their environments; and they have stressed the importance of looking at future as well as immediate needs.

Philosophy and Practice

The theoretical constructs described earlier have combined with social and political positions to influence practice in numerous ways. In order to consider the effect of these beliefs and events on practice, we will look at three questions that must be answered by any home visiting program and any agency that funds such programs:

TABLE 2.2: Philosophical Positions on Family Support

Who is the Client?

Child	Family
Individual	Family System
Encapsulated	Ecological
Handicapped	Universal

How is the Client Served?

Restrictive	Broad
Predetermined	Negotiated
Standard	Individualized
Exceptional	Normalized
Deficit	Strength
Treatment	Prevention

What is the Role of the Helper?

Expert	Collaborator
Problem-Solver	Facilitator
Decision-Maker	Negotiator

Who is the client?

How is the client served?

What is the role of the helper?

In Table 2.2, we have identified points of discussion and debate under each of these three questions. For the most part, we have seen a shift over time from those philosophical positions listed on the left side of Table 2.2 to those on the right side. Some of these shifts may be more evident in the writings of our times than in actual practice, but many of these philosophical positions have also been incorporated into public policy as part of PL 99-457 that addresses the needs of families with handicapped children.

Who is the Client?

A fundamental issue in clinical work is the question, "Who is the client?" Answers to this question are essential to service providers because decisions about client identity influence intervention plans, funding sources, the qualifications of the service provider, and measures used to evaluate the programs. Several shifts in conceptualizing and identifying the client that have occurred during the past decade include a shift from the child to the family and from an individual family member to the family as a system. Shifts have also occurred from an encapsulated view of the family to an ecological or environmental view, and from thinking of handicapped or at-risk individuals as the only type of client to considering most individuals as needing help in times of stress.

Historically, the question of "Who is the client?" has had a more straightforward answer. The client was the adult or child in need of help, an individual typically described as having some type of handicapping condition or being at risk for some problem. As noted in Chapter 1, the child was typically removed from the family under stressful home conditions or when the child needed treatment. When the focus shifted in the 1960s to home care for exceptional children, the child was still primarily the focus of attention.

Zigler and Freedman (1987b) believe that the seeds for this shift to a family focus originated in the policies of Head Start that called for the family's "maximum feasible participation" in the services that were offered. Practical concerns also influenced this shift, for when home-based services were provided for a handicapped child, the visitor could work with the parent of the child as often, or even more often, than she worked with the child. This shift from the child to the family reaffirms the family's preeminent role and responsibility in childrearing, as well as the child's dependence on the family for survival.

Though we have described a shift to a family focus, it is important to recall that at the beginning of this century the practice of visiting nurses, teachers, and social workers all emphasized the importance of considering the needs of all family members; in nursing, in particular, elements of a family focus can be seen across the century (Whall, 1986).

As one begins to visit with families, it becomes clear that complex interactions exist among family members, and some of these relationships may be associated with difficulties. The relationship between mother and child, for example, needs attention when the mother fails to establish a caring relationship with the child. Complex and disruptive interactions can occur between siblings and a handicapped child. At times, the entire family may have needs. Viewed in this way, one can see that when serving the family, the question of "Who is the client?" becomes complex, introducing the possibility of multiple clients within the family and of a change of clients within the family over time. Thus, in addition to focusing on the handicapped child, one can focus on other family members, on dyadic interactions between any two family members, or the entire family as a system (Bailey, 1988).

When placing this concept of multiple clients within the framework of family systems theory, in which changes in one family member potentially influence changes in another family member, one can see the development of possible dilemmas. An intervention designed to help one family member could have a negative influence on another member (Margolin, 1982). Helping a woman seek a job could cause marital problems if her spouse doesn't want her to work.

Consistent with the shift in recognizing the child as a member of the larger family has been the parallel shift toward viewing the family as part of a larger network of extended family, neighborhood, and community (Bronfenbrenner, 1979). This view is supported not only from a systems theory position, but also by the empirical data referred to earlier that documented the strong effects the immediate social supports in a person's life can have on his or her mental and physical health. This acceptance of an ecological theory approach is captured by Weissbourd (1983), who noted:

> We are no longer "child savers." We realize that concern for the child's well-being means focusing not just on the child and his development, but also on the child in the context of his family, the community in which he lives, and the social institutions and government policies which affect family life. (p. 8)

This shift to considering the larger environment of the family also has a direct implication for home visitors and the programs for which they work. Both the program administrators and visitors have responsibility for interacting with other community agencies because, at times, the causes of problems reside within the community, and an advocacy role needs to be assumed. In some professions, such as social work, there is a long history of client advocacy and of working with community agencies.

As seen in Table 2.2, another major characteristic is whether the concept of client is limited to a child or adult with handicapping conditions or if the concept of client can refer to the general population. Services to clients can be classified under three headings: (1) programs serving families with existing difficulties or established risk, (2) programs serving families and children with specific characteristics that place them at risk for later problems, and (3) programs serving all families during times that are judged to be universally stressful. Though programs addressing these three objectives can be dated back to the early beginnings of home visiting and can be seen in current national and international efforts as noted in Chapter 1, most often the focus has been on those with existing difficulties or at-risk groups. There is, however, increasing interest in programs designed to serve all families during common times of stress, with prenatal care and the birth of a first child receiving the most attention as a home visiting service for the general population.

In summary, the answer to the question, "Who is the client?" has broadened over the past decade, emphasizing the importance of family needs as well as those of individual children. This broader focus, however, does not make decisions necessarily easier when faced with prioritizing services or addressing conflicting needs within a family. Rather, it forces the home visitor to consider the needs of the family as a whole and those of individual family members, as well as those of a child whose characteristics may have led to the initiation of services. Based on such considerations, the home visitor makes a judgment of what seems best at that time, given problem objectives, family needs, and resources. Whenever possible, such judgments should be in collaboration with the family. Decisions on the provision of services often cause ethical dilemmas for home visitors, and these are discussed in more detail in Chapter 8.

How is the Client Served?

Traditionally, home visiting services have consisted of treatment or intervention for specific problems and have often been restricted to the predefined needs of children or adults. Presently, there is interest in providing a more broad-based approach that makes it possible to respond to critical needs of all family members and a negotiated service that involves families in identifying their needs, priorities, and preferences for service procedures. There is also more emphasis in individualized services rather than standardized ones. These three shifts all have in common a recognition of the preeminent role each family should have in the determination of services.

Though there is a trend toward offering more comprehensive services for families, the family's right to negotiate services as well as the need to individualize services implies that not all families will want or need a broad-based approach. In some situations, particularly characteristic of private home visiting services, a specific contract will be written between the visitor and the family, specifying the services that will be provided. Consequently, service providers need to remain aware that when we speak of broader services, some families may want help only with a specific problem, such as the care of a chronically ill child. Broader services are not better services if they do not meet the families' needs.

There is also increasing interest in providing earlier intervention for problems that could be prevented, rather than intervening in these situations after the problems have developed. This interest in prevention is reflected in the increased attention to programs beginning for children in infancy rather than at ages 3, 4, or later, and in the interest in providing support to all families during the prenatal, early infancy period.

Another direction in services is building on family strengths rather than responding only to deficits. Programs for the handicapped or exceptional populations are also placing emphasis upon the most natural way of helping families, from promoting support networks to helping families learn how to include handicapped members in the family's ongoing activities. These last two shifts in direction are reflected in the principles underlying PL 99-457, namely that services should be "provided in as normal a fashion and environment as is possible," and such services should "promote the integration of the child and family within the community" (Johnson et al., 1989, p.9). These principles promote natural social supports and are consistent with the views described under the section addressing the need to consider the family as part of a larger community of extended family, friends, and community.

In summary, current views of how the client is served reflect a change from narrowly focused interventions for specific handicapping conditions to a broader conceptualization of family services, with a focus on prevention, family strengths, and normalization.

What is the Role of the Helper?

For most of this century, the home visitor has been the "expert," whether she has been a professional or paraprofessional. With presumably more knowledge or experience than her client, she came prepared to solve problems and make decisions, and she carried out her role as an individual, not as a member of a team.

Shifts in the home visitor's role have resulted from changes in the view of the family. No longer seen as a passive recipient, but rather as an active participant, the family is encouraged to define its own needs, decide on priorities, and state preferences for services. This means that the visitor must be a collaborator, a facilitator, and a negotiator. Though these roles have not been prominent in the past, they are now recommended by many professionals. We need to recognize that the changes in the roles of the visitor do not imply less competence on the part of the visitor. Indeed, to carry out the roles of collaborator, facilitator, and negotiator, the visitor must be an expert in the helping skills, as well as competent in the particular content of her program and in the knowledge and skills of her profession. The shift from the "expert problem-solver" means that she does not come in prepared to offer immediate answers to predetermined problems. Even in the health care field, where we tend to think that there is less client involvement in the designation of services, families should still be involved in identifying their concerns and goals.

The principles underlying PL 99-457 also have relevance for the role of the visitor. One underlying principle calls for service providers to re-examine their traditional roles and practices to assure that they promote mutual respect and partnerships. The focus on families, as opposed to individuals, is seen as "a profound shift of perspective for many professionals whose training and practice has equipped them to work primarily with children and whose role with families has been primarily an instructive one" (Johnson et al., 1989, p.8). Dunst, Trivette, and Deal (1988) identify eight roles that practitioners may find useful as they reconsider older patterns of interacting in light of current goals. These roles are the empathetic listener, teacher/therapist, consultant, resource, enabler, mobilizer, mediator, and advocate. These roles all continue to recognize the helper as a person with special skills and competencies. The shift in focus is not on less competence on the part of the visitor, but on incorporating family competence in decision-making and problem-solving.

These shifts in the roles of visitors are essential in order to respond to the shifts in client population and program focus that have already been mentioned. Differences in both clients and services can be discussed at many levels, but it is the visitor in the field who must be prepared to meet these new challenges. A person who has been educated to address the specific needs of handicapped children should not be assumed to have the skills necessary for working with parents on a broad range of parent needs and priorities. It is easier to describe the advantages of family-focused intervention than to identify the skills necessary for such services and to assure that appropriate training and supervision occur for those providing these services. Additional training issues will be discussed in more detail in Chapter 10.

Current Client Characteristics

The shifts in views about clients, service providers, and helping roles tell us about current beliefs, but not about current practice. In this section, we will present information from the national survey on home visiting described in Chapter 1 regarding current characteristics of those who receive home visiting services (Roberts & Wasik, 1989). These data reflect a variety of current societal judgments concerning the most appropriate timing for intervention efforts. Program directors who completed the survey were asked to identify the primary and secondary child and parent characteristics of the population they served. One in five programs reported providing services for nonhandicapped children. This finding is notable, given the current interest in specialized funding. Similar percentages of programs (12% and 13%) were reported as serving children who had been maltreated, were at risk for school failure, were physically handicapped, or were developmentally delayed.

Survey data also describe the primary characteristics of the parents involved in home visiting programs. The largest category was comprised of low-income families (30%), followed by parents in the general population (20%), and maltreating (abusive/neglectful) parents and parents of physically handicapped children (10%) each. Fewer programs focused primarily upon drug or alcohol abusing parents (5%), single parents (4%), teenage parents (3%), or parents of low birthweight infants (3%). From these data, poor families appear to be of primary concern, as reflected by the number of programs that are provided for them. Thirty percent of the programs identified low income as the primary parent characteristic, and another 21% identified it as the secondary characteristic of their parent population. Thus, half of the programs reported low income as a salient characteristic of their parents.

There is also increased interest in providing services to younger children. It was not that long ago that Head Start was initiated, based on the belief that extra attention prior to school entrance could help ameliorate the detrimental effects of poverty. During the 1980s, we have seen major interest in providing services for even younger children, prompted by the belief that many childhood problems need to be addressed in the first few years of life. Survey data as seen in Table 2.3 indicated that the largest number of children served, 34%, are in the birth-to-age-three category (Roberts & Wasik, 1989). The next three highest categories are the birth to age 18, the 3- to 6-year-old categories, and birth to school-age.

The age of the child served, however, is a function of the primary parent characteristics. Programs that identify low income as the primary characteristic of their families more frequently serve children when they are ages 3, 4, or 5, rather than infants or toddlers (Wasik & Roberts, 1989a). This age group accounts for 45% of programs serving low-income families, a phenomenon that may be attributable to the large role the Head Start home visiting program has in providing services for children in low-income families. Eighty-five percent of all other programs report services for children as infants and toddlers. Programs for children at biological risk generally begin serving families as soon as the children are diagnosed, which is usually shortly after birth.

We anticipate that during the next decade, there will be an increase in services during both the prenatal/perinatal period and

TABLE 2.3: Percentage of Programs Serving Each Age Group and the Two Agencies Providing the Most Service for Each Age Group

Children's Age	Percentage of Total Programs	Agency	
Pre/Perinatal	3	72	Public Health
		15	Private Health
0-3	34	30	Public Health
		24	Public Education
3-6	20	70	Head Start
		20	Public Education
6-12	1	43	Private Social Service
		28	Public Social Service
12-18	1	40	Private Social Service
		28	Public Social Service
Birth-School	16	30	Public Education
		27	Public Health
K-12	2	46	Public Education
		32	Private Social Service
Birth-18	22	44	Public Health
		27	Private Social Service
Other	1	63	Public Health
		18	Private Social Service

SOURCE: Roberts, R. N., & Wasik, B. H., 1989. National home visitor survey: Agency affiliation, family characteristics, purposes, and services provided. Manuscript submitted for publication.

during the birth-to-age-three period. We believe that this shift in age group will occur in part from a recognition of the potential benefits of working with women during pregnancy and the benefits of working with children, especially those from low-income families, earlier in their lives.

Principles for Providing Home-Based Family Services

From our own experience with many home visitors in a wide range of programs, we have formulated five general principles that we find useful in focusing the work of the home visitor. These principles appear to have relevance regardless of the particular characteristics of the family or the specific goals of the program.

(1) *Family support should enhance the ability of families to work toward their own goals and deal effectively with their own problems.* This guideline is intended to help service providers remain continually aware that their work is to help the families they serve become more independent over time. Providing direct services for immediate needs or solving clients' problems for them may help alleviate present stresses, but such actions do not necessarily leave the clients better able to deal with future stresses. In our programs, we have asked visitors to evaluate their work with families on a continuous basis to assure that they are promoting the families' participation in a way that facilitates increased self-reliance and independence.

The home visitor will find wide variations in families' abilities to cope with their own problems. Some families may benefit from extra assistance at a stressful time in their lives, but their general coping skills may be very strong. Other families will require help beyond that of the primary objectives of a specific program. These variations are especially apparent in those home visiting programs that reach out to all families at a particular stage of family life, as, for example, during pregnancy.

(2) *Home-based intervention should be individualized, based upon an assessment of the social, psychological, cultural, educational, economic, and physical or health characteristics of the family.* In everyday language, the visitor must begin with the family where it is at that time. This principle is true whether it is the first visit or the twenty-first. The home visitor should evaluate family strengths and limitations and use that knowledge appropriately.

This principle of individualization may come in conflict with programs that have a predetermined curriculum if the home visitor is not allowed the flexibility to make judgments about the appropriateness of the specific curriculum for the family at any particular point in time. With the exception of some research studies that may be designed to evaluate a specific curriculum, the strength of home visiting lies in its capacity to plan interventions to meet the needs of each family.

(3) *A home visitor must be responsive to the immediate needs of families, as well as to their long-term goals.* Hungry children need

food. They cannot survive while their parents learn a trade and find employment. A sick child needs medical attention. An abused woman needs support and possibly shelter. Respite care or home-maker services may be more important at a particular time than focusing on long-term goals. The home visitor must be able to assess such needs, and know when to call for assistance, when to provide direct service, or when to help a family secure needed services through its own efforts.

(4) *A helping relationship should be a collaboration between the home visitor and the family members.* This concept is a relatively recent one in the practice of home visiting. Although earlier writers, such as Richmond, talked about the importance of discussing needs with families, many programs have been based upon a philosophy that the agency knew what was best for the families and provided the services that they were prepared to offer. This approach can be seen across the history of home visiting regardless of the profession involved. A collaborative relationship, however, emphasizes the importance of families working cooperatively and actively with home visitors.

It should be recognized that families may have needs that the home visitor is not prepared to handle, but she still needs to respond sensitively and in a supportive manner in such situations. A home visitor, for example, who continues to talk about infant development when a parent has just told her that she is about to be evicted from her apartment will have difficulty maintaining the confidence of the parent. The parent will probably not attend to the infant development content, and the visitor may find that the parent is less interested in future visits.

(5) *The family should be recognized as a social system, understanding that intervention efforts directed at one individual within the family can influence other family members and can influence the overall functioning of the family.*

This guideline should be used by the visitor throughout her work as she evaluates the consequences of possible changes on each family member. Who will this affect? Do the negative costs outweigh the benefits? Attending to possible consequences can help the visitor and family plan ahead to reduce any adverse situations.

In summary, these working principles can function as a set of criteria for the home visitor by which she evaluates her work with families. These principles can provide a basis for discussion with clients or supervisors when considering recommendations for assessment or intervention procedures. These guidelines can also facilitate decision-making on the part of the visitor when faced with a choice of direction.

Problem-Solving Approach for Home Visitors

Jahoda (1958) was one of the first to identify the importance of the relationship between problem-solving skills and mental health. In the 1960s and 1970s, several other individuals began to write about the close relationship between problem solving and mental health, including D'Zurilla and Goldfried, who emphasized the importance of teaching individuals a strategy for dealing with real life social and personal problems (D'Zurilla & Goldfried, 1971; D'Zurilla & Nezu, 1982; Goldfried & Davison, 1976). Spivack and Shure have also had a major effect on the field during the last 20 years (Spivack & Shure, 1974; Shure & Spivack, 1972; 1978). Results of several studies they conducted with a variety of populations support a relationship between problem solving and adjustment. The clinical literature shows that helping individuals to solve problems is a basic part of most therapeutic procedures (e.g., Peterson, 1968; Haley, 1976, 1987; Forgatch & Patterson, 1989).

Of increasing concern to professionals is the relationship between problem solving and the adjustment of the family. Concern in this area has led some writers to suggest that the absence of conflict-resolution skills can lead to the dissolution of the family (Patterson, Weiss, & Hops, 1976). Others have written that failure to use effective problem-solving skills in childrearing can lead to serious emotional and behavioral problems in children (Kelley, Embry, & Baer, 1979). Problem-solving has been used in many intervention programs for families (i.e., Robin, 1979; Robin & Foster, 1989; Blechman, 1974), teachers and parents of young children (Shure & Spivack, 1972; 1978), and parents of handicapped children (Intagliata & Doyle, 1984). In the problem-solving approach we have used, home visitors are to help families identify concerns and goals, set priorities, and develop a plan for working toward resolution. This approach is consistent with other theorists and practitioners who have called for a focus on client-identified concerns.

In any home visiting program, it is very important that the goals of the program coincide with the procedures that are used by the home visitors. Otherwise, the procedures could encourage behaviors and activities on the part of clients that are incompatible with the program goals. We are particularly concerned about the relationship between philosophy and procedures as it relates to enhancing parent coping, independence, and problem solving. Though these parent goals have been frequently promoted as desirable, it is possible for home visitors to use strategies that are incompatible with promoting these goals.

To assure that home visitors use procedures compatible with program goals, it is important first to be aware of the consequences of using different helping models. The particular helping model used by the helper, either implicitly or explicitly, or assumed by the client influences the helping outcome (Brickman, Rabinowitz, Karuza, Coates, Cohn, & Kidder, 1982). A model that promotes the home visitor as the expert who solves issues is not compatible with promoting independence. Second, it is important for programs to assure that home visitors receive the training necessary to implement the program goals.

We have developed and used a problem-solving approach in home visiting because we believe problem solving is an essential component of individual well-being, family functioning, and parenting, and we believe that the use of this model can enhance a family's ability to independently address its own needs.

In the course of our daily lives, in both personal and work settings, all of us have goals we want to reach, and we experience problems or stresses we would like to change. Problem-solving strategies can be used to reach goals, meet challenges, or deal with stresses and problems. It is one way of coping with life's events. Given the same stressful circumstances, one person may cope by denial, while another copes through effective problem solving.

In addition to this general problem-solving approach, we have also focused on specifically teaching parents about the problem-solving process so that they will have a better understanding of the processes and strategies involved in thinking through a problem and carrying out proposed solutions. This program, *Problem Solving for Parents* (Wasik, 1984), goes beyond helping parents with current problems to helping enhance their own ability to deal with future concerns.

This model was based in part upon an assumption that the day-by-day situations parents have to deal with are often as complex and demanding as those of many professionals and that the preparation and training given to many professionals in problem solving is appropriate for parents. Problem-solving skills have been seen as an important part of physician training in helping doctors learn how to diagnose patient illness (Elstein, Shulman, & Spratka, 1978) and have been incorporated into the training of psychologists (Wasik & Fishbein, 1982). Other professions, such as social work, also have a history of using problem solving for training (Kadushin, 1976; Perlman, 1957). These skills have been a part of the preparations of teachers in order to help them learn how to handle their professional problems (McGuire & Babbott, 1967). Nursing training has also recommended a problem solving approach (Miles, 1986).

A second assumption of this program is that teaching parents problem-solving skills helps to assure that parents will have many of the necessary skills for developing positive parent-child relationships. The *Problem Solving for Parents* program is particularly suitable for working with families in the home. It has been used in several home visiting programs in a number of states and has been implemented with parents across a range of income levels. It has been used with diverse populations, including families with alcohol problems, depressed individuals, single parents, teenage parents, and parents of handicapped children.

The seven steps of the model were selected because each is an important part of the total problem-solving process, and at any of these steps, individuals can have difficulty proceeding with a problem solution (Wasik, 1984). The steps used in the model are listed and defined below:

1. *Problem definition* describes a problem situation. A situation is defined as a problem when its resolution is not automatic.
2. *Goal selection* describes what a person wants to happen.
3. *Generation of solutions* identifies a number of alternative responses that may lead to resolution of the specific problem.
4. *Consideration of consequences* identifies the positive and negative consequences of any solution in relation to time, money, personal, emo-

tional, and social effects, and in terms of immediate and long-term effects.

5. *Decision-making* weighs the proposed solutions and consequences, determining which one is best for the individual at that time. Decision-making involves consideration of a person's priorities and values.

6. *Implementation* carries out those actions called for by the proposed solution.

7. *Evaluation* reviews the outcome to determine whether it met the goals.

Integrating a Problem-Solving Approach with Current Philosophical Positions

The problem-solving approach presented here is extremely compatible with the emphasis upon helping families learn ways of becoming more independent and self-reliant. In the problem-solving approach, one does not simply help clients resolve present difficulties; rather one helps them learn a strategy for dealing with future concerns.

Earlier in this chapter, we discussed a philosophical shift in the role of the home visitor from that of an expert problem-solver to that of a facilitator. It is important to consider this shift in relation to using a problem-solving model. It is very important to recognize that the shift from the expert role to a consultant or facilitator role is at the point of defining problems and setting goals. In the past, service providers often defined their clients' problems and then provided solutions. The current philosophical shift is to assure that the client or family actively identifies its own needs and goals. When a family has difficulty doing so, the visitor needs to be able to facilitate this process. In some situations when someone is having difficulty focusing in on a difficult situation, the home visitor may be more directive in identifying a problem, but her goal remains to help the family ultimately take on this responsibility.

In considering solutions to problems, however, home visitors will likely have more knowledge about many topics than the family and will be in a position to offer help. The shift in philosophy to a facilitator does not mean such information will not be shared. Rather, it means that clients will be encouraged to generate solutions on their own and consider consequences. In decision-making, the visitor will at times need to say what she thinks is the best thing to do, or even ask specifically that something be done; in general, however, she will encourage the family to make its own decisions. Helping clients obtain more independence in effective coping and decision-making takes place over time. In the early stages, more direction may be necessary as one "does for" someone else, while later, the visitor becomes less directive as the client assumes more responsibility. One program described how its services to families changed over time: at first, "doing for," then "doing with," and, finally, "cheering on."

Summary

In this chapter, we have discussed philosophical shifts over time, noting that some shifts bring us back to positions held at the beginning of the century, especially the renewed focus on the entire family. Such shifts should help us keep in perspective our current views and remind us of the need to learn from and build upon the work of others in the field.

Though it is helpful to review past and current philosophical positions, when different positions are recommended as policy, they should not be implemented in a way that fosters rigidity in services. Using the facilitator role of the visitor as an example, with some clients at some times, the most effective and professionally accountable position may be for the visitor to assume a very directive role and to monitor client cooperation closely. The recommended shifts in roles should not conflict with good practice. Overall, however, the current philosophical views appear to be grounded on an appreciation of the importance of each individual, a recognition of individual and family beliefs and values, and a commitment to promoting family participation in all aspects of the helping process.

3

Illustrative Home Visiting Programs

Though literally thousands of home visiting programs exist throughout the country, the typical home visitor does not have the opportunity to visit or learn about these other programs. Furthermore, most visitors are not aware of the wide range of families served through home visiting and the breadth of services offered to these individuals. In the 1988 volume on exemplary prevention programs by the American Psychological Association, several programs involving home visiting were selected for inclusion, namely the Prenatal/Infancy Project, Project CARE, and the Houston Child Development Center (Price, Cowen, Lorion, & Ramos-McKay, 1988). The Harvard Family Research Project has provided information on the development of state-sponsored family support and education programs, including information on state-funded home visiting programs (Hausman & Weiss, 1987; Weiss, 1989). Other sources of information on home visiting programs include several recent reviews of research programs (i.e., Halpern, 1984; Ramey, Bryant & Suarez, 1985), as well as summaries in books (e.g., Weiss & Jacobs, 1988) or manuals prepared by programs (e.g., Missouri Department of Elementary and Secondary Education, 1986).

Our purpose in this chapter is to present information on several programs to illustrate the considerable diversity in the field on a number of dimensions. We included programs with different funding sources, including state, federal, and private foundations. We selected programs that employed professionals as home visitors and ones that employed paraprofessionals. We also selected programs that illustrated restrictive versus universal inclusion criteria, that took place in many different locations, and that served families with a range of characteristics. Each program summarized in this chapter has produced written materials on its procedures and has the possibility of replication. There were many home visiting programs with exemplary characteristics from which to choose to illustrate the diversity in the field. The projects we selected to describe are the following: (1) Prenatal/Early Infancy Project, (2) Project CARE, (3) the Infant Health and Development Program, (4) Missouri's Parents as Teachers Program, (5) Hawaii's Healthy Start Project, and (6) the Head Start Home Visiting Program. For each of these six programs, we have described their purposes, philosophies, services, participants, home visitor credentials, and, when available, information on program effectiveness.

The Prenatal/Early Infancy Project

The Prenatal/Early Infancy Project was a home visiting program designed to prevent a number of maternal and child health problems through home visiting by nurses. Only first-time mothers were recruited, though the emphasis was upon young, unmarried, or poor mothers. The program specifically focused on improving prenatal health habits, infant care-giving skills, social support, use of community services, and informal community supports (Olds, 1988b; Olds et al., 1985; Olds, Henderson, Tatelbaum, & Chamberlin, 1986).

The theoretical foundations of the Prenatal/Early Infancy Project were based on several psychological theories, including the cognitive development theory of Piaget (1952), attachment theory as proposed by Bowlby (1969), and social learning theory as proposed by Bandura and Walters (1963). The project was also strongly influenced by the ecological theories of Bronfenbrenner (1979) that emphasized the importance of family, friends, and community. Olds also notes another philosophical position that he refers to as "commonsense" psychology. This philosophy was to guide the work of home visitors by having them assume that, in general, parents would respond appropriately during pregnancy and in caring for their infants and young children.

Because the purpose of the program was to prevent a wide range of maternal and child health problems, the mothers were recruited using the three factors identified as being predictive of such problems: being a teenage parent, poor, or unmarried. Because it was not clear that one of these variables was more important than another, the presence of any one of the three factors was sufficient to include a mother in the research sample. To reduce the possible stigma associated with a program that focused on young, single, poor parents, any first-time mother was invited to be part of the service delivery sample, including those without any of the three risk factors.

The project focused on first-time mothers for three reasons. It was believed that (1) they would be more receptive to help, (2) they would be able to use the knowledge and skills they learned in future pregnancies, and (3) there was a higher likelihood they would return to school or work if they only had one child to care for. To be able to measure the mother's health during pregnancy, women were recruited early in their pregnancy, at less than 25 weeks of gestation. None of the women had previous live births. They were recruited through a variety of health and human service agencies, with 500 women interviewed and 400 enrolled. Of this number, 85% met at least one risk factor, and 23% had all three risk factors (Olds, 1988a).

The location for this project was a semirural county in the Appalachian region of New York State in a community in which a range of health and human services was available. Prenatal care was accessible through nine obstetricians, and a free clinic was sponsored by the health department. The community was characterized by high rates of reported and confirmed cases of child abuse and neglect.

The home visitors were all registered nurses who were employed through a nonprofit private agency. Personal characteristics were emphasized in the employment of the visitors. All nurses were to be parents themselves because it was believed that parenthood experiences would be invaluable in home visiting. Also, maturity and judgment were used as selection criteria.

The Prenatal/Infancy Project was designed as a randomized clinical trial, with families assigned to one of four groups. The first group served as a control group and received no treatment services; however, at 12 and 24 months of age, these children were screened for sensory and developmental problems by an infant specialist. The three remaining groups all received the same screening, as well as one of three treatment conditions. Group 2 families received free transportation for prenatal and well-child care at local clinics and physicians' offices. Group 3 families not only received screening and transportation, but they also had home visits by nurses every two weeks during pregnancy. Group 4 families received all the services of Group 3, plus home visits by nurses throughout the first two years of the child's life.

The services of the Prenatal/Infant Project can be described under these main headings: educating the parent, involving informal support systems, and encouraging linkages with formal systems. Parent education included two major components: prenatal education and infancy education. Nurses were also to encourage parents to make decisions concerning their own education or job training, employment, and future childbearing. When these topics were discussed, the woman's primary support person was especially encouraged to attend. As examples of specific objectives, nurses were to help women improve their diets during pregnancy and monitor their weight gain; eliminate the use of cigarettes, alcohol, and drugs; learn the common signs of pregnancy complications; and prepare for labor, delivery, and the early days of infant care.

Information on infancy was divided into five development periods across the first two years of life, with the home visitor describing to the mother her responsibilities and the child's needs during these time periods. Specific objectives related to child development were addressed, including helping the parent understand the child's temperament and encouraging social, emotional, cognitive, and physical growth.

The primary procedure for encouraging informal support was to have the mother identify family members and friends she could count on for help. Based on her discussions with these mothers, the home visitor identified the mother's sources, who were most often the client's own mothers, husbands, or boyfriends. The home visitor then encouraged the mother to include these individuals in the home visits. When they did participate, the home visitor encouraged them to be supportive of the mother in ways ranging from accompanying her to the hospital to later helping with the infant.

It was also the home visitor's role to encourage appropriate contact with the local health and human service agencies. One way she communicated with the medical care provider was by sending written reports to the obstetricians and pediatricians providing the care. Case conferences and phone calls were also used to facilitate communication.

The Prenatal/Early Infancy Project has been evaluated by comparing families in the different groups. Assessments were made during pregnancy and at periodic intervals after the infant's birth to obtain information on maternal and child health. Even though the program ended when the children were two years of age, the children and their families continued to be evaluated until the children were four so that the long-term effects of the program could be evaluated. The results of the evaluations showed that during pregnancy, women who received home visits had more informal supports, improved their diets more, and smoked less. The very young mothers had significant increases in infant birthweight, and there was a lesser incidence in preterm delivery for those who smoked. Of particular significance was that for those women with all three risk characteristics (poor, unmarried, teenaged), there was a reduction in verified cases of child abuse and neglect (from 19% to 4%). Important changes were also obtained in areas of adult social behavior. White women in the home visiting program who did not have a high school education returned to school more rapidly. Also, unmarried white women in the home visiting program were employed for a longer period of time, had fewer subsequent pregnancies, and waited longer before the birth of a second child (Olds, Henderson, Tatelbaum, & Chamberlin, 1988). Based on this study, having nurse home visitors during the prenatal period and the first two years of a child's life can be seen as having important benefits for children and mothers. At the present time, a replication of this project is being planned for Memphis, Tennessee. This replication study should provide valuable data on the generalizability of these results from one setting and population to another.

Project CARE

Project CARE was designed to determine the effects of two intervention programs initiated during infancy on the cognitive performance of high-risk, low-income children. The goal of intervention was to increase the likelihood of school success. Project CARE is an acronym for the Carolina Approach to Responsive Education. We developed and implemented Project CARE at the Frank Porter Graham Child Development Center of the University of North Carolina in cooperation with two other colleagues, Craig Ramey and Joseph Sparling. This study has been supported by grants from the Special Education Program of the U.S. Department of Education; the Administration for Children, Youth, and Families, and the National Institute for Child Health and Human Development.

The major purpose of Project CARE was to test the hypothesis that cognitive performance of children would differ as a function of the intensity of the intervention program. For the most intensive intervention group, a family education home visiting program was combined with an educational day-care program; the less intensive intervention group only received the family education home visiting program. It was believed that children in the family education plus day-care program would perform higher than children in the family education group, and both groups would perform higher than the control group.

The Project CARE philosophy is based on a biosocial systems theory of development (Ramey, Bryant, Sparling, & Wasik, 1984). It is consistent with other ecological and systems theory models of development, such as those discussed by Bronfenbrenner and Crouter (1983) and Sameroff (1983), and emphasizes the need to consider parent variables, child development, and environmental conditions in developing intervention programs.

During a 17-month period in the late 1970s, 65 families were identified for participation in Project CARE. All eligible families had infants judged to be at risk for delayed development. The selection of families was based on a High Risk Index (Ramey & Smith, 1977), which included weighted scores for mother's educational level, father's educational level, family income, father absence, poor school performance of siblings, and eight other weighted factors. In the research design, families were randomly assigned at the birth of the child to one of the three groups; the Child Development Center plus family education group (16 children) the family education only group (25 children), and the control group (23 children).

A review of the demographic characteristics of the three groups showed that the groups were comparable. The average age of the mothers at the child's birth was approximately 22 years and of the fathers, 25. The level of education of the mothers and fathers varied from an average of 10 to 11 years of completed schooling across high-risk groups. The IQ scores of mothers were in the mid-80s. When the children were 54 months of age, 93% of the original families were still participating in the program.

Project CARE took place in a university community in North Carolina that is characterized by the availability of many community resources. As a result, the Project CARE control group may have had more services than would be available in other communities to families on a routine basis.

Home visitors had backgrounds as day-care teachers, social workers, or nurses. Their educational credentials ranged from high school diploma with certification as a day-care teacher to master's degree. Several home visitors served as both day-care teachers at the Child Development Center and as home visitors. Others were full-time home visitors. Home visitor training was conducted throughout the program. The more intensive training occurred during the first year of the program, with a focus on implementing the child curriculum and the parent problem-solving program, as well as on topics of child management and the logistics of managing home visits. Training manuals were used to supplement weekly training meetings (Wasik & Ramey, 1982). Intensive weekly group supervision was a part of the training during the initial part of Project CARE, complemented by periodic individual supervision.

The services Project CARE offered varied in intensity across groups. Children in the control group received iron-fortified milk and disposable diapers, and they participated in periodic assessment sessions. Children in both the intervention groups received family-focused home visiting. The frequency of home visiting averaged about two-and-a-half visits per month for the first 3 years and about 1 per month from ages 3 to 5, lasting about 1 hour per visit. The major child curriculum resources were *Learning*

Games for the First Three Years (Sparling & Lewis, 1979) and *Learning Games for Threes and Fours* (Sparling & Lewis, 1984), which emphasized activities that support both the intellectual/creative domain and the social/emotional domain of the child. Language stimulation received special attention and focused on promoting verbal interaction modeled on what a nurturant and developmentally encouraging mother might establish with her child. All learning activities were presented in gamelike episodes and were integrated into the child's day. Adults were helped to interact positively and constructively with their child through the use of such specific adult behaviors as modeling and prompting the child.

A parent problem-solving curriculum designed to help parents learn a strategy for effective resolution of day-by-day parenting concerns was also used by the home visitors (Wasik, 1984). Home visitors gave parents opportunities to discuss and work on specific concerns in their own lives, and they used these ongoing concerns to introduce the problem-solving curriculum and to discuss the stages in the problem-solving process (i.e., problem identification, goal selection, generating alternatives, considering consequences, making decisions, evaluating problems, implementation, and evaluation). Each home visitor used both real and hypothetical examples to help parents understand the procedures and she encouraged the parent to think through her concerns, to generate alternatives, to make decisions, and to carry through with appropriate actions. Parents were given materials illustrating the problem-solving process.

Children in the most intensive intervention group as well as the home visiting program participated in the Child Development Center and began attending the center between 6 and 12 weeks of age. The Center was open from 7:30 A.M. to 5:30 P.M., and all children routinely attended until at least 3 P.M., though most participated for a full day. In this setting the children received care from professional caregivers, who focused on enhancing the children's social and intellectual development through a developmentally appropriate curriculum (Sparling & Lewis, 1981, 1984, 1985a) and planned environment.

Parent groups were also conducted, and parents in both intervention groups were invited to attend. The groups served as a parent support setting in which information could be shared with one another and knowledge about child development and community resources could be provided.

Assessments of intellectual performance were conducted at every six-month interval beginning in infancy. Beginning at 12 months of age and continuing through the age of 5 years, children who participated in the Child Development Center *and* whose families participated in the home visiting program performed the highest on measures of cognitive performance. Their scores at 5 years of age strongly suggest that they would be at lower risk for school failure. Children whose families participated only in the family education home visiting program did not perform differently from children in the control group on measures of cognitive development (Wasik, Ramey, Bryant, & Sparling, in press). Although the potential family benefits of home visiting cannot be assessed simply through measures of child cognitive development, two other measures, the Home Observation for Measure of the Environment (HOME) and a measure of parent attitudes about children, did not show treatment effects. We also believe that for children from low-income families, home visiting may need to be supplemented with other services to positively affect the child's intellectual performance. In this study, the fact that positive effects were not found for child cognitive development is consistent with the results of some of the findings in the field, but inconsistent with other research. Differences may be accounted for by the fact that services in Project CARE were initiated after the child's birth and may have been less intensive. The results of this study indicate that not all programs will meet their goals and, especially in the area of child cognitive development, additional research is needed to determine those services most likely to affect positive change.

Infant Health and Development Program

The Infant Health and Development Program (IHDP) was designed to study the effects of early intervention with low birthweight infants and their families. It was a randomized clinical trial that took place in eight medical institutions located in diverse urban settings throughout the country, funded by the Robert Wood Johnson Foundation (IHDP Research Consortium Group, 1989).

IHDP was based upon both theory and research related to the cognitive, medical, and social development of low birthweight infants. The content of IHDP and the way in which it was delivered to parents and children were based on Project CARE, the early intervention program for children from low-income families described in the preceding section (Ramey, Bryant, Sparling, & Wasik, 1985). The model that guided the IHDP intervention was a biosocial systems model developed to take into account salient factors affecting the growth and development of young children (Ramey, Bryant, Sparling, & Wasik, 1984). This model is an extension of a transactional model of infant education that describes family systems, family functioning, and the process of family and individual change (Ramey, Trohanis, & Hostler, 1982; Sameroff & Chandler, 1975).

The model proposes four major areas of influence: (1) the biological and social histories of the child and caregivers, (2) the current status of individual family members (e.g., child and caregiver), (3) the transactions that occur among individuals within the family and between individuals and forces outside the family, and (4) the future status of family members and their relationships. It was assumed that the transactions of greatest educational importance were the young child's social interactions with adult caregivers. For this reason, the focus of the intervention was on the parent-child interactions in the home and the teacher-child interactions in a center-based program.

The families in this study had infants born in 1985 whose birthweight was 2,500 grams (five pounds) or less. Though 4,551 infants met this initial criteria, additional criteria excluded infants whose mothers lived outside a prespecified catchment area, whose gestational age was less than 37 weeks, or who were members of a multiple birth greater than two. A number of other administrative, infant, or maternal exclusions were also used (e.g., language barrier, severe neurological abnormality, enrolled in another program). The design of this study also called for 2 weight groups: infants weighing between 2,001 and 2,500 grams and those weighing less than or equal to 2,000 grams.

The eight sites selected for the IHDP program were located in the following eight cities: Little Rock, New Haven, Miami, Boston, New York, Philadelphia, Dallas, and Seattle. Each of these sites had a large teaching hospital that was the setting for the recruitment of the families for the study. The ethnic composition differed from site to site, though, overall, about 50% of the participants were black, 14% Hispanic, and the remainder were white or of other ethnic backgrounds.

All home visitors had a bachelor's degree or its equivalent, primarily from the fields of education, social work, and nursing. Training in basic clinical skills was part of the in-service training of home visitors and was provided through workshops, role playing, supervision, and written materials. All home visitors from the eight sites attended annual 3-day training meetings at the Frank Porter Graham Child Development Center at the University of North Carolina, and were supervised by an education director at each site. Several training materials were developed for use by the home visitors, including the *Handbook on Home Visiting* (Wasik & Lyons, 1984) and a handbook on teaching parents problem-solving skills (Wasik, 1984).

The training program was guided by many of the beliefs we have presented in the next chapter of this book, namely the importance of competence in basic helping skills and techniques, as well as knowledge and skills regarding specific child or parent curriculum materials. The importance of providing supervision was stressed, and supervisors met periodically to discuss both the content and structure of in-service training and alternative supervisory procedures.

Infants were randomly assigned to either an intervention (n = 377) or follow-up group (n = 608). Groups were balanced by birthweight, gender, maternal age, maternal education, and maternal race (black, Hispanic, other) at each site. Both groups received pediatric follow-up and social support services. Only the intervention group received the comprehensive early education program (Ramey, et al., 1985). The program components were the same as the ones in Project CARE: home visits, attendance at a child development center, and parent group meetings. The content of the program consisted of parent support, parent problem solving, and learning activities and play materials for children.

Home visitors met with families weekly from the time the child was discharged from the hospital until age one, at which time the child entered the child development center. Home visits were provided twice a month throughout the remainder of the program.

Home visitors were to be guided by the following program goals: (1) to provide information to parents that would make it possible for them to make better decisions about their child, (2) to provide health care information and encourage parents to use appropriate resources in the community as needed to maintain the child's good health, (3) to provide emotional support to parents during stressful times, (4) to help parents learn ways to enhance their child's intellectual, physical, and social development, (5) to help parents learn more effective ways to cope with the stress that results either from the responsibilities of parenting or from other events in their lives, (6) to help parents learn more effective communication skills so that they could be better able to accomplish their own goals in life, and (7) to help parents learn positive ways of dealing with their child's behavior.

Home visitors used a general problem-solving approach in working with parents that encouraged active participation on the part of the parents in addressing their own concerns. Home visitors also used the specific problem-solving curriculum for parents developed by Wasik (1984); this parent program is briefly described in the preceding section on Project CARE.

A curriculum written for low birthweight infants, *Early Partners* (Sparling, Lewis, & Neuwirth, in press), as well as *Partners for Learning* (Sparling & Lewis, 1984), were essential components of the home visiting program. The materials were designed to help parents encourage the growth and development of their child. The child development center, established at each of the eight sites, met the licensing requirements for each respective state, as well as additional standards and procedures established as part of the IHDP. Children attended the centers from ages one to three.

The three major outcomes of this study focused on the cognitive, behavioral, and health development of the children. Cognitive development was measured with the Stanford-Binet Intelligence Scale, behavioral competence was assessed using the Child Behavior Checklist for Ages 2-3, and health status was assessed with three dimensions: morbidity, functional status, and maternal perceptions of the child's health (IHDP, 1989). Results will be forthcoming in the *Journal of the American Medical Association* in 1990. The scope, design, and findings of this study make it important in the home visiting literature. Furthermore, though home visiting was only part of the total IHDP and its effects cannot be separated from other program effects, this study has significance for the field of home visiting by making more publicly visible the use of home visiting as a part of early intervention for low birth-weight infants.

Missouri Parents as Teachers Project

The Missouri Parents as Teachers Project (PAT) is a statewide program designed for all families with children under the age of three. It is based, in part, upon a demonstration project initiated in 1981 that is called the New Parents as Teachers Project, or NPAT (Pfannenstiel & Seltzer, 1985; Weiss, 1989).

The Missouri program had its roots in 1972 when the Missouri State Board of Education adopted early childhood education as a priority. At that time, it identified the role and responsibility of the public education system that was relevant for the child's pre-school years. The philosophy of the program was influenced by work in the 1950s and 1960s in the fields of psychology, education, and medicine that called attention to the importance of the first years of life for the child's cognitive, language, and emotional development. NPAT was also influenced by the early education programs of the 1960s that had emphasized the importance of working with the family to improve the child's development, rather than focusing only on the child and excluding the family from intervention efforts (Missouri Department of Elementary and Secondary Education, 1986).

The Harvard University Preschool Project study of early development directed by Burton White provided a basis for the NPAT curriculum (White, 1975). Abilities that were emphasized were those considered the foundations of educational ability: language, curiosity, social skills, and cognitive intelligence. The NPAT project stressed the importance of the prenatal period for parents, parent support groups, and an individualized educational program for each family. Periodic screenings for children were an important program component. The project was guided by the philosophy that a partnership between parents and the school during the early years could enhance the likelihood for school success for young children.

Four school districts participated in the original NPAT demonstration project, selected on the basis of competitive proposals to assure the representation of urban, suburban, and rural communities. After the demonstration project, the program was extended statewide. We will describe the demonstration project here because it was the model for the statewide effort and because evaluation data are available.

The families were recruited from a wide range of backgrounds, with the restriction that only first-time parents could participate in the NPAT demonstration project. A comparison group with a similar range of characteristics to the children in NPAT was obtained in order to evaluate the results. The mothers in NPAT were about 26 years old at the time of the child's birth, and the fathers were about 28. The mother's and father's educational level averaged two years beyond high school, ranging from tenth grade to postgraduate degrees.

Between December 1981 and September 1982, 380 families were recruited to participate. Only first-time parents were selected based upon prior findings that such parents are the most motivated for this type of educational program, and because program effects could be evaluated more easily with this population. Families were recruited with procedures designed to assure that all socioeconomic strata, parental ages, and family characteristics were represented.

To evaluate the demonstration project, a random sample of the original participants and a comparison group were selected to match as nearly as possible the characteristics of the families in the intervention program, resulting in a quasi-experimental research design.

The results of the evaluation study demonstrated a number of important outcomes. First, children in the NPAT program scored significantly higher than the comparison children on the intelligence scale of the Kaufman Assessment Battery for Children. They also scored significantly higher on the achievement measure of the Kaufman and on the Zimmerman Preschool Language Scale. Additional findings showed that parent participation was positively correlated with a child's intelligence, achievement, and language ability. NPAT children were also rated higher on positive social development and had their hearing tested more often than those in the comparison group. Of particular note are the results showing parent participation was significantly related to children's intelligence, achievement, and language ability. Parents who participated more frequently in home visits were more likely to have children who were rated higher on prosocial behaviors, including coping abilities and interacting with adults.

Of particular significance is the fact that Missouri has now initiated a statewide home visiting effort for parents. State funding was authorized for developmental screening beginning at age one, as well as for parent education beginning at the birth of the child. Under the current implementation procedures, families are not limited to first-time parents. An evaluation project is now underway with 25 school districts to provide information on its effectiveness.

In the current statewide PAT program, home visitors, called parent educators, have backgrounds in child development or early childhood education, and parent education. These are the same credentials required in the demonstration program. Emphasis is placed upon selecting home visitors who can maintain a close relationship over many months with a wide variety of families and who are themselves parents. The actual experience of parenting was considered to provide knowledge about children that cannot be duplicated by academic study or work experience; thus, parenting experience is considered essential in the selection of home visitors (Missouri Department of Elementary and Secondary Education, 1986). Home visitors are responsible for planning and making home visits, participating in recruitment and screening activities, and assisting in parent group meetings.

Home visits are referred to as "personal visits," and the home visitor is to individualize the program for each family. Visits are held monthly and last about an hour. The PAT program has developed a set of well-organized materials for home visitors that describe objectives and procedures for visits made during the prenatal period and throughout the first three years of life.

The home visitor keeps records on all home visits and on any issues brought up by parents. She also records her own impressions or comments and plans for the next home visit. These reports are considered essential for monitoring both the child's and the family's progress. The reports are also routinely used during staff discussions focused on the best ways to provide educational guidance to families.

The following services are provided by the home visitors: provision of information on child development and guidance before the baby is born to help expectant parents prepare for the important job of being parents; provision of information about things to look for and expect as the child grows and develops; and guidance in fostering the child's intellectual, language, social, and motor-skill development. There are also periodic checkups of the child's educational and sensory development (hearing) to detect possible handicaps that can interfere with growth and development. If serious problems are discovered, help is sought from other agencies or professionals. In addition to the home visits, there are monthly group meetings with other new parents to share experiences and discuss topics of interest. By implementing this program, Missouri has obviously taken a proactive preventive statewide effort that can potentially reach all young children and their families.

Hawaii Healthy Start Program

The Healthy Start Program is a home-based intervention program designed to prevent child abuse and neglect and to increase parent competence in high-risk families. The area selected for the project was the Ewa area of Oahu, part of a mental health catchment area with a high incidence of confirmed reports of child abuse. The ethnic mix is representative of Hawaii, and the area has few social service resources. This program is a pilot demonstration project of the Hawaii Family Stress Center, administered through the Maternal and Child Health Branch of the Family Health Services Division of the Department of Health. The original pilot project continues to operate in the Ewa area, though several similar programs have now been established on the other Hawaiian islands (Sia & Breakey, 1985).

The Healthy Start Project is based upon several assumptions, the first of which is that the most effective way to prevent child abuse or neglect is to intervene with parents at the birth of a new infant. It is also assumed that children at risk for child abuse and neglect are at risk for emotional and mental health problems and developmental delays. The failure of bonding to occur between parent and child is seen as the most predictive risk factor. This belief has led to a focus on facilitating positive parent-child inter-actions as part of the intervention. It is also assumed that to successfully prevent child abuse and neglect throughout early childhood, it is necessary to provide follow-up services from birth to the age of five years.

The goals of the pilot project included a number of specific child and family objectives; the first being the screening and identifica-tion of all high-risk families in specific census tracts. Once the family was in the program, the goal of the intervention was to enhance parent skills through home visits, group meetings, and ongoing family support. Case management was also an objective and included referrals to a primary care physician and assistance with housing, legal aid, or other services as needed. Developmen-tal screening was conducted on each infant. The general proce-dures used within Healthy Start were those found to be effective in other home visiting programs, adapted as appropriate for the Hawaiian populations.

Healthy Start's target families are those at-risk for child abuse or neglect. The records of mothers of newborns are screened in the hospital to determine demographic risk factors, such as single parent or low income. If any of 16 different factors are present, a personal interview is conducted with the mother (and often, the father) in the hospital. Information from the interview is used to complete the *Family Stress Checklist*. If the score is above the at-risk criterion, then the mother is invited to be a part of the program.

Home visitors, who chose to call themselves Family Support Workers, are paraprofessionals selected for their nurturing quali-ties and successful experience in parenting. A month's initial training is provided to them, with ongoing extensive in-service training. The home visitors are also trained to use the Nursing Child Assessment Satellite Training (NCAST) scales and are certi-fied in their use. Information gained from the NCAST on mother-child interaction enabled the home visitors to see areas of concern or progress with their families. Gaining competence in the use of this measure has been seen as providing a validation of compe-tence and skill for the home visitors.

Home visitors meet with families weekly, first working on es-tablishing rapport and trust. With the supervisor, the family sup-port worker develops an individualized plan for the family, with case goals based upon problems identified by the initial risk assessment or defined by the family. If necessary, the home visitor tries to link the family to a physician for the infant. During the home visits, she demonstrates play activities from the two curriculum resources, *Hana Like*[1] *Mother-Baby Book* and the *Hawaii Family Support Worker Baby Play Book*, to try to produce positive parent-child interactions. In addition to parent-child activities, the visitor is to refer the family to other agencies for financial or housing concerns, to arrange for or provide transportation to physician appointments, and to provide informal counseling and emotional support.

Evaluation of the Healthy Start Program has focused on its two main goals, improved parenting and decreased child abuse and neglect. Parenting has been evaluated with periodic administration of the NCAST Home, Feeding, and Teaching scales. Attempts have been made to evaluate possible reduction in abuse and neglect by using census tract data. However, the definition of child abuse has changed during the last few years in Hawaii, influencing the reporting of child abuse and neglect and making it difficult to compare current rates with prior rates of abuse and neglect. Also, the census data are influenced by individuals moving into and out of the catchment area.

Because the Healthy Start Program was not specifically developed as a research program, definitive conclusions cannot be drawn about its effectiveness. Nevertheless, it appears to be a cost-effective program that may be effective in reducing the incidence of child abuse and neglect. This project is an excellent example of a service program for which evaluation data would be extremely valuable and that provides support for the importance of funding resources to plan and implement systematic studies of program effectiveness.

Head Start Home Visiting Programs

Since its beginning as a summer center-based program for five-year-old children in 1965, Head Start, a project of the federal government, has expanded to offer a variety of options for providing health, social, and educational services to children and their families. One option is a home-based program that became available following the positive evaluation of a demonstration program that showed a home-based program, referred to as Home Start, had the same benefits as the center-based Head Start program (Love, et al, 1976). These Head Start home-based programs are seen as facilitating continuity between center-based programs and the actual conditions of family life (Zigler & Freedman, 1987b). Also, when center-based programs cannot be established in communities, home-based programs provide an alternative way to reach families. Communities now determine which type of program best fits their needs, and they may select a center-based program, home-based program, or a combination of programs (Boyd & Herwig, 1980; Wolfe & Herwig, 1986).

The philosophy of the Head Start home visiting program is based upon the importance of emphasizing parent participation by the staff, and establishing a positive interpersonal relation between the home visitor and family so that there can be an effective exchange of information. The program philosophy also emphasizes that parents are primarily responsible for their children's development. Parents have the right to determine whether they will accept any services that are offered to them or their children. The Head Start staff assume a secondary role in the life of the child; their role is not to teach the child, but to facilitate the parent's role as the teacher of the child. The home visitor accomplishes this role by focusing on the parents' teaching, interaction, and problem-solving skills, with the objective of enhancing the parents' skills and confidence in parenting.

Head Start has described a number of advantages for providing services to a family in its own home; the first being that it provides an opportunity for individualized instruction and makes it possible for learning to occur in the natural environment. Home visiting also makes it possible for the helper to observe directly the parent-child interaction, thus providing important information for helping many parents become better managers of their child's behavior. Such information may be particularly important when working with parents of children with handicapping conditions. Home-based programs also have the advantage of intervening early in the development of problematic situations, and thus serve a prevention role. Furthermore, they provide unique opportunities for involving the parents and other family members in the educational program of the target child, and they can facilitate interactions between the parent and center-based programs.

Children who are between the ages of three and five from low-income families are eligible for the program. Ten percent of the positions in each program are available for families above the income guidelines, and an additional 10% of the positions are reserved for children with handicapping conditions. Families are recruited for the program through a variety of procedures, including newspapers, local schools, and direct contacts of potentially eligible persons.

The home visitor qualifications reflect the interest of Head Start in employing individuals from the community in which the program is offered. The minimum qualifications include: being at least 18 years of age; having a high school diploma or GED; having a valid driver's license, insurance, and a working automobile; and being willing to drive a Head Start vehicle. Home visitors also have experience in working with adults and preschool children for at least one year, or have a two-year degree in a related field. Important interpersonal characteristics for Head Start home visitors include being adaptable, nonjudgmental, resourceful, energetic, dependable, friendly, and confident. Preference in employment is given to past or present parents of a Head Start child (Wolfe & Herwig, 1986).

Home visitors are expected to perform a variety of activities in addition to working with parents in the home. These include, but are not limited to, assisting in recruitment, encouraging attendance at parent meetings and providing transportation if necessary, assisting families as necessary in arrangements and transportation for medical and dental appointments, providing health checks, and food preparation skills. The excellent publications prepared for Head Start home visitors provide detailed information on actually conducting home visits and on materials and activities for young children and their families (Boyd & Herwig, 1980; Wolfe & Herwig, 1986). Head Start also provides training through institutes and training centers.

Head Start's home visiting program illustrates the continuing national commitment to provide services for children from poverty families. Because of the program's widespread use throughout the country, additional evaluation data are needed to help ensure that the most effective procedures are being implemented. The scope of Head Start's home visiting program provides an excellent opportunity to evaluate systematically a variety of variables related to home visiting, such as the frequency and duration of home visiting and the content and scope of the services.

Conclusions

From this diverse set of home visiting programs, several features stand out. First, the characteristics of the programs demonstrate the range of populations served by home visiting, including preventive programs and programs for children with existing risk conditions. The Infant Health and Development Program identified families who had a child with an existing physical condition associated with problems in development, namely low birthweight. Project CARE and Head Start identified families based on variables associated with children's failure in school, and Healthy Start identified families based on characteristics predictive of child abuse and neglect. By working with pregnant women, the Prenatal/Early Infancy Program successfully prevented some of the conditions in pregnancy associated with child developmental problems. The Missouri effort, following its initial demonstration program, is providing universal home visiting to all parents throughout the state.

These programs also illustrate the diversity in selection criteria for employing home visitors. Though both the Prenatal/Early Infancy Program and the Missouri program required individuals to be parents themselves, one required that the home visitors be nurses while the other required backgrounds in child development. Both the Hawaii Healthy Start Program and the Head Start home-based program emphasize hiring individuals from the community. Project CARE had home visitors with diverse credentials, ranging from certification as day-care teachers to master's degrees in social work. Clearly, home visiting can be provided by individuals with different educational backgrounds and training.

It is instructive to note that in the written materials we reviewed on each program, all emphasized the importance of maturity and judgment as home visitor characteristics. Some sought to ensure this competence by requiring that the visitors also be parents, while others required a minimum amount of prior experience before an applicant could be employed as a visitor.

Several programs, including the Infant Health and Development Program, Project CARE, and Head Start, also provided a center-based program for some or all of the children in the program. Such combinations may be particularly advantageous when addressing the cognitive development needs of children from low-income backgrounds. Center-based, child-focused programs, however, are designed to address the needs of children and are not necessarily an essential part of programs whose objectives are to promote positive maternal health during pregnancy or to enhance infant development during the first six months of life.

Another characteristic these programs had in common was an emphasis upon training and supervision. All programs provided for an in-service training time, and most provided home visitors with written training materials. In most of these programs, supervision of home visitors was identified as an important program component.

One distinguishing feature of the three research programs we described is that all met relatively rigorous criteria for the experimental design of an empirical study. In each one, the families were randomly assigned to either an intervention or a control group prior to the initiation of the study. This procedure helps to reduce bias that would likely result if families selected their group assignment. These randomization procedures are typically not possible in programs focused on service delivery. Missouri and Head Start had funded demonstration projects prior to making their programs more widely available. Such evaluation studies add considerably to the empirical support provided by those research studies designed to evaluate more rigorously the effects of home visiting. These efforts, however, are expensive in time and effort, and have not been commonly included as part of service programs.

In summary, the programs described herein illustrate that home visiting programs can be implemented by a wide range of agencies, both federal and state, as well as public and private, all of which view home visiting as an important family service. They serve families with diverse needs and employ home visitors with a wide range of educational credentials. The programs we've described all have a number of exemplary features that can be useful to individuals developing new home visiting programs.

Note

1. *Hana Like* is a Hawaiian expression that means helping hands.

4

Personnel Issues Related to Home Visiting

Competent home visitors are essential for effective home visiting; consequently, their credentials, professional training, and supervision all require serious consideration. In this chapter, we will discuss these personnel issues as they relate to the employment of home visitors. We will also discuss guidelines for the hiring process. Though many home visiting programs that function as part of larger administrative units may have existing personnel procedures, we have found that many home visiting programs have little overlap with other administrative units and, as a result, they need to develop their own personnel procedures. Furthermore, we have found that even within large organizational structures, such as local and state government or universities, where relatively comprehensive personnel guidelines exist, such procedures often need to be modified to recruit the kinds of people needed by home visiting programs and to provide for their ongoing professional development.

Interrelations of Program Components

Home visitor credentials, professional development, and supervision are closely interwoven, not only with each other, but with other aspects of home visiting, such as program goals, resources, and information from program evaluations. Questions about whether to hire professional or paraprofessional visitors or to have paid or volunteer staff are issues directly related to program goals and resources. Home visitor characteristics are also influenced by the populations served and the complexity of services that can be provided in the home.

Some programs require a home visitor who is particularly skilled in enhancing child development and supporting families. Others need individuals with specific knowledge and skills related to medical conditions or to particular handicapping conditions of children. As a result of these different program needs, no single set of educational credentials is appropriate for all home visitors; rather, each program must match its needs with the criteria it sets for its home visitors.

The credentials of the individuals who are recruited and employed will influence the amount of training and supervision that is required. Individuals who have graduated from advanced professional training programs may need less in-service training, professional development activities, and supervision in comparison to individuals with little or no academic or experiential preparation for home visiting. On the other hand, even professionals with advanced educational degrees often have not received intensive training in working with families in the home.

Sometimes a poor match between program goals and home visitor competence results from a lack of financial resources to pay for qualified home visitors. A program may have excellent goals, but if its program salaries and benefits differ significantly from the expectations of interested applicants, programs are likely to have trouble filling their positions with qualified visitors.

Program evaluation can provide information important to consider in hiring and training home visitors. Program directors need to establish ongoing evaluation information of the home visiting program to determine whether or not home visitors are reaching their goals or to what degree the goals are being met. Such evaluations should specifically address the roles of home visitors. If a program is not reaching its objective in a particular area, administrators need to consider the possible factors that might be interfering with successful home visiting. Are the goals unrealistic for the resources? Is additional training necessary for the home visitors? Are family needs more complex than had been anticipated? Because the effectiveness of home visitors is a critical factor in the success of any program, information from evaluations can lead to revisions in hiring credentials or to the implementation of additional in-service training.

The interrelationships we have described above between program components and home visitors can determine a program's overall success. Awareness of these relationships before employing staff should increase the likelihood that there will be a good match between program goals and home visitor qualifications. In the following sections, we will discuss issues and make recommendations concerning home visitors in the areas of credentials, professional development, and supervision. We will then discuss hiring procedures and make suggestions for the employment process.

Credentials

What are the credentials considered essential for effective home visiting? Most program directors establish criteria related to education, interpersonal characteristics, and experience. Some programs may also include age, gender, and ethnic characteristics as considerations when hiring visitors. Issues related to each of these credentials are discussed below.

Educational Credentials

A wide range of educational credentials can be found among those employed as home visitors. According to the respondents in the national survey of family home visiting programs by Roberts and Wasik (1989), over 50% of the programs reported that they required at least the bachelor's degree for employment. Of the public education agencies conducting home visiting programs, 75% reported a bachelor's degree as the minimal educational requirement. These education levels reflect the general four-year degree requirements for teachers as well as for many nurses. The entry level into the field for social workers can be at the bachelor's or master's level.

Among Head Start programs, 45% reported that the high school diploma was the minimal educational level; almost 17% reported the Associate of Arts; and 24% reported the Child Development Associate degree as the entry-level requirement. The lower requirements for Head Start home visitors are similar to survey results showing that programs serving low-income families generally have a lower educational requirement for their home visitors than other programs (Wasik & Roberts, 1989b). This phenomenon most likely relates to the philosophy of many such programs to encourage the employment of people from the population that is served as a way of establishing rapport and credibility with families. Such programs often put a high premium on matching the sociocultural background of the visitors with that of the families in the program. Also influencing this practice is the fact that such programs have often viewed the home visiting experience as a job opportunity and training for the individuals employed as home visitors.

Programs may set a general educational level that all visitors must meet, and not require a specific professional background. The Infant Health and Development Program, for example, recommended that individuals have a bachelor's degree, but it accepted individuals with a range of education backgrounds, including education, nursing, and social work (IHDP Research Consortium Group, 1989).

Professional, Paraprofessional, or Lay Visitor

For our purposes, we have defined professionals as those who have earned credentials in a recognized field, such as education, nursing, or social work. We will use the term lay visitors interchangeably with the term paraprofessionals, consistent with some of the literature in the field (e.g., Larner & Halpern, 1987). We are aware, though, that in some volunteer programs lay visitors may be a cross section of community members and include individuals with a wide range of education and experience.

The issue of whether to employ professional or paraprofessional home visitors is possibly more relevant to home visiting than to other disciplines because both professionals and paraprofessionals have served as home visitors throughout the past century. Furthermore, many programs employ a combination of professional and lay workers, making the more relevant question one of how best to meet the needs of each group in the areas of professional development and supervision, and how best to capitalize on the unique skills of each type of person.

We believe decisions about the type of visitor are critical to each program's overall goals and must be carefully considered. Though researchers have attempted to determine the different merits of professional and paraprofessional workers (e.g., Durlak, 1979; Carkhuff & Truax, 1963), some programs strongly recommend professionals (e.g., Olds, 1988b) and others, paraprofessionals (e.g., Heins, Nance, & Ferguson, 1987). The determining factor is usually the program's specific goals. Other variables that need to be considered are how complex the families' needs tend to be and the role and responsibilities the home visitor may have within the agency itself and in coordinating services among agencies. At the present time, such decisions are most often made based upon the need for specific training (e.g., nursing) or the commitment to hire people from the community. The former decision usually results in hiring professionals; the latter often results in hiring paraprofessionals. An alternative used by many programs is to employ home visitors at two levels and to have the home visitors work in teams. Team work could include either a professional-level home visitor supervising a group of paraprofessionals, or it could call for different home visitors to provide services at varying times according to a family's needs.

Interpersonal Characteristics

Home visiting is demanding work that is best carried out by mature individuals who have had life experiences that enhance their own capacity to help others. The importance of interpersonal and communication skills, maturity, and judgment appear continually in the literature on home visiting. Because these characteristics are so essential to the success of the home visiting process, it is extremely important that programs select individuals who already possess basic competencies in these areas. Olds (1988b) wrote of the home visitors in the Prenatal/Early Infancy Project:

> We decided it was important to hire nurses who were parents themselves and who displayed considerable life experience and wisdom in addition to their formal training. Although it is possible to educate helping professionals in methods of forming effective therapeutic relationships, we believed that it was even more important to find individuals who had demonstrated a wealth of personal experience

that would help them relate effectively with the family and make sound judgments in the field. (p. 21)

In writing about the Resource Mothers Program, an organization that employs nonprofessional women to reduce the hazards associated with adolescent pregnancy, Heins, et al. (1987) described the Resource Mothers as women who combined warmth, successful parenting experience, and knowledge of community resources.

In Chapter 5, we will discuss ways of improving interpersonal and communications skills, as well as specific clinical or interviewing skills. However, we strongly believe that home visitors should have at least satisfactory skills in relating to others at the time of employment. Otherwise, training will become excessively lengthy and intense and may still not be able to achieve the level of skill required of home visitors. Later in this chapter we will discuss procedures that can help in the selection process.

Experience

Relevant previous experience of applicants should also be a major consideration in evaluating credentials, as it serves several functions. It allows the applicant to make decisions about her own work objectives and to have determined whether there is a good fit between her personal objectives and work in a helping profession. Previous experience also provides an opportunity for an employer to consider the applicant's performance in similar work situations. Such experience need not be limited to paid employment. Volunteer work in community, government, religious, educational, or health organizations can be relevant and beneficial. Home visitors themselves who work in family-focused programs have stressed the need to have considerable prior experience in working with children, as well as experience in implementing intervention procedures.

Age

The age of the home visitor applicant is also a relevant characteristic to consider when recruiting home visitors. Setting a minimum age can be one way of assuring an acceptable degree of maturity. The age of home visitors has been a concern primarily in programs that hire people with less than a high school or college degree and, consequently, have the possibility of employing individuals who are younger than 21. Because programs that employ people with a bachelor's degree will find that almost every applicant is at least 21, we will direct this discussion to the younger paraprofessional worker.

With few exceptions, we recommend that 21 be the minimum age for employing home visitors. We recognize that reaching a certain age does not assure maturity, but we also know that quality home visiting calls for strong interpersonal skills, judgment, and the ability to keep life events in perspective. The success of home visiting also depends upon the family's ability to have confidence and trust in the visitor, a situation more likely to develop if the visitor is perceived as a competent, knowledgeable, and reasonably experienced individual.

When would hiring a younger home visitor be desirable? It may be that young men or women should be employed if their youth might serve to open doors and facilitate communication with young clients, as it could in a program for school dropouts. A program designed for pregnant teenagers or young mothers might also choose to employ women who are similar in age to, or slightly older than, the clients. Though there are some programs where youth might gain some advantages, in general we believe that younger home visitors have not had the opportunity for the breadth of experience or the time to develop the maturity that is most helpful in the home visiting role. We urge programs that do employ very young home visitors to provide them with frequent and close supervision.

Gender

Almost all of the home visiting positions in this country are filled by women. In one program we directed, women were the only applicants for the visitor position; in another, a women-only hiring rule was created because the program focused on maternal and child care. In Richmond's 1899 book, *Friendly Visiting Among the Poor*, she referred to visitors as men though the vast majority of visitors then and now are women.

Should men be home visitors? Does it matter? We believe the gender issue is an important consideration, though, like age, it may be a more relevant issue in some programs than in others. For certain kinds of programs, we strongly recommend only women be hired. These situations include programs that provide visits to women who live alone, single women with young children, and women in programs focused on prenatal or postnatal care. Too many opportunities exist for misunderstandings in the community when a male home visitor provides home visiting services for a woman on a regular basis in her own home. The possibility for misunderstanding may also be true for visits to married women whose husbands would object to a regular male home visitor, especially if the husband were not at home. There are other times, however, when it may be particularly advantageous to have a male visitor as, for example, when working with male school dropouts or teenage fathers.

Ethnic Background

Ethnicity in relation to service providers has been defined as an umbrella concept that includes both cultural characteristics and social and racial distinctiveness (Jenkins, 1987). Religion, nationality, kinship patterns, and language can all be a part of ethnicity. Jenkins noted that ethnicity has particular relevance for those who work with families. Because early forms of family support were provided by family, friends, and others of a person's immediate community, the characteristics of helpers were similar to those who received their services. Only as support services became formalized and professionalized did we move away from this commonality between helpers and clients, leading to less recognition of needs stemming from ethnic concerns.

Jenkins (1981) proposed a typology to suggest how, when, and where ethnicity needs to be addressed in human service programs. These levels are the individual, group, and society level. She notes that there are no simple formulas or general prescriptions by which one can make decisions, but rather there is only a framework for evaluating decisions about ethnicity and the need to remain sensitive to family needs. She has described several programs in which matching the helper and the family on similar ethnic characteristics has been an important part of the programs' rocedures. Solomon, however, in her analysis of services for ninority groups, noted that matching on ethnic variables can nean the provision of services by less qualified individuals (1976).

We believe that the issue of ethnicity should be considered very eriously by each program. There is no uniform answer to the uestion of whether to hire visitors with characteristics similar to ne families who are served. Programs need to balance advantages nd disadvantages of ethnicity just as they should for other char- cteristics, such as age and education. New programs should onsider reviewing the effectiveness of the procedures used by ther programs serving similar groups. Furthermore, all programs eed to provide home visitors with training that assures each can nteract with families in a culturally sensitive manner.

rofessional Development

Program administrators need to provide for continual profes- ional development for their visitors. Such activities, often called n-service training, are particularly important because few educa- onal institutions provide this training (Weissbourd, 1987). Basic reparation of professionals is typically under the auspices of ollege and university administrations, but there are a few formal ducational experiences that specifically address the needs of ome visitors. Weissbourd noted that training programs related to ne family support movement generally lag behind the demands f current practice. The same can be said when speaking specific- lly of family support services in the home.

The training of paraprofessionals or lay visitors has almost lways been the responsibility of the employing organization. lany organizations employ some combination of professional, araprofessional or lay helpers, and responding to the needs of nese various groups can make training a complex activity. Indi- iduals enter home visitor positions with different educational ackground, different helping skills, and different content area nowledge, such as child development or nursing. We have por- ayed these characteristics in Figure 4.1 to illustrate differences mong individuals that need to be considered when making deci- ions on professional development activities. Two main levels of ducational backgrounds are shown: professional and paraprofes- ional. Yet, within these two levels, a wide variety of backgrounds

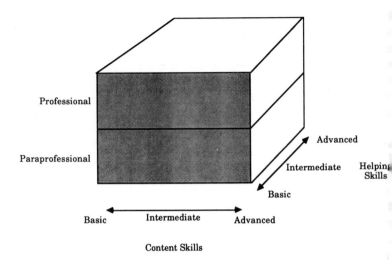

Figure 4.1: Illustration of the various backgrounds and skills
characteristic of home visitors

can be evident. At the professional level, a home visitor could hav
a two-year nursing degree or a master's degree. At the parapro
fessional level, she could have completed the eleventh grade o
could have attended college for two years. Furthermore, bot
salaried and volunteer helpers can have either professional o
nonprofessional backgrounds.

Decisions about training need to consider each of these majo
characteristics. For example, a teacher may have a relevant degre
in education but may not be knowledgeable of the specific curric
ulum used in a program and may have had very little preparatio
for working with families. A social worker may have had consid
erable experience in working with families in a clinic but may nee
to translate some of those skills into working with families withi
the home. A woman may have been a very successful mother bu
may know little about the issues involved in helping parents wh
have abused their children.

In providing for professional development activities, home vis
iting programs should consider existing educational opportun
ties in their community; for example, programs in technica
schools, colleges, and universities (Kubany, Roberts, Furund

Hosaka, & Matsuda, 1989). Home visiting programs should either seek opportunities for their staff in such settings or require such educational experiences before employment. Because most home visiting programs will likely have to provide program-specific or content-specific training activities, they should attempt to use other professional resources for more general training when available and appropriate.

An important resource for the training of home visitors who work with young children and provide parent support is the Child Development Associate (CDA) National Credentialing Program, a national effort to provide training, assessment, and credentialing of both child-care providers and home visitors (Home Visitor, 1987). The credentialing is competency-based, defining the skills needed by caregivers who work in center-based programs serving infants, toddlers, and preschool children; family day-care settings; and home visitor programs. Within the CDA credentialing process, home visitors are trained to provide home visits to families with children 5 years old or younger and to support parents in meeting the needs of their young children. Training is available at over 300 colleges and universities, as well as by day-care and Head Start centers. This credentialing process serves as an initial entry level for many individuals, but we caution that the demands of many programs will necessitate more extensive training.

Program Training Procedures

Training programs need to be designed to provide home visitors with skills and knowledge necessary for their work. The procedures used in such training should maximize the learning process of the trainees. In this section, we will present recommendations for staff training and for the content of a basic home visiting training curriculum. Ideally, the trainees will be active participants in defining the specific content areas and procedures that may best serve their training needs.

We strongly recommend three interrelated training procedures in the training of home visitors: (1) role playing, (2) experiential learning, and (3) peer teaching. Role playing allows the trainee to take turns being the helper, helpee, and observer (Egan, 1975). We have found role playing to be an effective part of our procedures for teaching clinical skills, and have seen role playing prompt home visitors to provide feedback and encouragement to their peers. Because role playing calls for active and physical learning, it is seen as particularly helpful for paraprofessionals (Pearl & Riessman, 1965), but we have found it valuable regardless of a visitor's educational background. Role playing also allows supervisors to gain information about strengths and limitations that can be used to individualize additional training.

Home visitors also learn by actively trying new procedures or behaviors in their own lives. This experimental learning is especially important for helping others learn a problem-solving process. In two programs we conducted in which a problem-solving approach was used, home visitors, as part of their training, first learned the problem-solving processes and then had opportunities to practice these processes on both professional and personal levels in a supportive training environment. Egan (1975) elaborated on the importance of such training, noting that since trainees "are eventually going to place demands on others to live more effectively, I believe that they should begin by placing these kinds of demands on one another" (p. 155).

The third useful training procedure is peer teaching, referred to as the "helper principle" by Pearl and Riessman (1965). This is the process of having more experienced individuals assist and teach beginners in the field. Peer teaching has gained increased acceptance and is used in many training settings. Peer teaching is frequently a part of group supervision settings.

Numerous other writers have described detailed procedures appropriate for training programs and for mastering curriculum objectives (e.g., Mager, 1962, 1972: Mager & Pipe, 1970). Some procedures have been stressed as especially appropriate for paraprofessional training, including on-the-job training, an active participation rather than a lecture approach, and a team approach to build *esprit de corps*. For home visitors, the components of effective training described by Gambrill and Stein (1983; 1978) are particularly relevant. They have described 20 components of effective training programs, listed in Table 4.1. Use of a guide such as Table 4.1 can help assure that training is relevant and presented in ways that are easy to master. The guide helps prompt a focus on mastery of objectives, and it can also serve as a basis for evaluating the outcome of training. Often staff may present training programs or

TABLE 4.1: Components of Effective Training Programs

_____ 1. Outcomes to be achieved through use of new skills are clearly described.

_____ 2. Skills required to achieve these outcomes are clearly described.

_____ 3. Intermediate skills are described.

_____ 4. Clear criteria are identified for assessing whether each skill is present, and for monitoring process.

_____ 5. Each trainee's initial repertoire is evaluated in the situation in which the skill will be used.

_____ 6. Objectives are directly related to required on-the-job tasks.

_____ 7. A step-by-step learning format is used.

_____ 8. More advanced material is withheld until mastery of earlier steps is achieved.

_____ 9. Models of effective performance are presented.

_____10. Models of inappropriate behavior are presented.

_____11. Desirable behaviors are clearly identified during model presentation.

_____12. Trainee attention to modeled behavior is arranged.

_____13. Practice opportunities are offered.

_____14. Immediate feedback on performance is offered based on previously identified criteria on each trainee's initial skill levels.

_____15. Constructive feedback is provided in which progress related to specific behaviors is first noted (see Chapter 9).

_____16. Opportunities for model presentation, practice, and feedback are offered as necessary.

_____17. Arrangements are made for trainees to gradually assume responsibility for evaluating their behavior based on specific criteria.

_____18. Trainees have opportunities to train others in skills they have learned.

_____19. A monitoring system has been designed and implemented so that outcomes achieved through the use of new skills can be tracked on the job.

_____20. Individual worker-supervisor agreements are made for specific performance changes.

SOURCE: Gambrill, E. D., & Stein, T. J. (1983). _Supervision: A decision-making approach_ (p. 145). Beverly Hills, CA: Sage.

particular topics, such as child management, spouse abuse, or nonverbal clients, that include excellent coverage of content but that do not focus on specifying the objectives of the training, identifying the skills required to attain the objectives, or determining ways to monitor new skill acquisition.

Basic Knowledge and Skills

In developing training programs, administrators should assure that they build on the existing knowledge and expertise in the field. Training of home visitors needs to be individualized according to program goals, family characteristics, and home visitor credentials. We also believe that there is a core of fundamental knowledge and skills that should be a part of all home visiting programs. Table 4.2 provides an outline of these fundamental areas, which are elaborated upon below.

History. People who work in various fields are often interested in the history of their field, and such knowledge can help provide a sense of pride and professionalism. We have found home visitors to be interested in the historical aspects of this field and in learning about other home visiting programs elsewhere in the country. Making this type of information available during the early weeks of employment helps visitors place their work in perspective. Those who come from professional areas, such as social work or nursing, may know the history in their own field, but will likely not know of the breadth of home visiting across disciplines. Those who do not have a professional background in a particular area are especially interested in the history because it helps them see their work in relation to other efforts in society while also providing a sense of professional identity. Additional information on the history of home visiting beyond that presented in Chapter 1 of this book is available by Holbrook (1983) on social work, Buhler-Wilkerson (1985) and Monteiro (1985) on nursing, and Levine and Levine (1970) who present information on the history of both visiting teachers and social workers. Interesting accounts of home visiting in Europe are available in books by Wagner and Wagner (1976) and Glendinning (1986).

Philosophy. Program directors need to present information on their program philosophy and goals so that expectations for home visitors are clear. Program philosophy provides information on

TABLE 4.2: Basic Content of a Home Visitor Training Program

I. History of Home Visiting

II. Philosophy of Home Visiting

III. Knowledge and Skills of the Helping Process

   1. Basic and advanced clinical skills
   2. Professional and ethical issues

IV. Knowledge of Families and Children

   1. Prenatal/perinatal development
   2. Child development
   3. Child management
   4. Family Systems Theory
   5. Health and safety
   6. Special issues (e.g., child abuse and neglect alcoholism, drugs, spouse abuse, chronically ill child)

V. Knowledge and Skills Specific to Programs

   1. Program goals and procedures
   2. Record-keeping and documentation
   3. Curriculum

VI. Knowledge and Skills Specific to Communities

   1. Cultural characteristics
   2. Health and human service resources
   3. Other pertinent community resources
   4. Transportation issues

---

the major beliefs and values that govern program policies and procedures. It typically includes information on the type of clients to be served and the type of services to be offered. A program might state its philosophy in the following way: "It is our objective to help reduce the incidence of child abuse and neglect in this county. We believe poor parenting skills are a major contributor to child abuse, and we plan to work collaboratively with families to help them reduce the incidence of abuse."

Of particular importance in program philosophy is the role home visitors are to play. We have mentioned that historically many programs promoted an authoritarian role, one in which the visitor was the expert who typically worked with one family member. This approach, however, is seen as interfering with active parent participation and, consequently, many programs have shifted to an approach in which the visitor is a collaborator and facilitator with parents. To accomplish this philosophical shift, home visitors must be taught how to perform in the role of collaborator and facilitator.

Programs that are guided by specific philosophies should present material to their home visitors that describes those philosophies. In the Infant Health and Development Program, our philosophy of helping families was presented to home visitors through workshops and was described in a training manual. The Head Start Home Visitor Handbook is a good example of material that describes a program's philosophy (Wolfe & Herwig, 1986; Boyd & Herwig, 1980). Recent writings on the philosophy of parent support that are relevant for home visitors are the summary by Johnson et al. (1989) on the implementation of PL 99-457 and the edited volume, *America's Family Support Programs* by Kagan et al. (1987).

Knowledge and Skills of the Helping Process. Several areas of knowledge and skills are common across all home visiting programs, including basic and advanced helping skills, and professional and ethical issues. In this book, we have provided information on these topics that can serve as an introduction to these areas or as a general review. Training programs should supplement these materials with additional discussions, readings, and supervision. Additional resources on helping skills include books by Egan (1975), Cormier, Cormier, and Weisser (1984), and Benjamin (1975).

Knowledge of Families and Children. Knowledge of families and children is an essential prerequisite for those who work in family support programs. Previously, if one worked with handicapped children, it was possible to be an expert on particular handicapping conditions and not know much about families. Family-focused programs, however, require knowledge about the needs, strengths, and values of families. Helpers also need knowledge and skills specific for working with parents and with parent-child dyads. Knowledge about the stages of family development and basic information on family systems theory are also essential for understanding family needs and the implications of intervention programs.

Home visitors also need to have basic knowledge in the following areas: prenatal/perinatal development, child development, child management, health and safety, and life-span development, as well as information on special family needs, such as alcohol or drug abuse, spouse or child abuse, or handicapped children. Home visitors will not become experts in all these areas, but their knowledge must be sufficient to assure they can respond appropriately when visiting in a variety of clients' homes. Their knowledge base should allow them to recognize situations that call for additional services and be able to make referrals as necessary. For example, they may encounter mild depression among some of their clients, and the home visiting services may help alleviate some of the causes of the depression. However, the visitor needs to recognize more severe depression and know when she should call on other professionals or seek emergency assistance. In Chapter 7, we describe some of the issues important in working with families with special needs that illustrate the type of knowledge necessary for those who work with families over sustained periods of time.

Knowledge and Skills Specific to Programs. The directors of each home visiting program need to assure that visitors receive an adequate orientation to their program, becoming familiar with goals, procedures, record-keeping, documentation, and curriculum. Again, the *Head Start Home Visitor Handbook* and the *Serving Handicapped Children in Home-Based Head Start* are helpful models for the preparation of training materials.

Written materials provide an extremely valuable resource for informing home visitors of essential program procedures. Such materials can provide step-by-step instructions for what to do in specific situations, particularly those that might be dangerous. As an example of the kind of detail that might be provided by a program, the Hawaii Healthy Start Program provided its visitors with a step-by-step guide of who to call, who to speak with, and in what order telephone calls were to be made when the visitor suspected that a home situation was potentially unsafe for the care of a newborn.

Many programs have developed specific training materials and detailed guidelines for use by home visitors. Examples include the *Partners for Learning* curriculum by Sparling and Lewis (1984) that has been used with children from many different ethnic and social backgrounds, as well as with low birthweight infants and infants with cerebral palsy. The detailed curriculum materials of the Kupalani Project in Hawaii incorporated Hawaiian traditions into child and parent activities (Roberts, 1988), an example that other programs should follow when serving specific ethnic populations.

Knowledge and Skills Specific to Communities. Communities can and do vary considerably along many dimensions. Ethnic composition, income, employment rate, cohesiveness, values, resources, and safety are some of the important community dimensions that may influence home visiting. Several sources of information exist in each community for obtaining knowledge about its characteristics. Individuals associated with business and civic groups, as well as staff of other public or private service agencies, can often provide very useful information.

Summary

Though we have outlined what we believe are valuable components of any training program, we need to underscore that the most important guideline for training is that it should fit the program's goals and home visitor's needs. A second guideline is that training should be of sufficient duration and intensity to assure that home visitors are competent to meet the program objectives and feel confident of their skills in doing so. Such training needs to be an integral part of program budgets so that the necessary time and materials can be available.

Training also serves an evaluation role. Regardless of how carefully one conducts the hiring procedures, some individuals who are employed may not be appropriate for the job. Reasons can range from their initial misunderstanding of job demands to their inability to implement the program procedures. Trainees who do not exhibit a criterion level of skills and knowledge following training should not be continued in the position of home visitor.

Supervision

Supervision—a relationship with another person that fosters professional growth—should have a preeminent role in home visiting programs and be regularly provided for all visitors, though its frequency and intensity will vary as a function of needs.

Home visiting is a front-line, stressful position that can be lonely and at times frustrating. Visitors generally work alone and away from coworkers during a normal day, and thus do not have daily contact with peers. The work itself can be physically tiring and emotionally draining because home visitors continually encounter families facing many of life's most pressing problems (Barnard, Magyary, Sumner, Booth, Mitchell, & Spieker, 1988). Being able to discuss their specific concerns about families with other knowledgeable people is often very productive for home visitors and can also serve as a stress-reduction process. In describing the important role of supervision in social work, Kadushin (1976) made a similar observation: "There are few professions that come close to social work in developing in the worker the need for support, encouragement, reassurance, and restoration of morale—a need met by supportive supervision" (p. 35).

In addition to being critical for morale, supervision has also been described as essential for maintaining objectivity and professional competence (Hardy-Brown, Miller, Dean, Carrasco, & Thompson, 1987). In research programs, such as the Infant Health and Development Program, supervision also served to prevent "program drift"—a situation in which individuals tend to drift away from the specified objectives and goals.

Boyd defined supervision in a way that is relevant for home visiting, describing it as that aspect of training or practice that includes the "function of overseeing a trainee's work for the purpose of facilitating personal and professional development, improving competencies, and promoting accountability in services and programs" (1978, p. 27). Clearly, supervision is a multidimensional role.

Because programs vary in their goals for supervisors, to reduce ambiguities concerning expectations during supervision both the supervisor and the home visitor in any particular program should understand the supervisor's role. Ekstein (1972) described the supervisor's roles as administrator, teacher, and therapist. We believe that the nature of home visiting calls for supervision that includes support, teaching, program management, and evaluation. If the supervisor is mainly an administrator, then supervision may be focused solely on the caseload, transportation concerns, or working conditions. A supervisor who views her role primarily as a teacher may focus upon teaching specific techniques or content the visitor needs. A supervisor who sees her role primarily as therapist may emphasize the visitor's feelings and satisfaction with her work and provide emotional support. No one role is inherently more appropriate than another, and effective supervisors switch roles as needed.

Gambrill and Stein (1983) suggested that the many separate tasks of supervisors (administrative, educational, and supportive) are really closely related and that information gained from one task is relevant for carrying out another task. Some programs, however, have divided certain supervisory roles from the evaluation roles to enable home visitors to express their opinions or feelings within supervision without being concerned that these opinions or feelings could jeopardize their jobs. In the Hawaii Kupalani Project, for example, a consulting psychologist was employed primarily as a support person or therapist. She was not asked to provide an evaluation of the home visitors' work, thus reducing inhibitions that may have occurred otherwise.

We recommend that all home visitors have professional supervision. Clearly, the nature and intensity of supervision will differ, but all visitors should have a trusting person with whom they can discuss their experiences and can receive feedback and support. Those who practice independently or privately should seek out professional support groups to provide constructive opportunities for discussing day-by-day issues and to provide a resource for professional growth.

Supervisory Formats

Supervision can take place individually, in a group, or in the field. Each format has its advantages and limitations. Individual supervision can be more intensive, respond more fully to an individual's needs, and be more personal. Group supervision provides opportunities for learning from peers and recognizing that many problems in home visiting are common to other visitors. It is also an excellent setting for role playing and peer teaching. On-site or field-based supervision provides the supervisor with firsthand knowledge of the home and family situation and allows observation and feedback on the visitor's actual performance.

Some programs provide supervision in all formats. The most commonly reported supervision in family-focused programs is weekly individual supervision, followed by weekly group supervision (Wasik & Roberts, 1989b). On-site or field-based supervision is the least frequently used supervision format, possibly because it is the most time-consuming, and, hence, expensive. Programs should consider providing supervision in all these formats because each format has advantages. A program could, for example, provide weekly individual supervision, monthly group supervision and bimonthly on-site supervision. The format and frequency should be responsive to the needs of the home visitors and may change over time.

An example of a project that used several supervisory formats is the Families Facing the Future project in Pittsburgh in which individuals with no prerequisite skills or experience were employed. All visitors had three weekly opportunities for supervision, first with their direct supervisor in a one-to-one conference where personal issues, quality and quantity of work, or case discussion took place. Second, a group session was held with the program coordinator to discuss program policy, roles, and responsibilities. Other possible topics during group supervision were business issues or program problem solving. In addition to these supervisory sessions, the home visitors met with a mental health professional in the community as part of a weekly process group. This professional, selected by the visitors themselves, helped the visitors discuss interpersonal issues among themselves or with other staff or their clients (Mulvey, 1988). The supervisory variability in this project served to match the purpose of supervision with its format.

Evaluation in Supervision

Evaluation of visitors is a professional responsibility that may be a part of supervision, and is usually at least a yearly requirement of staff in many organizations. The stresses typically involved in evaluation can be reduced by assuring that individuals know what is expected of them and on what criteria they will be evaluated. If the evaluation occurs within a supportive environment and in a timely manner, it can give helpful feedback to home visitors and serve as an opportunity to improve their performance. Written evaluation forms that identify the person's responsibilities, program expectations, and the evaluation procedures help home visitors to understand the evaluation process clearly. Visitors especially need to know how evaluation information will be used. In some agencies, evaluations may directly influence salary raises from one year to another.

Supervisory Models

Several supervisory models have been proposed as a way of helping supervisors carry out their responsibilities. For social workers, Gambrill and Stein (1983) proposed a decision-making approach to supervision based upon the many decisions supervisors have to make and the ones they help others to make. To facilitate the supervisor's decision-making role, Gambrill and Stein presented a detailed guide for supervisors in the major areas in which they make decisions. In some areas, the supervisor may need to discuss decisions of the home visitor on selecting clients or identifying assessment and intervention actions. At other times, supervisors will be involved in decision-making related to service coordination, staff competence, and training programs.

A second model for supervision is that of problem solving, described by Wasik and Fishbein (1982) and Bartky (1953). In this model the processes of problem solving in general are viewed as synonymous with the goals of supervision. Supervisors use the processes as a guide to identify strengths and weaknesses of the supervisee and to help the supervisee improve his or her professional problem solving skills.

It is not surprising that models of supervision would mirror models for practice in the profession itself because supervision has much in common with the helping relationship established between a helper and a client. It is important for supervisors to select a model or philosophy that guides their work. To be maximally effective, their beliefs and procedures should be compatible with those the home visitors are expected to use with families.

Hiring Procedures

Because the interview is so important in the employment decision, specific recommendations for the conduct and content of the interview are provided here. Employment procedures should involve, at a minimum, a review of the applicant's résumé, an interview, and information from references. In this chapter, we will focus on the interview process. Though we have identified a number of areas about which the interviewer needs to obtain information, the interviewer should make sure he or she does not dominate the interview by too much talking, but rather makes sure the applicant has ample opportunity to describe his or her background and experiences and ask questions about the position.

Interviewing

A well-conducted interview should provide information to help the program directors decide whether they want to employ the applicant. Interviews also serve to provide the applicant with an opportunity to find out enough about the position to determine whether she wants the job. We recommend that the personnel interviewer do the following: (1) assure that all important program goals are explained and understood by the applicant, (2) assure that the visitor's specific work responsibilities are identified, (3) assure that all expectations concerning supervision, evaluation, and professional development are identified, (4) provide salary, other staff benefits, and information, and (5) assess the interpersonal characteristics of the applicant. Each of these areas is discussed below.

(1) Program goals. The goals and objectives should be made clear in the interview. Even when program directors are very knowledgeable about the goals and objectives of their program, it is easy for another person to misunderstand what the program is trying to accomplish and what his or her role will be. Because many programs serve families with a multitude of needs, it is important to identify areas that are excluded from program responsibility.

(2) Visitor responsibilities. It is very important for all programs to make sure that specific home visitor responsibilities are discussed during the interview. As one example of what can happen when responsibilities are not initially defined, we worked with home visitors who became concerned when they learned, *after* they were employed, that they would be responsible for providing their own transportation to the homes of clients. The implications of this expectation were too important to have been omitted in the interview.

The following areas of visitor responsibility or work conditions are also ones that should be discussed during an interview. In addition, programs will want to add items specific to their situations.

(a) *Work setting.* Information about office space and working conditions for those times when the home visitor is not in the field should be specified. Since visitors are often out in the community, programs may assign limited space or may assign several visitors to one office. Though there are understandable reasons for this practice, information on the office space conditions should be provided; ideally, the facilities would be shown to the applicant.

(b) *Report preparation.* Information should be provided on the expectations for report preparation or program documentation. When possible, the applicant could be given completed examples of the types of reports required by the program.

(c) *Work hours.* The home visitor should be made aware of the program expectation for general work hours and for work at other times, for example, attending evening parent group meetings or making weekend or evening home visits. Most programs expect some evening hours, and this expectation needs to be clear during the interview process so that future misunderstandings can be reduced.

(b) *Work expenses.* On-the-job expenses of the home visitor that are reimbursed by the program should be identified. In particular, information should be provided about mileage reimbursement, car insurance, or other transportation expenses.

(3) *Supervision, Evaluation, and Professional Development.* The degree of autonomy with which the visitor can function should be described in the interview, and the program expectations for the home visitor's involvement in supervision should be explained clearly. This explanation should include information on the frequency and type of supervision. If on-site supervision is part of the program, the home visitor should be made aware that her field performance will be observed and by whom.

Program evaluation procedures for home visitor performance should be specified, particularly if the program has a probation period. The applicant should be told what work will be reviewed and the criteria on which her work will be evaluated. She also needs to be informed of the type of evaluation procedures that are

TABLE 4.3: Interpersonal Rating Scale for Interviewing Home Visitor Applicants

	Not Adequate	Adequate	Good	Excellent
Rapport	1	2	3	4
Warmth	1	2	3	4
Motivation	1	2	3	4
Self-Confidence	1	2	3	4
Tolerance	1	2	3	4
Flexibility	1	2	3	4
Maturity	1	2	3	4
Calm/Reflective	1	2	3	4
Cultural Sensitivity	1	2	3	4
Empathy	1	2	3	4

used, when evaluation occurs, and how she will be informed of the evaluation results.

Any expectations for ongoing professional development, including costs and time, should be identified. If the program requires attendance at weekend or evening professional training sessions, applicants should be informed during the interview so they can determine whether the job requirements are ones they are willing to accept.

(4) *Salary and Other Staff Benefits.* The program needs to describe the salary and staff benefits, including vacation time, sick leave, and any other benefits (for example, health insurance, life insurance, retirement, and tuition fees for continuing education). If written policies exist, these should be made available.

(5) *Interpersonal Characteristics.* To help determine interpersonal characteristics, we strongly recommend that part of the selection process include a carefully conducted interview. We also recommend that a rating form be completed immediately after the interview to provide qualitative judgments on the applicant's interpersonal characteristics and to facilitate a comparative evaluation of multiple applicants. We have constructed an interview rating form, seen in Table 4.3, that provides a guide for evaluating applicants during the interview process. In this rating form, we have included those interpersonal skills identified most often in the field as important characteristics for home visitors. Programs may also want to have more than one person conduct interviews

with the same applicant. The collective judgments of the interviewers should facilitate accuracy in hiring decisions.

We also recommend that during the latter part of the interview, the applicant be presented with additional interview questions on home visiting in order to provide information on the applicant's attitudes and beliefs about children, families, and home visiting, as well as information about how the applicant might respond in difficult situations related to home visiting. We recognize that what a person says he or she might do in a particular situation is not always consistent with what they would actually do, but these questions will help assess an applicant's beliefs, ability to problem-solve, ability to respond under stress, and resourcefulness.

Table 4.4 contains several sample interview questions that could be used to prompt information useful in making judgments about an applicant's potential effectiveness as a home visitor. There are three categories of questions: children and families, home visiting situations, and the home visiting position. Although several interview questions are listed, an applicant would be asked to respond to only some of these. Interviewers may want to substitute examples that are directly pertinent to their own communities, population, or content.

Interviewers need to know how to interpret an applicant's responses in such interview situations. The interviewer is not necessarily looking for one "right" answer because several different responses could be acceptable. In listening to the applicant's response, the interviewer may want to consider its reasonableness, its potential effectiveness, its sensitivity to the family, and whether or not it suggests resourcefulness and willingness to consider alternative options.

Summary

We have discussed three components of home visiting programs most directly related to the visitor: credentials, professional development, and supervision. We have also made suggestions for the hiring process. The component that has received the most attention in the home visiting literature has been the area of credentials, specifically focused on employing professional or paraprofessional visitors. This issue is grounded in the traditions and

TABLE 4.4: Sample Interview Questions

Children and Families

Directions: The interviewer should lead into these questions with an appropriate introduction so that the applicant does not feel like this is a
"test" where he or she must give one "right" answer. For example,
as a lead-in to some attitudes questions, the interviewer could
say, "Our current home visitors have different backgrounds in their
work with families. What experience have you had?"

Have you had experience with unwed mothers? Teenage mothers? What did you think about the experience?

How do you feel about mothers of infants who are on welfare?

What do you believe about the number of children a person
should have? Could you elaborate?

What kind of person makes a good mother?

Should a baby be picked up if he is crying, or should he be left
alone?

What do you think about the timing for toilet training children?

What do you think is most important for fathers to do when caring
for infants?

What do children need the most from their families?

Home Visiting Situations

Directions: As a lead-in to this area, the interviewer might say, "Many home
visits proceed in a fairly routine manner, but sometimes problems
occur. What would you say or do if you arrived for a home visit
and found that:
  – The mother had a number of noisy friends visiting her?
  – No one was there?
  – No one was there for the third visit in a row?
  – The whole family was watching television and you couldn't
    hear the parent talk?
  – The parent was drunk?
  – The mother had lost the materials you had left her and did not
    remember what you had done the last time?
  – The mother was sad and crying?
  – The father had left the baby alone with a seven-year-old child?

(Continued)

TABLE 4.4: Sample Interview Questions (Continued)

How would you handle the following situations?

- The baby has a runny nose, and the mother hands him to you for a "hello" kiss.
- The baby's older brother and sister want you to play with them.
- You must miss a visit but the family has no telephone.
- The mother gives her children soda pop and potato chips for lunch instead of nutritional foods.
- The toys you had left on loan are broken.

The Home Visiting Position

Directions: These questions are designed to obtain information on values related to home visiting and whether there is a good match between the applicant and the position. The interviewer should select two or three questions that best fit the particular interview situation.

What would your ideal job be like? Could you tell me why this job interests you? Are there some parts you would not like?

Could you tell me why you think you would be good for this position?

What do you think the benefits of this program might be for the clients? For you?

What would you do if the program director asked you to convey some information with which you disagree?

How would it affect you if you had to make visits in the late afternoon, at night, or on weekends?

history of home visiting, in which both professionals and paraprofessionals have provided family support in the home. We do not recommend one over the other. Rather, we strongly endorse a philosophy of matching credentials to program goals and procedures. Such matching may lead to creative models for service delivery in which professional and nonprofessional home visitors work together in teams.

Home visiting is a process used by many different professional groups and service agencies and serves a multitude of needs. One strength of home visiting is its diversity. While we endorse such diversity, we also strongly endorse rigor in selecting, training and

supervising home visitors. If administrators and practitioners believe that home visiting has the potential for effectively helping
families, then the corollary must be also accepted, namely that
home visiting has the potential for being ineffective or even harmful. To ensure the most effective services, careful attention must
be devoted to all aspects of the employment of home visitors and
future research efforts should direct attention to improving the
hiring and training process.

5

Helping Skills and Techniques

At the heart of home visiting is the relationship between the home visitor and her client, a relationship established for the purpose of providing some type of help over a period of time. This relationship is so basic to home visiting programs that the program objectives cannot be met if a good interaction is not established. It is a process through which one can assess family priorities, convey information, provide support and encouragement, be an advocate, and promote self-reliance and effective coping. Its importance has been supported in research by Beck and Jones (1973), who found a strong, highly significant correlation between the outcome of treatment and the quality of the helper-client relationship. Hollis and Wood (1981) have described it as a powerful tool in the field of social work, noting that "successful treatment depends heavily on the quality of this relationship" (p. 284).

The helping relationship itself can be defined as having three basic elements: a person seeking help, a capable or trained person willing to provide help, and a setting that permits help to be given and received (Hackney & Cormier, 1979). A major purpose of this relationship is to facilitate behavioral changes that can bring about a higher level of satisfaction and self-confidence. The home visitor's role in this relationship is to help her clients clarify their goals and work toward obtaining them.

Many synonyms exist for the helping relationship: psychotherapy, counseling, casework, crisis intervention, and education
being among them. There are a number of writers, however, who
have distinguished the procedures of the helping process from
crisis intervention and psychotherapy (Brammer & Shostrom,
1982; Cormier, Cormier, & Weisser, 1984). Psychotherapy can be
defined as an intensive introspective analysis that focuses on
self-understanding and addresses long-standing behavior problems, dynamics, or personality traits. It is generally of long-term
duration. Crisis intervention is an action-oriented effort to provide immediate help in an emergency situation and is usually time
limited. In a helping relationship, the focus is on problem solving,
decision-making, and adaptive coping (Brammer & Shostrom,
1982), and the helping goals can be defined as developmental,
educative, and preventive in nature. Because of the diversity of
professions and programs using home visiting, any one of the
three interventions could be found in home visiting programs.
Many social workers are trained to provide therapeutic or psychiatric casework that could also be described as psychotherapy.
Almost all home visitors will be involved in crisis intervention at
some time; we have seen the need for crisis help arise in every
program we have conducted. Though these other interventions
may occur, we believe that the characteristics of the helping relationship best capture the type of interactions appropriate for most
home visiting situations.

To be effective as a helper, a number of skills and procedures are
essential. The home visitor must be a reasonably competent clinician; that is, she must be able to listen carefully to the meaning of
what the family tells her; she must be sensitive to verbal and
nonverbal communication from the family about its desires and
goals; she must be able to assess difficulties the family is encoun-
tering that interfere with effective problem solving; and she must
be able to promote those skills, knowledge, attitudes, and environmental conditions that contribute to effective coping. In describing these skills, we are aware of a paradox that currently exists in
the field: The role of the home visitor is often described as enabling
parents to learn to cope more effectively and to learn problem-
solving and decision-making skills, but few programs are providing the training necessary for home visitors to carry out these
objectives. In this chapter, we will first discuss four sets of charac-

eristics and skills essential for effective helping relationships: helper characteristics, basic helping skills, specific helping techniques, and behavioral change procedures. A problem-solving approach will then be presented as a model that incorporates these four categories of helping skills into an integrated process for providing home visiting services.

Helper Characteristics

Most home visitor programs identify *communication* and *interpersonal skills* as essential characteristics for their home visitors; program directors say they are looking for "a warm, caring person" when describing the personal characteristics of home visitors. Though these terms are general, one can identify specific behaviors that capture these characteristics of helpers.

One of the more generally accepted and useful descriptions of helper characteristics was proposed by Rogers (1951, 1957) and has been used by Truax and Carkhuff (1967), Egan (1975, 1982), and Cormier, et al. (1984). These characteristics are considered the critical abilities needed to establish an effective helping relationship: (1) empathy, (2) respect, and (3) genuineness. Empathy is the ability to understand and relate to another person's feelings and actions as though they were one's own. Respect is the ability to regard another person with worth and dignity (Rogers, 1957). Respect involves a commitment to the client, an effort to understand the client, nonjudgmental attitudes, and warmth. Genuineness is the ability of a person to convey sincerity and to be congruent in one's words and actions.

Cormier and her colleagues have elaborated on these three characteristics in a clear and instructive manner. Because their presentation seems particularly helpful for home visitors, we have incorporated it into Table 5.1. For each characteristic, they have presented a definition, described the purposes of the characteristic, and then made specific suggestions for the type of helper behaviors that can convey these important elements. They have included guidelines from the writings of Carkhuff (1969), Egan (1982), Rausch and Bordin (1957), and Seay and Altkreuse (1979).

The information in Table 5.1 describing helper behaviors can be used during training, for self-evaluation, for supervisory feed-

TABLE 5.1: Fundamental Helper Characteristics

Condition	Purposes	Guidelines for Use
Empathy (The capacity to respond to the client's feelings and experiences as if they were your own; the ability to communicate accurate understanding of the client)	1. To establish rapport 2. To show understanding and support 3. To demonstrate civility 4. To clarify problems 5. To collect information	1. Concentrate with intensity on the client's verbal and nonverbal messages 2. Use silence to assimilate the material before responding 3. Formulate and deliver a verbal response that is equivalent to the message expressed by the client 4. Make the verbal response concise 5. Use language that is similar to that used by the client 6. Respond in a nonverbal manner that is congruent with the client's feelings
Respect (The ability to see a person with worth and dignity; consists of commitment, understanding, nonjudgmental attitude, and warmth)	1. To communicate a willingness to work with the client 2. To communicate interest 3. To communicate acceptance of the client 4. To communicate caring to the client 5. To provide an outlet for and to diminish the client's angry feelings	1. Reserve specified amount of time and energy for client's use 2. Interact with client without "hurrying" 3. Indicate, with questions or comments, interest in and efforts to understand the client 4. Convey understanding of client without overt approval or disapproval 5. Comment on positive aspects or attitudes of client 6. Express differences of opinion with comments that support rather than criticize client's ideas 7. Support verbal expressions with appropriate nonverbal behaviors of respect and warmth
Genuineness (The ability to be yourself without presenting a facade)	1. To reduce the emotional distance between interviewer and client 2. To increase the identification process between interviewer and client, thereby providing rapport and trust	1. Be congruent; make sure verbal messages, nonverbal behavior, and feelings are consistent 2. Be aware of any inconsistencies in your messages and behaviors 3. Avoid overemphasizing your role, position, status, or authority 4. Be spontaneous—do not constantly ponder what to say, and yet at the same time be tactful 5. Express genuineness and supporting nonverbal behaviors, such as direct eye contact, smiling, and leaning toward the client

back, and as suggested areas to observe and discuss during role-playing experiences. For example, one guideline for empathy is that the helper should use language that is similar to that used by the client. This guideline is particularly important for assuring that the helper conveys to the client that she understands what is being said to her, and that she does not introduce erroneous meanings by using different words. During a role-playing situation, a home visitor could practice identifying and using key words introduced by a person playing the role of client. Using audio tapes of home visiting situations can make it possible for both the home visitor and supervisor to determine how responsive the visitor is to the client's words. Many of the other behaviors listed in Table 5.1 can be focused on in a similar manner.

Fundamental Helping Skills

A number of specific skills and techniques are fundamental across the helping professions. They include those verbal and nonverbal communication behaviors that set the tone of an interaction and that help one person assist another in accomplishing a goal or dealing with some difficulty. Many people attracted to the helping professions already have some of these skills, but to be most effective, they need continuing practice on the specific techniques and strategies described below. Supervision from a skilled individual is essential in order to receive appropriate feedback on style and skill.

We believe that an understanding of these skills provides the home visitor with information on how she can interact with families in a way that is constructive, supportive, and effective. Visitors who have poor communication skills cannot establish the necessary relationship needed to help families. Visitors who are not sensitive listeners will not know what their clients' real needs are. Visitors who cannot support, encourage, model, or prompt desired actions of their clients will not be helping their clients reach their goals. And visitors who are not knowledgeable of basic behavioral change procedures cannot be effective in helping clients deal with day-by-day concerns.

The basic helping or interviewing skills we will discuss are: (1) observing, (2) listening, (3) questioning, (4) probing, and

(5) prompting. These skills help assure clear communication be
tween the visitor and client and allow information to be obtained
that is essential for developing intervention programs. There are
other more advanced clinical skills, such as interpreting and con
fronting, but we consider them to be beyond the scope of this
chapter.

During any visit with a family, the objectives of the verbal
interactions may change. Some of the time, the visitor will be
obtaining information useful in understanding the family's situa
tion or in planning with the family how to cope with a particular
stressful event. At other times, the visitor will use the interactions
to provide emotional support or will encourage a person to keep
working on a difficult task. Some people are more adept than
others at shifting from one purpose to another, but as a visitor
gains more experience with different types of verbal interaction,
she will become better at shifting, for example, from a questioning
mode to a listening mode, and better at knowing when these
changes are appropriate. Knowledge of the various clinical skills
and how they can be effectively used to accomplish the goals of
home visiting can enhance a home visitor's effectiveness.

Observation

Observation may be the most important clinical skill needed by
the home visitor. Observation allows her to obtain information
essential in understanding the clients she is serving. Home visit
ing provides unique opportunities for observation. In contrast to
a clinic, hospital, or school setting, home visiting provides the
opportunity for an ecological assessment of individuals and their
families and communities. From the time the home visitor begins
her trip to the client's home, she should be aware of the broader
environment in which the client lives, noting such things as access
to other community services (including transportation, medical
and educational agencies), the safety of the neighborhood, and
recreational and cultural opportunities. Such information will
help the home visitor put into perspective her later discussions
with the client and also provide a knowledge base that she can
draw on when making suggestions about resources.

Once in the home, observation takes on additional importance.
The organization of the home and the resources available to pro

vide for basic living enable the home visitor to understand more about her client's strengths and coping strategies, the material resources available to the client, and the limitations imposed by her home environment. For example, when working with parents of a developmentally delayed child, the visitor may note that there are very few children's materials in the home and may question about the parents' knowledge of child development. She may find that the initial hypothesis she drew from her observation of the home was supported during interviews with the parents. She would then likely have discussions with the parent that would be different from those she would have had if she had found the home equipped with many child-appropriate materials, including books, toys, and play equipment.

Assessing the resources through observation in the home is particularly important for those providing medical assistance. Being aware of physical barriers in the home, for example, may help the visitor understand why a person may have difficulty complying with a medical routine. A broken refrigerator would help explain why a mother was not keeping milk available for her children and could alert the home visitor to other potential health problems.

In addition to information on environmental and physical resources, home observation provides a particularly advantageous situation for noting how the family members interact with one another. Often in clinic visits, professionals interact with only one member of the family. Through home visits, one can see how family members contribute to each individual's overall well-being or dysfunction, and may obtain clues for what might be done to assist the family. Observation also makes possible program documentation or other record-keeping required by many programs.

Systematic observation, a more formal procedure used both in research and in practice to record actual behavior (Wasik, 1984), also has a place in home visiting. It is used when more objective information on the actual occurrence of events is desired. Under some circumstances or for some purposes, it may be extremely helpful for the family if the visitor actually records how often a specific behavior occurs as part of the process for deciding how to deal with the behavior. Such procedures are particularly valuable for helping families learn how to manage their child's behavior. They are often a part of many programs that help parents learn to manage the behavior of hyperactive children. Systematic observation is also employed to help parents who abuse their children to learn positive, effective behavior management techniques. Helping a parent change from a punitive, primarily negative way of handling a child to a more positive, reinforcing way of interacting can be facilitated by self-recording procedures, such as teaching parents to count the number of times they respond positively or negatively to their child. Helping a parent learn to record the words that a child with a speech problem says during part of the day may be an important part of an assessment procedure for speech difficulties. Having a parent learn to record the number of times a particular physical therapy routine is carried out could be very important for increasing compliance with a treatment program.

Overall, observation skills can serve as a basis of information for many intervention decisions made during home visiting. Such information, however, should always be obtained in a manner that remains sensitive to and respectful of the fact that one is a visitor in the home of the family, and such information should not be used to make value judgments on life-styles.

Listening

The ability of the home visitor to be an effective listener is critical to establishing rapport, building trust, and learning information necessary to provide assistance. It is important to listen to both the words and the meaning of the client's discussions in order to help determine the client's concerns, priorities, and resources, as well as her strengths and limitations in coping with her own life. Careful listening provides the home visitor with important knowledge about the client's emotional status, and can help the home visitor gauge changes in the client's emotional well-being from one time to another.

Several guidelines can be used to improve home visitors' listening skills. First, the visitor can make sure she has allowed the client ample time to respond to questions, to talk about what has happened since the last visit, to describe things of importance to her, or to discuss particular goals. Second, the visitor should attend to her own body language and words to assure they convey a message of support and interest in what the client is saying. Contradictory messages, such as acting restless while encouraging a member of the family to talk, can discourage and confuse that person.

Third, while listening, the visitor needs to be mentally alert, sorting through what she is hearing so that she can respond to any information or unspoken message the client is sending to her. Inattentiveness is a frequent cause of misunderstanding, and a home visitor should work to reduce the likelihood of misunderstandings by careful attending. A home visitor can ask herself questions while listening, such as, "Is this concern similar to ones I have heard this father talk about before?" or "Is this reaction similar to the one this person had several weeks ago? If so, what did we learn from that event that can help now?" The importance of listening is underscored by the evaluations of families who positively evaluate their home visitor by saying, "She really listened to me," or "She heard what I said."

Questioning

Questioning is part of the verbal interchanges that naturally occur between individuals, and can have a particularly facilitative effect during the verbal interactions of the home visitor and family members. Long, Paradise, and Long (1981) have presented an excellent description of the role of questioning in the helping process. Although the use of questions in interviewing procedures has been discouraged by some (e.g., Egan, 1975; Gordon, 1974), clearly there are advantages as well as disadvantages in using questions. Concerns about the use of questions are based in part upon the overuse of questions by the unskilled interviewer and, in part, because the inappropriate use of questions can hinder the communication between the helper and the client. However, when used appropriately, questioning has an extremely important role to play in facilitating the interactions between the visitor and her clients. For this reason, it is important for the visitor to learn the appropriate use of questions, and to learn how to avoid using questions in a way that interferes with good communication.

For our purposes, we selected a set of questions that seem particularly suitable for the home visiting process, namely (a) those that help begin the interview, or initial questions, (b) open-ended questions, (c) facilitating questions, (d) clarifying questions, and (e) focusing questions. Familiarity with these different types of questions and skill in using them will enhance the ability of the home visitor to be more effective with clients.

(a) *Initial questions.* A home visitor beginning with a new client needs skills that help start the interview, establish rapport, and begin to build trust. The appropriate use of questions during this early time period can help make the client and the home visitor feel more at ease, and can help convey to the client that the visitor is there to offer help in a nonjudgmental way. Questions asked during this time should encourage the client to talk about topics of his or her choice. To facilitate the initial visits, the home visitor may suggest topics related to the nature of the visit. For example, in a program providing visiting for parents of low birthweight babies, many home visitors found that asking questions about the birth of the baby was a good way to engage a mother in discussion during the first interview. The home visitors found questions like the following to be valuable: "This was your first child. What was it like for you?" or "Could you tell me about your baby?" A mother who is somewhat nonverbal might respond more easily if she is asked to tell about a typical day with her newborn.

(b) *Open-ended questions.* Open-ended questions are especially useful during the initial interview because they do not restrict the kinds of responses the client can give to the visitor. Using the example of the visitor with the parent of a low birthweight infant, the visitor might ask the parent the following: "What were some of the things you had to change in your life during the first few days you were home with your baby?" Questions asked in this manner will encourage the client to talk more than an initial direct question focused on feelings, such as, "Did you feel disappointed that your baby was born early?"

Open-ended questions also allow the visitor to learn from the client what events and feelings are important to her, and allow the client to influence the content of the interaction. In the first question above (in which the visitor asked about changes in the parent's life), the parent may respond with a wide range of examples and, in the process, convey feelings that are important to her. The second question stated above would most likely not be appropriate during an initial interview, especially if there were no reason to suspect such feelings of disappointment.

(c) *Facilitating questions.* Facilitating questions require active listening. They are most often asked for a specific purpose. A good facilitating question can solicit missing information or clarify previously discussed material. "It can help start an interview or clarify client behavior. A facilitative question communicates understanding and respect. Most importantly, it helps the client better understand him- or herself" (Long et al., 1981, p. 73).

Facilitative questions attempt to focus on the important element of what is being said while avoiding details that might detract from the main point. If a caregiver for a physically ill person were to tell the visitor, "I am so confused by all the equipment, I don't know what to do," the visitor should pick up the caregiver's concern by possibly asking, "Tell me what is confusing to you." In this way, the home visitor can learn directly from the individual what is troubling her or him. In contrast, if the visitor had responded, "It is really very simple to operate; let me show you," she may be missing what the individual is trying to tell her. At some point later in the same visit, the visitor's response might well be to demonstrate how to use the equipment, but if she were to respond too quickly with a solution to a perceived problem, she may prevent the caregiver in the home from elaborating on his or her real concern. She may also miss an opportunity to engage the individual in creative problem solving.

(d) *Clarifying questions.* Clarifying questions facilitate communication by providing additional necessary information, by providing examples, and by defining multiple meaning words that the client has used. These questions are particularly appropriate during the initial visits in the home and at any other time when the client is discussing situations that are open to different interpretations.

A clue to when clarifying questions may be in order is when the client uses vague words or words that can have more than one meaning. For example, if a Head Start home visitor is discussing learning activities with a child's mother and the mother says, "Things are all mixed up," the visitor might not know what the word "things" refers to or what "all mixed up" means. She could begin by asking, "Could you tell me what things are mixed up?" Once the visitor has an idea of the areas of concern, she would then want to clarify what "all mixed up" meant to the client. Clarifying questions in this example help prevent the Head Start visitor from jumping to conclusions about what is meant by "things are all mixed up." It could be that the child development materials were confusing to the mother, or it could be that she was concerned about the child's transportation to the Head Start center. It could even refer to a major life event in the mother's life, such as an unexpected pregnancy.

Visitors should be careful not to use clarifying questions too frequently or in ways that interfere with what their client is trying to say. At times it might be better to wait for clarification rather than ask a question.

(e) *Focusing questions.* Home visitors will find that it is often necessary to help many clients focus on specific concerns. Such clients may feel overwhelmed with a number of problems or may not be able to identify on their own what is troubling them about a situation. Focusing questions are particularly important in helping clients identify problems, set priorities, or identify goals. It is usually relatively easy to recognize when clients need help in focusing. They may tend to identify many problems without prioritizing them; they may use vague language to identify concerns; or they may not be able to say what is troublesome about a particular situation. An example of identifying problems while not prioritizing them is a new mother who might say, "Nothing is going right. The baby cries, she gets up at night, and I'm tired. I miss my job." To help this mother begin to focus, the home visitor could try to get her to identify what she most wants to work on by saying, "There are several things right now that seem to be bothering you. Which one would you like to talk about first?" or "What would help you most today to talk about?" If the visitor believes that it is too difficult for the client to focus, she may offer a suggestion, such as, "You have mentioned the baby's crying a couple of times before. Would you like to talk about that now?"

An example of using focusing questions with clients using vague language might be the father who is abusing his teenage son and who says, "He does everything wrong. Nothing is right. He can't seem to follow directions. He keeps me upset." In this situation, focusing questions could help the parent identify particular times, situations, or behaviors that are troublesome as a way to help the father identify the specific concern. Questions like, "Could you give me an example of the kind of behavior that upset you?" might begin to help both the father and the visitor identify specific areas of concern. Once these areas are identified, it becomes possible to discuss how serious the situations are and to determine whether or not action should be taken.

(f) *Redirecting questions.* Redirecting questions can facilitate shifting the discussion to a topic that the visitor believes is important to discuss. This type of questioning might be used when the visitor believes the client has wandered from her initial concerns and is discussing unrelated or tangential matters. They may also be used when the visitor believes that the client is avoiding a difficult issue. If, for example, a young woman had mentioned health concerns with a pregnancy on two prior occasions but didn't mention those concerns again, the visitor might say, "Earlier, you told me you were concerned because you were still smoking and because your boyfriend wanted you to drink when you went out. How do you feel about those things now?"

When the visitor redirects, she is making a judgment about the importance of certain feelings or events in her client's life, so the use of redirecting questions should be judicious. Sometimes, though, this kind of questioning helps clients discuss difficult issues in their lives.

Probing and Prompting

Probing is an attempt to seek additional information; it is particularly important when there is insufficient information to understand client concerns or feelings or to help clients deal with problems. Probing could be used to help a client begin to consider the personal and family resources that might be available to help her in times of stress. Parents of a handicapped child may have been depending only on one another for support and relief. The visitor could help the parents consider extended family members, friends, neighbors, and respite care as alternative sources of support by asking, "Is there some member of your family who could help?" or "Earlier, you said your mother could not help because she was working. Do you think she could help you occasionally on a weekend?" Such questions help a client consider in more depth alternatives that may have been dismissed too quickly or not considered at all.

Prompting facilitates a particular behavior by either verbally encouraging it or through the use of physical prompts. Prompting is particularly useful when teaching new behaviors or encouraging the client to try actions she might be hesitant to try. A home visitor may, for example, place a mother's hands in the right position and guide her through a physical exercise to do with a handicapped child, or she may suggest that the family carry out an activity they have been planning to do together but may have needed encouragement to get started. Prompting a client to try something new can convey the home visitor's confidence in the client's ability.

Summary

The basic helping skills presented here (observation, listening, questioning, probing, and prompting) are ones that should be mastered by all home visitors in order to use the home visiting time constructively and productively. Interactions with families are not simply social exchanges, and the visitor must know how to use the verbal and nonverbal communications in clinically useful ways.

Specific Techniques

A number of specific techniques are also available to home visitors to use in their interactions with families. As with the basic clinical skills, these techniques are common across the helping professions. In this section, we will discuss three that we believe are particularly useful in home visiting: modeling, role playing, and the use of examples. All these techniques help the client to become better prepared to deal with some event in his or her life or to understand better the important aspects of a problem.

Modeling

Modeling is actually demonstrating for the client a specific behavior. It is a technique particularly advantageous when the client cannot seem to visualize herself carrying out a particular action or when she cannot seem to think of how to begin an activity. It is also useful when a client seems to lack the skills necessary for an action, or when she seems hesitant to try out a behavior. Modeling such situations could include showing how one might respond during a job interview, how one might ask a spouse to help with child care, or how one can comfort a colicky child. Modeling is an ideal teaching technique in many parenting situations, from showing how to burp an infant to helping parents who are learning physical therapy techniques with a child who has cerebral palsy. It is a prevalent practice of nurses and physicians in demonstrating appropriate medical care.

In most situations, once the visitor has modeled the behavior, she should then allow the client to perform the behavior. Doing so assures that the client understood what was modeled and that the client can match her behavior to that of the visitor. Such practice helps assure that the client will remember the behavior. It also gives the visitor the opportunity to correct any errors in the client's performance and provides the opportunity to reinforce and encourage the client's behavior.

Role Playing

In role playing, the visitor acts out one real-life role and the client acts out another, usually in order to help the client gain skill and confidence to deal with a difficult situation. This technique is particularly appropriate for those situations in which one has difficulty being assertive because of the newness of the situation. A parent may have been offended by the brisk manner of her child's physician, and she may be reluctant to ask the physician questions she has about her child's health. During role playing, the visitor can take on the role of physician and let the mother practice what it is she would like to ask the physician. In this example, there are advantages for the mother in trying out both roles. She can be the mother and ask the physician what it is she would like to know, or she could be the physician while the visitor models some of the questions the mother could ask.

Use of Examples

Using examples is a common daily event for people during their interactions with others, and is often used when one is explaining, describing, or teaching something to a second person. The use of examples is also pertinent for the visitor-client interactions. In general, examples should be relevant and fit with realistic experiences in the client's life.

Examples can be used to accomplish each of the following objectives. First, examples can help an individual see that others are experiencing similar difficulties. A visitor might say something like the following to a parent who was concerned when her child began kindergarten, "Many parents have these concerns. I remember a mother who told me that with each one of her five children, she felt some sense of concern as they began kindergarten." Examples can be used to provide information on a possible way of dealing with a difficult situation. A visitor might say, "Once when I talked with another mother about a similar situation, she told me that she had tried letting her child take a nap in the afternoon. Your situation is similar. Does her decision seem like it would work for you, too?"

Examples can also be used to help a client feel at ease with something she has done that may not have worked out or that she is not satisfied with. The visitor might say, "I remember a mother who tried three different ways to help her child learn to use the toilet before the child was trained. Like her, you may find that the second or third thing will work, even though the first one did not." Interesting stories told as examples are extremely valuable teaching aids because they not only teach some point, but they are often remembered when other discussion is not.

Behavior Change Principles and Procedures

The principles and procedures of behavior change also need to be a fundamental part of a home visitor's repertoire of skills. The procedures of behavioral change are based upon the principles of behavior modification and social learning theory (Bandura, 1969; 1977) that describe how behavior can be increased, decreased, or maintained, and how new behaviors can be learned. We believe that these principles are essential for anyone who will work with families. Home visitors who are not familiar with them and cannot use them in their work will not be as effective with many clients as they could be. These principles are especially important in working with parents.

The basic principles of behavior analysis address the effects on behavior of both the antecedents and consequences of the behavior. Though most attention has been focused on the consequences of behavior, especially positive consequences or reinforcement, it is important to recognize the effects on behavior of changing the immediate environment. This focus on changing the environment is frequently used to make homes safe for young children. We put fences around playgrounds to keep children safe, and we remove dangerous objects from their reach. A home visitor who brings toys or other activities for one child to work with while she talks to the parent and another child is changing the environment of the first child in a way that promotes constructive interactions. What we say to each other can also be an antecedent condition to behavior and can increase the likelihood that a behavior will occur. Parents who know how to give clear, unambiguous directions, for example, will likely see more cooperation on the part of their children than parents who give confusing, conflicting directions.

Behavior is also strongly influenced by its consequences. These consequences can be positive and reinforcing and will increase the likelihood the behavior will occur again, or the consequences can be negative and punitive and can decrease the likelihood that a particular behavior will take place again. Many parents naturally use positive consequences as, for example, when they praise and encourage a child who is learning to walk or talk. But as child behavior becomes more complex or problematic, parents often need help in knowing which behaviors to attend to, which ones to ignore, and which ones may need to be punished. Many parents unintentionally become negative in their interactions with their children and often need help in learning to change these unpleasant interactions into more positive and enjoyable ones (Patterson, 1976; Forehand & McMahan, 1981).

Teaching parents how to use reinforcement and punishment are both important in a parent training program. When home visitors are in the role of parent trainer, they also need to keep a broad perspective, recognizing that parents need to be able to integrate knowledge on child development and the child's environment with knowledge of behavior principles in order to make good judgments of when children's behaviors are appropriate or inappropriate. Furthermore, the guidelines we discussed earlier concerning home visiting in general are also important when teaching parents about child-management procedures. For example, the home visitor needs to keep in mind that the parents' needs may be interfering with their ability to respond to their children, and such a situation may need to be addressed. Home visitors also need to consider intervention procedures from a systems perspective, considering the effects on other family members. This recommendation is compatible with the views of Wahler and Dumas (1984), who have emphasized the importance of recognizing that a child's behavior is influenced by subsystems in which the child lives and that these system influences need to be considered in dealing with parent-child relationships. When taking a broader ecological view, one goes beyond asking what consequences could change a child's behavior to asking questions about environmental conditions. Such questions might determine whether the materials required for a task were available and whether the physical environment made it possible for a child to complete a required task (Embry, 1984).

Other areas of compatibility between the philosophy of home visiting in this book and parent training is seen in the writing of Blechman (1984), who emphasized the importance of problem-solving skills as a prerequisite for competence in parenting. In addition, Bijou (1984) and Embry (1984) have stressed the need to conduct parent teaching and training in the parent's home rather than in a clinic or other institutional setting, a tenet completely compatible with home visiting.

Project 12 Ways is a home visiting program that has demonstrated the effective use of behavioral change strategies when working in the homes of parents of abused and neglected children (Lutzker, 1984). This project has successfully helped parents increase home safety (Tertinger, Greene, & Lutzker, 1984) and increase the personal cleanliness of children (Rosenfield-Schlichter, Sarber, Bueno, Greene, & Lutzker, 1983). It has also helped reduce incidents of abuse and neglect (Lutzker & Rice, 1984). Becoming familiar with procedures used in studies such as these can provide home visitors with possible ways of working with other families.

Because we cannot present the detail necessary in this book for home visitors to master the knowledge and skills needed for using these principles with the families they work with, we urge the reader to obtain this information elsewhere as preparation for home visiting. Several excellent, comprehensive parent-training programs have been developed to help parents deal with many child-management problems. The procedures are especially important for many parents of children with handicapping conditions and parents who abuse or neglect their children. An excellent reference on many parent-training programs is Richard Dangel's and Richard Polster's book, *Parent Training*, which provides descriptions of several exemplary programs that could serve as the basis for parent training as part of home visiting services. We also recommend *Families* by Patterson (1975) and *Parents and Adolescents Living Together* by Patterson and Forgatch (1987).

Integrating the Helping Skills

In this chapter, we have discussed four categories of helping skills: helper characteristics, basic helping processes, specific techniques, and behavioral-change procedures. It is important for the visitor to have a guide or method for bringing together these skills. In Chapter 2, we presented a problem-solving model as one approach for guiding the work of home visitors. Here, we will use this problem-solving model as a framework for organizing these various characteristics and skills so as to help the visitor make the home visiting process a constructive one for her clients.

One of the important roles of the home visitor is to assess the beliefs of the client in relation to problem solving. Some families may have beliefs that interfere with their ability to orient to and define problems. Such families may believe that what happens in their lives is due to fate or luck and that their own behaviors are not important. Because beliefs can interfere with effective problem solving at any stage in the process, it is important to use knowledge of such beliefs when making decisions as to how to help a client.

The problem-solving model has seven stages that can guide the work of the visitor: defining problems, selecting goals, generating

TABLE 5.2: The Problem-Solving Plan

Problem identification	What is my problem?
Goal selection	What do I want?
Generating alternatives	What can I do?
Considering consequences	What will happen if?
Decision-making	What is my decision?
Implementation	Do it!
Evaluation	Did it work?

alternatives, considering consequences, making decisions, implementing decisions, and evaluating the outcomes. These steps are like a road map for the visitor, reminding her that there is a purpose to her interactions and helping her evaluate her own interactions with the client against a criterion of whether or not she is helping her client make progress toward her goals.

In Table 5.2, we have shown how each of the problem-solving stages can be written as a question or statement, illustrating what people can ask themselves as they think through each step or carry out some action. These questions, such as, "What do I want?" and "What can I do?" illustrate that problem solving is a cognitive or thinking process as well as an action or behavioral process.

Each of the problem-solving stages will be described in sequence, but it is very important to recognize that the process of solving problems does not always go step-by-step, and thus helping one work through problems should be approached from a flexible standpoint. Unexpected events might occur in a client's life, or the person may find out new information; as a result, they may change their minds about something they may have previously decided to do.

Problem Identification

Problem identification is defining or describing the troublesome issue or situation. It answers the question, "What is my concern?" Identifying problems helps to focus on the relevant aspects of a situation, eliminating those things that are not of concern. This clarification can sometimes lead a person to decide whether the concern warrants specific attention. It is important for home visitors to recognize that all problems do not need resolution, and that all problems cannot be resolved.

Parents cannot change certain handicapping conditions of a child, but they can find ways to make the care of the child less burdensome, or help the child learn things he or she can do successfully in spite of the handicapping conditions. At other times, it may be possible to change a problem, but the client may have learned to live with the situation and cope with it as it is and may not want to change.

In helping the client identify in specific words what is bothering her, the home visitor can enable her to describe how, when, and where the problem occurs. The home visitor can also encourage the client to talk about how she feels about the situation. At times, this process of talking and thinking about a particular situation can help a person evaluate how important it is for her and help her judge whether or not she can or wants to do anything about it.

Another very important part of identifying problems is deciding who "owns" the problem. Most of us at some time have probably worried about problems that were really the responsibility of other people, and we may have become upset worrying about needless things. Talking with another person can often help someone differentiate between problems they need to deal with and those they do not.

The home visitor can also help a client see that some problem situations do not really need to be addressed. Some problems will work out on their own. Others can become less of a problem if the client obtains new information. We see this particularly related to some child-rearing situations in which parents may make fewer demands on their children when they have more knowledge of child's abilities at different ages.

When discussing situations that clients want to address, it is important to obtain information on the severity and frequency of the concern. To obtain such information, the visitor may ask such direct questions as, "About how often does this situation occur?" and "How serious a problem is this for you?" Information on the generality of the problem is also important for making intervention plans. Visitors can prompt such information by asking, "How long has this been a problem?" or "Where does the problem usually occur?" One can probe for additional information by asking, "Does it occur during mealtime?" or "Is it a problem at work?" Such information may serve as a basis for selecting behavioral-change strategies at a later time, or may even help the client decide that the situation is not as serious as she thought it was.

Goal Selection

In some problem-solving models, goal selection is a part of identifying the problem. It has been listed as a separate process here because we have found that even when people can describe what is troubling them, many still have difficulty stating just what it is that they would like to have happen. By making goal selection a separate step, it causes a person to focus specifically on what they want. It also makes it possible for a person to describe what she wants in positive terms rather than negative ones.

A new mother may complain that she is tired all the time because her baby does not sleep through the night, thereby keeping her awake. In talking with her, a home visitor might find that at first the mother says that she wants the baby to sleep through the night, but she may want this primarily so that she herself can feel more rested during the day. The home visitor could then talk with the mother about ways the client may be able to get more rest for herself. If she is home during the day, she may be able to sleep in the afternoon when the baby is napping, or she may be able to arrange for someone else in the home to get up with the baby during the night so she could have a longer stretch of sleep.

Asking the question, "What do you want to happen?" is a straightforward way of having clients identify their goals and priorities, but some people will have difficulty doing so. Nevertheless, it is very important for home visitors to have families identify what they want; simply identifying a situation as troublesome is insufficient. Clients need to say that the situation is one they want to change, and they need to say what the desired outcome would be like for them.

Generating Alternatives

A person typically has a better chance of thinking of effective solutions to a problem if he or she thinks of more than one or two ways of handling a situation. A second or third choice may be better than the first; it may cost less, be more effective, or require less work. The client may also consider it more acceptable, or even find that combining more than one alternative to deal with a problem can be a good strategy.

The home visitor can suggest that a person think of two or three things that could be done in a particular situation before deciding on what action to take. She can encourage the individual to think of things that may not seem workable at first, with the possibility that a solution may become evident upon closer scrutiny. One should be careful, however, not to persist in generating alternatives beyond the point of productivity. Thinking of 8 or 10 alternatives would be confusing for many people. It is important to remember that all good solutions cannot always be figured out at one time. A parent may first need to find out what options are available, or she may need to address only small parts of a problem at a time.

Considering Consequences

There are many important reasons for considering the consequences of what one does before taking action. Thinking ahead about what might happen can allow a person to decide whether or not those are consequences or events she is willing to live with. Just thinking about them can help a person decide whether to go ahead in spite of the consequence or to determine how to minimize any negative consequences.

The home visitor can help in this process by encouraging a person to think about how much any particular solution will cost, how much time is involved, how the solution will affect the person, and how it will affect other people. The home visitor can encourage the client to think of short-term and long-term consequences and to evaluate the positive and negative features of different ones. The home visitor can also encourage the person to think of what will happen if she tries something and it fails. A person may not want to try a given solution for fear that it might not be successful. Yet, when talking about the situation, the client may be more inclined to go ahead, deciding that she is willing to deal with any negative aspects. In considering consequences, one has to be careful not to become too involved in considering all possibilities. It is very important, however, to consider all serious consequences of any action.

Decision-Making

To facilitate decision-making, home visitors can help people weigh the consequences of different actions and determine what resources are available. They can also help people consider their values and priorities and determine which alternatives best fit with these beliefs. The visitor can also help a client think about what is best for the client in a particular situation.

Many individuals can think through a problem situation, consider consequences, and discuss the pros and cons of the various actions they can take, but they may then have difficulty actually making a decision. They may be concerned with some of the possible negative consequences and avoid them by not making a decision. Through discussion, home visitors can help individuals see how important it is to make their own decisions, and discuss the consequences of leaving things to chance.

Implementation

For some people, figuring out the best thing to do is not the difficult part of resolving a problem. Rather, they have trouble taking action and carrying out their plan. Home visitors can help their clients see how they can reduce stress by taking care of difficult situations. The client can reduce the likelihood that some situations will become worse by taking action early, and make it possible to have time to attend to other things that may be of more interest or enjoyment by taking care of the problem situations.

Home visitors can help by encouraging a person to arrange for the necessary resources and procedures to carry out a plan, encouraging them to take action.

Evaluation

When a person tries to deal with a problem, it is important to consider her own success in a particular situation. If the client were able to accomplish what she wanted, she needs to be aware of her own efforts. If it is a situation she had struggled with, the home visitor can offer encouragement and praise. A client may make a decision that something did not work, but even if the goal was not completely met, it is important to consider the client's own success in a particular situation. The client could decide that the problem had been sufficiently dealt with and no longer needs attention, or a different alternative may need to be implemented.

Implications for Home Visitors

For a home visitor to implement a problem-solving approach, we believe several conditions are important. First, the home visitor must recognize problem solving as an important procedure for coping effectively with day-by-day difficulties and decisions, and she must be able to use it in her own life. This recommendation addresses the home visitor's own orientation toward life events. It is not easy to use or teach something that one does not accept or believe in, and problem solving is no exception. A home visitor's beliefs can facilitate her ability to help families help themselves. For example, if a home visitor believes that no matter what one does in life, some people will always have things work out poorly for them, she will be disinclined to promote effective problem solving.

Second, the home visitor must be knowledgeable about the problem-solving process. The more familiar a home visitor is with a problem-solving model, the more likely she will understand her families' problem-solving strengths and weaknesses. We believe that knowledge of problem solving helps a home visitor become adept at recognizing when a client might be having difficulty reaching a goal. She can also become adept at seeing how families cope and the barriers that may be preventing them from reaching what they want in their own lives.

Third, the home visitor must be knowledgeable about barriers to problem solving, be able to recognize barriers that confront other people, and be able to use this information to help others better understand how to use their own problem-solving strategies. Barriers to effective coping are numerous and vary considerably from person to person (Wasik, 1984). These barriers can fall under one of the following categories: cognitive, emotional, informational, social, language, communication, physical, and environmental. As examples of these barriers, a person could be too emotionally depressed to take any action, she may lack basic health-care information to respond appropriately to a sick child, or she may not be able to read or write. The barriers some individuals have to cope with may be more complex and stressful than those that other individuals face, but effective coping means each person must deal with his or her own unique situation. Home visitors must also recognize that some coping strategies, such as denial or procrastination, may not solve any problems, but they may help a particular person at a particular time.

In summary, problem-solving ability can be considered essential in order to function in a competent way in one's day-by-day life. Promoting these abilities in their clients can help home visitors integrate many of the goals and objectives of home visiting.

Summary

In this chapter, we have discussed four sets of characteristics and skills important for home visitors: helping characteristics (empathy, warmth, and genuineness); basic helping skills (observation, listening, questioning, prompting, and probing); the techniques of modeling, role playing, and use of examples; and behavior-change procedures. We then described problem solving as a strategy for focusing home visits and serving as a guide for the home visitor. The content of this chapter can provide a foundation for mastering these behaviors and skills, though more extensive written materials on clinical skills should also be incorporated into a training program, and appropriate practice and supervision should be included.

6

Managing and Maintaining
Home Visits

Successful home visiting takes planning, persistence, patience, and skill in getting along with people. It also requires the home visitor to have a thorough understanding of the objectives and materials used by her individual program. In this chapter, we will first focus on the three stages of home visiting: the first home visit, ongoing home visits, and the final visit. Salient issues involved in these three stages will be explored, as well as practical suggestions and philosophical approaches. Second, we will discuss some of the practical aspects of home visiting, including scheduling and timing, materials, safety, special circumstances, and confidentiality. Home visiting is a complex profession, requiring multiple skills and involving a myriad of issues. We have selected for discussion the major ones that appear to underlie the management of home visiting and maintenance of visits over time.

Much of the material we present in this chapter is derived from our experiences with a variety of home visiting programs and our association with the home visitors who served in these programs. The practical knowledge amassed by the home visitors we have known is considerable, and we have tried to capture it in sufficient detail that it can be operationally useful to new home visitors.

Stages of Home Visiting

The First Home Visit

The first home visit is the beginning of what may become a long-term relationship between a home visitor and her client. This relationship may extend over a period of months or years, although some programs are relatively brief in duration. Whether of short-term or long-term duration, this relationship, as described in Chapter 5, is the heart of the home visiting process. The first home visit requires special attention because it is the first step in establishing a positive relationship between home visitor and client and because it will, in large part, predict the quality and course of subsequent home visits (Berg & Helgeson, 1984). Consequently, the home visitor needs to engage the client's interest as soon as possible, and begin to establish the rapport that is crucial to the home visitor's continued presence in the client's home.

The first home visit should be brief, focused, and relaxed (Reschly, 1979). It should also cover the six components essential to a first visit: becoming acquainted, reviewing program purpose and goals, defining the home visitor's role and that of the client, clarifying client's expectations, beginning the establishment of rapport, and scheduling the next visit. Although we discuss these steps sequentially, adherence to an order is not implied and the steps will overlap. All of these components should be included in the first visit in whatever fashion suits the home visitor.

The first step is becoming acquainted with the client. This can consist of several simple exchanges between home visitor and client, including information or conversation that would be normal for any first dialogue between two people. Conversational talk about everyday happenings is appropriate here. This social interchange is an important part of establishing a helping relationship, especially in terms of allowing the client to see home visitors as the persons they are (Leahy, Cobb, & Jones, 1982). Another way home visitors can facilitate getting acquainted is to share their own enthusiasm about the home visiting program. This sharing often has the effect of inspiring more interest in the program for the client as well.

The second step is a review of the purposes of the home visiting program and the nature of the activities that will be completed in order to carry out the program. For this and subsequent home visits, a focus on program goals is important in structuring visits in a purposeful way (Wolfe & Herwig, 1986). A long time may have elapsed since the client first agreed to participate in the program, and she may have forgotten the specific details of the program. Reminding her about these details and program benefits may also help to stimulate her enthusiasm and interest.

In the next step of the first visit, the home visitor needs to explain clearly what her role will be; that is, she should define as clearly as possible her responsibilities and any limitations to her role. The sooner the limits and structure of the relationship are established, the sooner the visitor and client can focus on productive work together (Combs & Avila, 1985). This clarification of role may be repeated many times throughout the course of the home visiting program, or it may be sufficient to describe it only once. More than likely, role clarification will require repetition and reinforcement by the home visitor through her behavior in order for the client to clearly understand the home visitor's role. This process may indeed continue throughout the duration of the home visiting program. Some home visiting programs have narrowly defined roles for home visitors, while others may permit or encourage home visitors to be flexible and independent in creating their own role boundaries. In either case, clarifying what the home visitor perceives her responsibilities and limitations to be will help to diminish potential confusion about exactly what the home visitor will be doing.

The role of the client in the program should also be clarified. Enlisting the client as a partner in the home visiting venture rather than only as a consumer will establish from the beginning that this is a mutual relationship to which the client will be making important contributions (Wolfe & Herwig, 1986). The most obvious and most important contribution of the client is her continued availability to the home visitor. Without reasonable access to the client and her continuing cooperation, home visitors cannot perform their part of the helping process.

What the client expects from the program should also be explored during this first visit. Sometimes clients' expectations are not realistic; perhaps they misunderstood the program content or were misinformed. Finding out exactly what the client expects and correcting any misperceptions during this first visit can help eliminate a home visitor's working at cross-purposes with her client later on.

The fifth component of the first visit is the beginning of the establishment of rapport between home visitor and client. This is a gradual process that will develop naturally as home visiting continues. There are, however, steps a home visitor can take to enhance rapport, such as expressing sincere interest in understanding the client's needs and conveying a willingness to help. With some clients, the development of rapport can be achieved quickly; with others, it may take considerably more time and effort, depending partly on the purposes of the program, the personality of the home visitor and the personality and life experiences of the client. Building a working relationship with a client is likely, however, to take place over a period of time rather than to develop quickly.

The development of a trusting relationship will not be consistently progressive. Gains made in developing trust one week can be lost the next if factors have intervened in the meantime that threaten the trust that has developed. These factors may or may not relate to the home visitor per se, but may be events in the client's life that could lead her to feel suspicious of others' motives. For example, if she has been visited by a caseworker from the children's protective services agency for suspected neglect or her children, even though the home visitor's role has nothing to do with her children, the client may still generalize her anxiety, distrust, and fear to the home visitor.

In this first visit, as well as in later ones, home visitors should be sensitive to the privacy of the family and not ask intrusive questions that violate that privacy (Cansler, Martin, & Valand, 1982). Home visitors should focus their questions on factual data that they need to carry out program goals, especially during the first visit. A client may be eager to share information with the home visitor, but most likely this will not be the case. If she chooses to talk about very personal matters, a home visitor can listen and respond supportively. The visitor may need to redirect the conversation to program-related topics if it becomes too tangential. A home visitor should not probe into a client's personal life, especially during this first visit; doing so has the potential to destroy chances of developing a working relationship with a client. A client who has shared information freely may later feel that she shared more than she wanted to.

The final component of this first visit is scheduling the next home visit. Encouraging the client to choose a time that is convenient for her is important because the less the visit interferes with her schedule, the better the chances for completing it. The first home visit with the mother will usually last about 30 minutes, depending on program content. As soon as the home visitor believes that she has accomplished what she needed to, there is no reason to extend her visit. However, if the visit is going smoothly and the client seems to be enjoying herself, the home visitor may extend her visit accordingly. Leaving the client feeling comfortable and looking forward to the next visit is the primary goal of this initial visit. If the home visitor accomplishes this, she should consider her first visit to be successful.

Ongoing Home Visits

Home visiting can be envisioned as a process in which a home visitor and client learn to know and accept one another, work together to achieve mutually acknowledged goals, and then end their relationship. In this process of learning, joining, and parting, there are a number of issues that are particularly salient.

The first is the importance of focusing on the client's needs rather than on those of the home visitor. The home visiting program exists for the benefit of the client rather than for that of the home visitor. The home visitor engages in this work for professional reasons, and the experience certainly will produce personal feelings of satisfaction, pleasure, and frustration. In the course of home visiting, home visitors will experience times when their self-esteem is heightened, skills are improved, and insight is gained. However, these outcomes emerge as a result of serving the client rather than being sought directly by the home visitor.

Sometimes focusing on the client is difficult to accept and adhere to, as when the home visitor may want to pursue some action that would benefit herself but which would not particularly benefit the client. For example, a home visitor may be tempted to schedule a visit with her client at 4:00 P.M. so that she could end her workday by 5:00 P.M., whereas the client would prefer to visit at 6:00 P.M. after she has had time to rest from the day's work and be with her children. Or conversely, something that the client needs to do may be inconvenient for the home visitor or be at odds with the home visitor's beliefs. For example, one client insisted on remaining with her drug-dealing boyfriend in a high-crime area instead of being with her mother in a low-crime neighborhood because her boyfriend was indeed kinder to her than was her mother. The home visitor would have preferred to visit in a safer neighborhood but recognized that her client fared better with her boyfriend than she did with her mother.

A second point that is important to home visiting and related to this focus upon the client is the client's right to self-determination. The home visitor's role is to encourage and sustain her client as she makes her own decisions. This role can be hard to maintain sometimes, especially when the home visitor recognizes the client's actions as self-destructive or futile, such as the unwillingness to leave a dangerously abusive relationship. Encouraging and enabling clients to make their own decisions, however, increases their sense of competence and control over their lives. People learn by experience, and unless a client has the opportunity to make her own decisions, good or bad, she will not develop new competencies. As one home visitor supervisor, who had previously been a home visitor, stated, "by supporting clients, providing them access to community resources and by continuing to help them improve upon their skills, clients become increasingly able to make appropriate (better) decisions and to change destructive life patterns" (R. Shapiro, personal communication, July 1989).

One approach a home visitor can take to help herself accept the client's right to make her own decisions is to remind herself that the client is a separate individual over whom the home visitor cannot have control, nor can the visitor accept responsibility for her client's actions. Accepting the client as a valuable individual in her own right is widely considered the underlying basis for developing a helping relationship (Hollis & Wood, 1981). Thus, not only is the home visitor not responsible for her client, but acting as if she were responsible can be harmful to her client as well as to herself and the entire process of the helping relationship.

It is also helpful for the home visitor to remember to differentiate between her own values and life goals and those of her client, continually reminding herself that her goal is ultimately to help her client learn skills or program content. Indeed, those in the helping professions are believed to be most effective when encouraging their clients' self-exploration and self-direction in the course of the helping process (Carkhuff, 1984). The home visitor also needs to re-examine her own purposes as a home visitor, sorting out which are her needs and which are those of her client. This self-examination can be greatly enhanced by talking about it with the home visitor's supervisor.

A third aspect of home visiting that is especially important for the client is the issue of dependence/independence. In any professional relationship between two people, there can be a tendency for dependency to develop; sometimes this is temporary and appropriate, while at other times it is counterproductive (Hollis & Wood, 1981). In times of stress and crisis, for example, clients may depend on home visitors to help them make and carry out decisions in ways that would not be acceptable in less stressful times. For example, if a home visitor is at her client's home and a child is injured seriously while playing, the home visitor may take both mother and child to a clinic, whereas ordinarily the client would take her own child to the clinic. In one case, a deeply depressed client told her home visitor that she wanted to obtain professional counseling but needed help in finding an appropriate therapist and setting up an appointment. The home visitor responded by devoting the remainder of the visit to phoning and scheduling the first session for her client, though customarily the home visitor would provide resources and information, encouraging her client to initiate contact.

While occasional dependency may be acceptable, home visitors should avoid fostering unnecessary dependency to protect clients from losing whatever competencies they may already possess (Gray & Wandersman, 1980). Home visitors who sometimes allow or encourage clients to become unnecessarily dependent can harm rather than help their clients. One home visitor left a family party when a client called her and asked her for a ride. This was not an emergency situation, and the home visitor did not place appropriate limits on her role. Learning to find her own resources for transportation would have been more valuable for this client than depending on her home visitor to transport her. During an ongoing home visiting relationship, the type and amount of dependence will vary, with the ultimate goal being for the client to have no dependence upon the home visitor at all. Keeping this goal in mind helps home visitors judge what is acceptable dependent behavior and what is not. In making such a judgment, the question might be asked, "Whose needs are being met in the situation?"

A fourth aspect of home visiting that home visitors are sometimes frustrated about is motivation. Clients may not seem motivated to comply with the home visiting program's expectations or to work toward other life goals that the home visitor believes are important. Sometimes home visitors label this behavior "resistance" or "obstructionism." Whenever the home visitor feels frustrated by what seems to be a lack of motivation on the part of her client, she can ask herself, "Are these goals ones that my client wants to achieve, or are they mine or the program's?" If these are not the client's goals, the home visitor can ask herself, "Why not?" Perhaps they are not culturally acceptable or personally meaningful to the client (Pedersen, 1981). If such is the case, the home visitor needs to look at how the desired behavior will truly benefit the client. If in her judgment it will, she should try to find a way to present it to her client so that it is acceptable. If, on close inspection, it does not appear to be of value to the client, the expectation should be dropped. Resistance is often a message from the client that the home visitor is overstepping the boundaries of the relationship that has been established (Dorn, 1986).

If worried about a client's lack of progress toward stated goals, a home visitor may ask herself, "What barriers may be preventing my client from engaging in behavior to achieve these goals?" Perhaps helping the client to problem-solve in order to overcome or remove the barriers would enable the client to move toward the goal. Home visitors have often found that clients would like to pursue goals but are greatly hampered by lack of resources. This issue was discussed in the problem-solving section of Chapter 5, but it merits consideration in this context as well.

One response that is helpful for home visitors is to remember that they can choose how they respond to an apparent lack of motivation. If the client is not complying with a required goal in an involuntary program, such as one court-ordered for child abusers, the home visitor's response will be determined by program policy and legal procedures. If, however, the client simply does not want to attend parent meetings that are part of a voluntary program, for example, the home visitor may change her expectation for this client, or she may choose from time to time to encourage her client to attend the meetings while otherwise focusing her attention on other aspects of the program to which the client seems to be more responsive.

The fifth aspect of home visiting that can pose problems for home visitors is the type of relationship they have with their clients. As the home visitor-client relationship evolves, its quality and the elements that comprise it will change. For example, as a positive feeling develops between home visitor and client, boundaries that define the relationship can become blurred. The professional relationship between the two individuals can begin to have the look of a personal friendship. Through her professional role of delivering services to her client, a home visitor may become truly fond of her client and deeply committed to helping her. Although a prerequisite to developing a good working relationship and necessary to carry out program goals, this positive regard should not become confused with friendship. There is a balance between genuine professional concern and maintaining distance that is difficult to define and more difficult to achieve. Maintaining this balance is important, however, for several reasons.

The first reason for keeping this balance is that the home visitor needs to remain objective and not overidentify with her client if she is to be truly effective. The second reason is that the home visitor represents a specific area of expertise, and becoming personally too close can often diminish the recognition of this special knowledge in the eyes of the client and thereby also diminish what the client perceives as available expert help. A third reason not to become close friends is that the home visitor often serves as a role model for the client. There needs to be enough distance between client and home visitor so that the client can see the home visitor objectively as a model to guide behavior.

On another level, maintaining a professional relationship with a client serves as a measure of self-preservation for the home visitor. The circumstances of her client's life could become unbearable to the home visitor if she allows herself to become too emotionally involved, or if she begins to see herself as personally responsible for solving problems in her client's life. She can eventually feel overwhelmed by distressing situations she may encounter (Hardy-Brown et al., 1987). Focusing on understanding how the client may feel, rather than allowing herself to feel as she thinks the client feels and taking on the burdens of the client's life, will help a home visitor function professionally and effectively.

It may also be helpful for the home visitor to try to see herself as a mentor who cares about her client, empathizes with her difficulties, and delights in her success. The home visitor's goal is to help her client ultimately outgrow the need for home visiting services.

The final aspect of home visiting we would like to emphasize here addresses the primacy of the client's well-being. Home visitors need to recognize that clients may consider a visit in their home as placing them in a vulnerable position. It can establish an immediate sense of inequity between client and home visitor, no matter what the purpose of the program. There is some danger that clients also can feel overwhelmed by the expectations of a program and see these expectations as demands that they cannot fulfill. Although we are stressing the importance of encouragement and positive expectations on the part of the home visitor, these other factors must be expressed realistically in light of existing strengths and limitations. It is vitally important not to increase feelings of inadequacy that a client may have, however inadvertently this may happen (Gray & Wandersman, 1980).

A client can experience the same difficulty that home visitors can in terms of understanding the nature of her relationship to her home visitor. We have known clients who felt pressured to be friends with the home visitor. This belief is as inappropriate for clients as it is for home visitors to offer friendship to clients. Home visitors should be alert to this situation and help alleviate any pressure clients might feel to befriend them.

In this section, we have discussed several aspects of home visiting that home visitors have found significantly influence their ongoing work. The next section will address several issues involved in the termination of home visiting services.

The Final Visit

The successful termination of a helping relationship requires considerable skill on the part of the helper. Although some home visitor-client relationships may end unexpectedly, most terminations are anticipated from the beginning of the client's participation in the program. This phase of home visiting should be planned carefully because the experience of termination can influence how the client sustains what she has gained during the relationship with the helper (Levinson, 1977). It is also important because a satisfactory termination to one helping experience usually predisposes a client to seek help when she needs it again.

There are three different reasons for termination, the first one being predetermined, as, for example, when home visiting has been planned to take place for three months. The second reason occurs when the goals of the home visiting program are achieved. The third reason for termination occurs when the client no longer wants to participate in a program, as indicated by words or, more frequently, by uncooperative actions, such as repeatedly not keeping scheduled visits. The decision to terminate home visits under such circumstances is discussed in Chapter 8.

Termination is a process of letting go and moving on. Regardless of the circumstances for termination, certain dynamics are at play for the home visitor and the client. These include feelings ranging from grief to joy. With some clients, home visitors may be relieved to discontinue visiting in difficult circumstances. With others, home visitors may feel sad and experience feelings of loss. Home visitors need to be aware of the emergence of these feelings and expect to have to deal with them.

Clients' feelings may range from pride and satisfaction by the time they terminate home visiting to anger, sadness, or regret. Clients may show negative feelings through words or behavior, such as denial or withdrawal. The home visitor needs to be sensitive to the possible occurrence of such behavior, for example, when a client begins to cancel appointments or not be home for a scheduled visit. One home visitor was trying to schedule her final visit with a client who canceled three times in a row. It was not until the home visitor told this client that she was running out of available times to see her and wanted to say good-bye in person that the client was able to verbalize that she didn't want to say good-bye, and therefore tried to put off the inevitable by canceling the visits.

Much has been written about the termination of helping relationships, most of it focusing upon the negative aspects. However, one research study found that for the majority of clients and their helpers, termination was experienced as essentially positive (Fortune, 1987). Clients focused upon their accomplishments, expressed increased self-confidence, and were eager to try out new skills in future ventures that were acquired during the helping relationship. The helpers in this study felt that they had accomplished much with their clients, which increased their own self-esteem, and they expressed renewed energy to work with future clients.

Home visitors can prepare themselves and their clients for termination by taking specific steps. The first is for the home visitor to discuss impending termination with the client, identifying as specific a time as possible for it. The second step is to review with the client what she has accomplished during the course of home visits. This reflection on accomplishment can be a powerful source of self-esteem for the client. The third step is to talk about the future, including how to build upon goals already achieved. Helping the client to design a strategy for attaining future goals is an excellent method for focusing attention on the future, rather than on the past. When appropriate, the home visitor can help the family make a transition to other community supports.

To benefit the home visitor, reviewing the accomplishments of her visits with a particular family is part of her own self-evaluation. Often home visitors will be able to see clear accomplishments on the part of their clients. Success, however, must not always be judged in terms of client behavior, but in terms of the home visitor's professional development as well. With most clients, the home visitor has learned something of value for herself—a new skill or improvement of an existing skill. Self-learning for the home visitor might also be expressed as, "I never gave up; I learned that I can be persistent" or "I have learned a lot about a different culture."

The difficulty of termination is exacerbated if a home visitor has not maintained a professional relationship with her client. For a home visitor who has become overly involved, termination will be a painful experience. She may miss the relationship on a personal level; she may be worried about her client's welfare; she may feel the loss very intensely. While all terminations may involve some of these feelings, the home visitor who has tried to maintain a professional objectivity will be able to deal with these feelings more effectively than home visitors who have not.

In the Infant Health and Development Program, home visitors approached the termination of their relationships with their clients in terms of a transition rather than as an ending. Although this may seem to be an insignificant conceptual difference, in fact, many home visitors felt that viewing the completion of the program as a transition from one set of circumstances to a new set was very helpful for themselves as well as for their clients. It helped engender the sense of a beginning as well as a recognition of all that had been accomplished.

Participating in a helping relationship requires a certain amount of faith—in oneself, in those we help, and in the process (Combs & Avila, 1985). Home visitors often may not see clear evidence that they have helped their clients to change behavior or achieve desired goals, but what they have done may make some very important differences in their clients' lives. What may be of highest value in a home visitor's work may not be fully realized for a long time after the visits are over since the greatest accomplishments may be encouraging enough confidence, skill, or support to enable clients to think and feel differently about themselves (Schectman, 1986) and ultimately to change their behavior. Believing that their efforts have not been in vain will help to diminish the regrets home visitors may have about leaving a client and can help to terminate the relationship with more ease.

Practical Aspects of Home Visiting

Scheduling and Timing

The scheduling of home visits is fundamental to a home visitor's work. Factors that need to be taken into account when scheduling visits include the purpose of the visit, the planned content of the visit, the location of the family's home, the level of ease or difficulty in contacting and working with the family, and the time available. It is helpful for home visitors to try to adhere to a planned schedule for their own convenience and that of the families with whom they work. Home visitors in long-term programs will probably find that scheduling on a weekly basis provides sufficient lead time, although frequency of visits depends on the goals of the program, the needs of clients, and the responsibilities of the home visitors. When scheduling their visits, home visitors need to allow time for other responsibilities, such as meetings, supervision, community liaison and advocacy work, documentation of services provided, and other tasks, all of which must be worked into the schedule (Wolfe & Herwig, 1986).

Scheduling home visits requires flexibility; well-made plans can be interrupted due to factors beyond the control of either the client or the home visitor. Home visitors need to build enough flexibility into their schedules to adapt to changing situations and to maintain enough psychological flexibility to handle these changes witout excessive distress. A useful approach is to plan carefully, but to expect that changes may be made that will interfere with the execution of these plans.

Home visitors must be sure to allow sufficient time to travel to their client's homes and to complete planned activities. It is helpful, if one's schedule allows, to make a trial run to a client's home prior to the first home visit in order to ascertain the length of time needed to get there and the most efficient route. Making this practice run will help assure a timely arrival for the first home visit. It will also help to orient the home visitor to her client's environmental setting, a procedure that can be very useful in preparing the home visitor for the circumstances in which she will be working (Berg & Helgeson, 1984).

Sometimes the time and distance between clients' homes will be the major consideration in scheduling visits. In fact, home visiting programs that cover large catchment areas will sometimes assign home visitors to families based on geographic location in order to reduce travel time. While this practice may not be as desirable as assigning visitors based on the best match with family needs, it illustrates the significance of travel time as a consideration. Allowing enough time between visits ensures that a delay in finishing one visit will not cause delays for subsequent visits that day. Many programs require that each visit be documented before beginning the next visit. If this is the case, the time and place for accomplishing this task should be taken into account when setting the daily schedule. Many visitors, looking for suitable places to complete their documentation, become "regulars" at coffee shops, libraries, and other convenient spots located between their clients' homes.

Another aspect of timing is becoming knowledgeable about traffic flows: the pattern and duration of rush hours, construction delays, bridge openings and closings, one-way streets, and other situations that have a bearing on travel time. For home visitors who work in congested urban environments, planning visits according to traffic patterns may become *the* deciding factor in arranging their schedules. Keeping a current city or county map at hand is one simple, but quite useful, tool because even home visitors who are working in familiar surroundings may not always be knowledgeable about some of their clients' neighborhoods.

In addition to environmental considerations, timing of home visits should also reflect the needs of home visitors and their clients. For example, home visitors should be aware of their own energy level at specific times of the day and try to maximize visits during their more productive hours. Home visitors may also want to consider the optimal time for scheduling visits to their most difficult clients. Some visitors may want to alternate between visiting clients who require more energy and time with clients who require less. Other visitors may prefer to schedule all of their most challenging clients during one part of the week. We know visitors who chose to schedule all their most difficult clients early in the week when they felt they had the most energy. Others tried to schedule these clients first in each day so that they could reward themselves with seeing their easier clients later in the day. Scheduling is a highly individual matter, but it is important that home visitors become aware of their own preferences and needs so that they can arrange their schedules to maximize their effectiveness and promote their own well-being. Handling a difficult caseload on a very inconvenient schedule can lead to burnout. In addition, an exhausted home visitor will not be in optimal condition to provide the quality of services that clients deserve.

Clients, like home visitors, have preferences for visit times, and, ultimately, their needs will be the most salient consideration when scheduling home visits. Clients will vary widely in their life circumstances. Some will have predictable schedules and home lives that will easily accommodate regularly scheduled home visits. Other clients will have less organized lives, some bordering on chaotic, and regularly scheduled visits will not be acceptable or possible. Learning clients' preferences, habits, and life-styles very early in the home visiting program will help the home visitor plan her visits accordingly.

Because home visits take place in the client's personal living space, the home visitor should show respect for her clients' privacy when scheduling visits by accommodating to their schedules as much as possible. For example, some clients may not want visits scheduled near meal times. Some mothers may not want visits when children are napping; others may specifically prefer the visit while their children are asleep. The dedication of some clients to specific television programs, particularly afternoon soap operas, is another variable worth considering when scheduling home visits. It is wise not to interrupt these or other favorite activities. Visitors who arrive at these times may be welcomed to come inside, but may be expected to wait until the end of a television program before beginning visit activities or discussion. On the other hand, some home visitors have found that briefly watching certain television programs with their clients prior to engaging in program activities provided a useful common ground for building rapport, particularly with clients who did not interact easily.

For parents who work, scheduling an optimal time for a home visit becomes more complicated. After a day's work, both parent and home visitor may be tired, and each may be feeling the pressures of impending evening activities. Neither parent nor home visitor may want the home visits in the evening. If, however, these are the only weekday times available for a visit in the home, it is preferable to arrange other acceptable options whenever possible, such as weekend visits or lunchtime visits at the workplace. In the Infant Health and Development Program, the percentage of all home visits that took place after 5:00 P.M. ranged from 10% to 25% across sites, an arrangement that most home visitors found to be manageable both for themselves and for parents.

We would like to end this section on scheduling by returning to the key element underlying the topic: flexibility. It is necessary for home visitors to find a reasonable balance between achieving specific program goals on every visit and responding to their client's immediate needs. Even after a home visitor and client have arranged a good schedule, the planned purpose of the visit may not be accomplished. There may be days when a client is simply not able to benefit from the planned purpose of the visit. She may be concerned with the threat of eviction, loss of employment, or a child's illness. Under such circumstances, the home visitor should attend to the client's concerns and discuss ways that she can offer help. She may need to help the client reach other service agencies; she may need to listen to the client's problems and offer emotional support; she may need to encourage active problem solving. Trying to impose a home visitor's purposes upon a client when she is clearly not receptive may jeopardize the continuation of the relationship. As one home visitor phrased it, "Flexibility is the key. That was what kept me sane, remembering that nothing was cast in stone, and that I could really trust my instincts" (M. Vinton, personal communication, July, 1989).

Materials

Being well prepared for a home visit enables home visitors to optimize their time with their clients. Having all materials prepared ahead of time allows the home visitor to concentrate on planned activities. This is true for standardized materials as well as for those that must be created for each visit. Depending on the program, materials may include activity cards, pamphlets, toys, and books, as well as recording instruments, evaluation measures, or referral forms. Any form that requires prior completion or materials that need to be organized should be fully prepared before the home visit. It is not unusual for visit planning to take as long as the actual visit, especially if materials must be gathered or made. For some families, it is a good idea to bring copies of materials used during the most recent visit in case the materials have been misplaced or damaged.

Devising an organizing system suitable to the requirements of the program, the home visitor's preferences, and the protection of materials is a practical and important aspect of home visiting. Materials should be organized so that they can be located and used easily. Because home visitors may use many different sets of materials for several clients while traveling from home to home and because they must keep other forms or materials organized at their agency office as well, the need to maintain an adequate organizational system is clear. Neglecting this task can result in loss of time, missed opportunities for effective visits, and considerable frustration for home visitors. We have seen visitors keep a cardboard file box in the trunk of their cars for case-by-case storage of recent and current paperwork. They then transfer older materials to the main office files and add new materials for upcoming visits to their current file box.

Special precautions should be established to protect confidential materials from being lost, damaged, or inadvertently combined with nonconfidential materials that may be distributed during a visit. The issue of confidentiality requires emphasis where written materials are concerned. It would be a serious breach of confidentiality to allow confidential written materials about one client to be seen by another client, either by design or by mistake. A separate container or secured system for confidential materials must be maintained both en route to and during home visits, as well as in the permanent system in the home office.

Children in the Home Visit

In family-support home visiting programs, children will often be the focal point. For many of these programs, home visits are initiated because of the needs of one child. Even when the home visit program is targeted to one child, however, there may often be additional children in the home during the visit. If so, home visitors will have to consider these children's needs. Home visitors should involve the parent in devising a basic strategy for dealing with such children during visits. This might be a plan for the children to be cared for elsewhere, to have special activities for children to occupy their attention, or to incorporate all children into the visit activities.

Home visitors have used a variety of approaches to handling children during home visits. For example, they have agreed with the children on a specific time period during which the children will occupy themselves, either with their own activities or those brought by the home visitor. If the children entertained themselves for the agreed period of time, the home visitor then spent time with the children and gave them special attention. In especially difficult situations, another home visitor has accompanied the regular home visitor and kept the children occupied during the visit.

At times, it may be necessary to help the parent arrange for the children to be absent during a home visit or to conduct the visit somewhere other than in the home. This may be called for when the parent wants to discuss something that children should not hear, such as marital difficulties, or when the needs of one or more children require almost constant adult attention.

Particularly when considering children in the family, the visitor needs to keep in mind the concept that the family is a system and that all members will be affected by factors that directly affect one member. The birth of a handicapped child, for example, could profoundly influence the parents' interactions with their older children and with one another. The diagnosis of a serious condition such as autism or cancer, will bring about changes in family needs and interactions. The siblings of sick children need opportunities to talk about their feelings and have their questions answered. Home visitors must be sensitive to the dynamics of the entire family and incorporate their needs into home visiting procedures.

Handling Special Circumstances

Although most home visits occur in a smooth, orderly fashion, home visitors should be prepared for those that do not. Blaring televisions, children's friends, and curious neighbors may all be part of the home milieu. Home visitors have worked with parents to find creative ways of handling diverse situations, such as meeting on the front stoop or at a restaurant, or having an older sibling agree to entertain the younger ones. If distractions and chaos persist over a long period of time, the home visitor and the family need to discuss these impediments to the home visiting program and find a reasonable method for resolving them.

Frequent mobility of clients is another occurrence that many home visitors find troublesome. If the move is planned and the home visitor is aware of it, she may have to adjust her visiting schedule. However, some families frequently move without notifying the home visitor, creating problems in locating them. It is helpful to arrange with the family at the beginning of the home visiting program how to reach them if they move without notice. For example, the home visitor can get the name, address, and telephone number of a specific relative or neighbor who will generally always know where the family is living and can serve as a contact person. Frequently updating this contact information and maintaining a tracking plan can save home visitors many frustrating hours.

Safety

Knowing how to maintain personal safety is essential in home visiting. Home visitors will not achieve program goals if they are distracted by danger or fear; thus, heroic home visiting will gain little, if anything, in the long run. In order to ensure the safest conditions for home visiting, we recommend that home visitors follow guidelines to protect themselves adequately. Because home visitors work in diverse settings in all areas of the country—some in rural, isolated areas, some in inner cities, and some in suburban areas—and because the populations that home visitors serve are diverse, safety concerns will vary within and across programs. However, several basic safety guidelines are applicable to all home visitors.

The first, and perhaps most important, safety guideline is that home visitors use common sense and follow good judgment. If a home visitor feels unsafe, she probably is; therefore, she should take whatever action is necessary to protect herself. Sometimes home visitors feel guilty about being suspicious of their clients' friends or feeling uneasy in their clients' neighborhoods, and this may lead them to ignore their personal sense of feeling threatened. Ignoring their own concerns, however, puts them at risk and is not advisable. On the other hand, if the home visitor is merely unfamiliar with the client's setting or is visiting in a cultural milieu much different from her own, she should examine the source of her uneasiness before she concludes that she really is unsafe. It is probable that once a home visitor becomes familiar with what is at first strange to her, she will be better able to discern real danger.

The second guideline is that home visitors should always make certain that their supervisor or other responsible staff knows their visit schedule. This schedule should include the name of the client, the date and time of the visit, and the expected time of return. If home visiting is taking place in particularly dangerous environments, programs may devise a monitoring system, such as having the home visitor call in when her visit is complete. When telephones are not available, we recommend the purchase of a two-way radio communication system. As mobile phone units become more affordable, all home visit programs should consider using them, especially programs in rural areas or dangerous urban neighborhoods.

A third guideline for safe home visits is knowing the neighborhoods where home visits take place. As home visitors become familiar to the people who live in the neighborhood, their safety will increase. Learning the layout of the immediate area surrounding clients' homes and the usual types of activities that occur there will provide the home visitor a baseline from which to judge potential danger.

A fourth guideline is to avoid dangerous neighborhoods at night. If this is impossible, arrangements should be made for an escort. One program with limited resources hired an escort, who was available during specific late-afternoon and early-evening hours. Visitors could then schedule certain visits when the escort could accompany them. Another option in this situation is to ask the client or one of her trusted friends to meet the visitor at a previously agreed-upon location and time and then accompany the home visitor into the home, escorting her to her car or other transportation when the visit is over.

The fifth safety guideline is to learn the safest route to and from the client's home. If the most direct route is not on the most well-lighted or patrolled streets, the choice should always be safety first. Parking in clients' neighborhoods may also present safety problems. The only available parking may be at a distance from the client's home or in an area where vandalism is likely to occur. If safe parking cannot be arranged, home visitors may want to consider the use of a paid driver. One program hired a driver who drove visitors whenever traveling to the homes of clients posed a transportation safety problem and then picked them up when the visit was over. Another home visiting program serving a high-risk urban community hired a full-time driver who escorted home visitors to all of their visits.

In addition to the above guidelines, there are several other factors related to safety that home visitors should consider. Most home visitors will be using automobiles for their work. Maintaining an automobile in good condition is clearly a necessary safety precaution for home visitors who must travel long distances and for visitors who must travel through potentially dangerous neighborhoods. Simple safety measures like having enough gasoline in the car for any given working day should be attended to. Because program materials, including confidential ones, may be kept in automobiles, it is imperative that they be secured against theft as much as possible.

The security of personal possessions should be considered when home visiting. To begin with, home visitors should limit carrying or wearing valuable possessions at work. Having more money than is necessary to get through the day is usually inadvisable. Accessories, such as expensive purses and jewelry, are generally not appropriate for home visiting. While it is a rare event, the theft of money or other items from home visitors has occurred, and a great deal of effort was necessary to overcome the ill feelings that ensued. It is much more desirable to prevent such incidents from happening than to have to deal with them once they have occurred.

If a home visitor feels frightened during a visit, she should assess the gravity of the immediate situation and leave if she considers herself to be in danger. Circumstances that may require this response include violence in the home, drug use and drug dealing, evidence of firearms, or the presence of acutely intoxicated or otherwise out-of-control individuals. If the home visitor encounters any of these circumstances during her visits, she should discuss them with supervisory staff and explore alternatives for ensuring her safety. In some circumstances, home visits may be discontinued or changed to a site that is safer than the client's home.

Another precaution is related to the presence of illness in the home. If the home visitor discovers that a family member has a contagious disease, she should exercise judgment about exposing herself to this illness. When confronted by potentially serious communicable illness, such as measles or influenza, home visitors may want to seek consultation with medical personnel about the advisability of visiting in the home. Home visitors will sometimes need to reschedule a visit due to illness in the client's family. Some programs, such as the Head Start home visiting program, have specific procedures for visitors to follow when confronted with illness in clients' homes (Wolfe & Herwig, 1986).

In this section, we have summarized several issues relating to safety that should be addressed in any home visiting program. The basic guidelines underlying our suggestions about safety are that home visitors should use common sense and trust their own judgments, try to prevent dangerous situations from developing, and keep supervisory staff aware of the conditions under which they are visiting.

Dress

Each community and client population has its own standard of dressing, and the home visitor should be sensitive to these standards in her own dress. Remembering that how they dress can influence their relationship with their clients will help home visitors avoid looking overdressed or wearing clothing that is obviously costly. Clothing should be professional, although the degree of formality can vary. Dressing appropriately for the activities planned for the visit is a useful guideline. For example, if the visit requires home visitors to play on the floor with children or conduct physical therapy, clothing should be appropriate for these activities. Home visitors who are nurses or other health professionals may wear uniforms as part of their work.

Maintaining Contact

It is important to establish reliable methods of communication, for a lack of communication between home visitors and clients can create serious difficulties in carrying out a home visiting program. On the other extreme, contact could become so frequent that it becomes an invasion of privacy for either the home visitor or the client. Each program or visitor should set their own limits to prevent this from happening.

Home visitors must make sure that their clients know how to reach them and that they know how to reach their clients. Such communication is facilitated if the client has a telephone, but some clients will not have phones. If the client does not have a telephone, the home visitor will need to devise another method for reaching her client. This may involve the use of neighbors' telephones or a system of leaving notes at the client's home. One home visitor, after many failures, found that supplying her client with addressed, stamped envelopes and stationery to inform her of cancelled visits or unanticipated moves was an effective method to stay in touch. It may be appropriate in some situations for home visitors to give their clients their home telephone numbers. Whether or not this is done may be specified by program policy.

Confidentiality

Home visiting offers professional services to families on a potentially more personal level than other service-delivery systems and, because of this, maintaining appropriate confidentiality is critical. The initial goal home visitors must achieve in order to be successful in their work is to gain their clients' trust. Conveying to a client that the information the home visitor learns about her and her family will be kept confidential is a part of this process.

Every program will have its particular policies and procedures to ensure confidentiality. These will depend on the nature and purpose of the program. However, the following guidelines describe the general extent and nature of the confidentiality that home visitors are expected to keep. Home visitors should not discuss clients by name unless they are doing so with their supervisor or in a case conference with team members. They should always make certain that the setting in which they discuss clients is appropriately private, never discussing clients in public places.

If home visitors are engaged in helping to link one of their clients with other community services, they must obtain their client's permission to do so beforehand. If the client has given permission for the home visitor to share confidential information with specific agencies or individuals, the home visitor should limit the information to that which is essential for the specific situation involved. Issues concerning confidentiality are among the most difficult dilemmas with which home visitors contend and will be further discussed in Chapter 8.

Summary

We have focused herein on various aspects of the process of home visiting, including the practical details of everyday practice and the stages of the process itself, from initiating home visits to ending them. Although home visiting encompasses a wide array of complex issues, being aware of them and preparing to manage such issues can increase home visitors' skill, self-confidence, and satisfaction significantly. In the next chapter, we will address several specific situations that many home visitors will encounter in their day-to-day work.

7

Visiting Families in Stressful Situations

Many families participating in home visiting programs are well-functioning families that might benefit from home visiting services designed to meet one specific need. Other families, however, may not be functioning effectively because of unusual stresses, poor psychological or physical health, inadequate coping skills, insufficient social support, or a lack of adequate environmental resources. Home visiting programs for such families may need to provide more specialized or intensive services, and home visitors who serve these families will need specific skills and knowledge to work effectively with them.

Several guidelines are important in home visiting with families facing stressful circumstances. First, the home visitor needs to be aware that many kinds of problems can occur during home visiting. Second, she needs to understand that these conditions influence multiple family variables and often have a profound and pervasive influence on all family members. Third, the visitor needs to be able to recognize the signs or behaviors indicative of these problems in order to carry out her role as a responsible helper. Fourth, she needs to know which factors in the situation are most important and immediate and how to respond to them appropriately. Finally, she needs to recognize that other resources may be necessary to help address the problem and to be able to enlist available resources as needed. She especially needs to be aware of existing support systems within the community that are also available to provide help, and she must know how to facilitate access to these supports.

We caution home visitors to remember that the existence of a problem does not mean that the family accepts it or is ready to address it. Indeed, enabling a client to recognize that she has a problem and to decide to work on it may be a more formidable task than subsequently helping her to address the problem. Lest home visitors feel overwhelmed with the problems they do encounter, it is critical that they accept the fact that all problems cannot or need not be addressed, either by the visitors or their clients. Furthermore, they need to recognize that progress will often be effected in small increments.

In this chapter, we have identified some of the serious family problems that home visitors may encounter, including child abuse and neglect, family violence, substance abuse and drug dealing and adolescent parenting. For each of these situations, we will present information relevant to home visiting and suggestions for working with families affected by these problems.

Child Abuse and Neglect

Relevant Theory and Research

Although varying descriptions of child abuse exist, most agree that it includes some form of physical injury or sexual abuse. The concept of neglect is much more difficult to define, and its identification is greatly complicated by the existence of differing value systems and styles of parenting. For the purposes of this book, our definition of neglect will include the deprivation of basic needs—shelter, clothing, medical attention, food—and severe emotional deprivation resulting from inadequate human caring and protection. The term *maltreatment* includes both concepts of child abuse and child neglect.

Since 1976 when the first nationwide survey of child maltreatment was initiated, the number of reported cases has steadily climbed. By 1985, 1,928,000 cases of child abuse and neglect were reported nationally, compared to 669,000 in 1976. These data represent a 12.95% increase each year since 1976 (Statistical Abstract of the United States, 1989). Incidence of child abuse for black and white children is almost identical, but it is significantly higher for all families of extremely low incomes (U.S. House of Representatives, 1984).

An ongoing debate focuses on whether the incidence and prevalence of abuse and neglect is increasing, or whether improved and mandatory reporting procedures, at least for child abuse, are simply bringing more cases to public attention. Whether child abuse or only the reporting of it is increasing is not of primary importance to those in the helping professions; rather, the challenge is to develop effective prevention and intervention procedures.

Although there is increasing knowledge about the relationship between social, environmental, and psychological factors and child abuse, no single factor or constellation of factors invariably leads to child abuse. For example, child abuse is often associated with poverty, yet clearly not all persons living in poverty abuse their children. Abusive parents were often victims of child abuse, but not every parent who was abused as a child in turn abuses his or her own child. Conversely, some parents of high economic and educational levels, who appear to function adequately and to have ample resources and social support, abuse their children. Because there are no clearly causative factors that determine whether child abuse will occur, we caution home visitors not to hold preconceived ideas that abuse will always be found in one situation and never in others. Nevertheless, there are patterns of behaviors and circumstances that are known to be potentially associated with child abuse, and home visitors should learn to be vigilant when these conditions exist in families they are visiting.

Research has also shown that abusing parents share certain characteristics. These include low self-esteem, social isolation, and a reluctance to seek or accept help (Fraley, 1983). Abusing parents tend to have a poor understanding of child behavior and development, leading to unrealistic expectations of children; they also have a history of being abused themselves (Steele, 1980). In one study of 439 parent-child dyads, the maltreatment of children was found to be most highly associated with parental rejection and lack of warmth toward children, even when income level was factored in (Herrenkohl, Herrenkohl, Toedter, & Yanushefski,

1984). Abusive parents are frequently ill-equipped to handle the daily stresses and decisions necessary to good parenting; they often have poor problem-solving skills (Azar, Robinson, Hekimian, & Twentyman, 1984). Many have a strong belief that punishment is the proper avenue for child discipline; they also have a strong aversion to "spoiling" their children (Fraley, 1983). Home visitors in programs with which we have been associated have also reported to us that parents in high-risk neighborhoods often sincerely believe that it is their responsibility to "toughen up" their children, who must survive in a harsh environment; physically severe discipline seems to them the logical approach in achieving this goal.

A number of researchers have found that parents who abuse their children are socially isolated; they have few social relationships and do not seek support. Frequently they live in neighborhoods where there is little support available (Warren, 1980.) Polansky, Ammons, and Gaudin (1984) found that mothers who neglect their children describe themselves as being significantly more lonely than do nonneglectful mothers, and they had fewer significant others to provide practical or emotional support. Jackson (1984) described neglectful mothers as tending to withdraw from professionals and warding off relationships; such behavior resulted in feelings of frustration and rejection among professionals who tried to establish working relationships with them. One study of client characteristics found that although it usually requires between 7 and 18 months to treat abusive families, it is extremely difficult to keep such families in treatment for this long (Berkeley Planning Associates, 1982).

Although the risk factors described for child abuse are generally well defined, those for sexual abuse are not so clearly understood. Finkelhor and Baron (1986) describe the circumstances that seem to give rise to sexual abuse as different from the circumstances associated with physical abuse. They found that children appear to have a higher risk of being sexually abused if their natural father is not living with them, especially if their mother has a male partner. Furthermore, their risk of sexual abuse is greater if there is a significant amount of marital conflict or if the child has a difficult relationship with his or her mother. In our experience, we have encountered a situation that others in the field have also noted—a mother will sometimes protect a male partner from outside efforts to stop his suspected sexual abuse of her children, continuing to allow her children to be victimized (J. Crooms, personal communication, July, 1989).

Certain children are more likely to be abused than others (Finkelhor, Hotaling, & Yllo, 1988). These are children who, for a variety of reasons, present additional problems for parents—for example, chronically ill, premature, or low birthweight infants, and hyperactive and handicapped children. Adopted children, children born during times that are particularly stressful for parents, and unplanned or unwanted children also fall into this category (Steele, 1980).

Implications for Home Visitors

What is known about child abuse and neglect has clear implications for home visitors. Families who mistreat their children are known to have difficulty establishing relationships and remaining in treatment, yet they are clearly in need of services. Home visiting offers a number of advantages in working with such families. The most obvious advantage is that home visitors seek out their clients rather than require or expect them to come to an agency or office. For families who need support but do not seek it, such a service seems more appropriate and more promising of positive outcome than agency-based services.

Another advantage to home visiting is that home visitors can diminish clients' isolation through contact with them and can help them to establish both the formal and informal support networks that they need. One striking example of this that we know of is a client who once abused her child but, through the help of her home visitor, did not repeat such behavior. Three years later, she told the home visitor, "You were the person who saved my life that first year because I could count on your coming every week even when I saw nobody else" (M. Hartley, personal communication, June 1989).

As described previously, abusive parents often lack knowledge of children's development and needs, and have poor skills in managing their children's behavior. These parents frequently harm their children out of ignorance. By educating parents about their children's real capabilities and needs at given ages, home visitors can help change the unrealistic expectations parents have of their children. Conveying such basic information has been shown to help prevent child abuse (Garbarino, 1987).

Home visitors need to be attuned to signs that child abuse or neglect may be occurring. These signs might include unexplained cuts, burns or bruises, or an unusual number of "accidents." Exceptionally timid or frightened children may also be an indication that abuse has occurred. One home visitor's suspicions were aroused when her client's young son became inconsolable when he spilled his milk. This home visitor subsequently discovered that her client had been severely beating this child whenever he spilled his food. In other cases, a child might appear malnourished or much smaller than other children of the same age, be inadequately clothed for weather conditions, or not receive available health care when sick.

Because home visitors are in clients' homes frequently, they are more likely than other professionals to become aware of the possibility of child abuse and neglect. Unless some evidence of maltreatment is present, however, we urge home visitors to discuss their concerns with parents cautiously. If the home visitor has established the rapport and trust needed to interact with a parent over a period of time, the parent is less likely to want to disguise or hide what is happening, and discussions about child maltreatment can usually be accomplished without jeopardizing the relationship. The guiding principle here is to investigate and explore what is happening with an attitude of sincere concern rather than judgment. Home visitors must be clear that they want to help the parents as well as protect the children. Most parents do not want to injure their children, and if help is offered to them in a nonaccusatory manner, most will want to accept it. However, parents must also be told that their home visitor will have no choice but to obey the law and report suspected abuse. Home visitors should not mislead parents into believing that they will overlook the parents' behavior because of their relationship with the family.

One example of a successful response to child abuse occurred when a home visitor reluctantly reported her client, a single, professional father, for breaking his daughter's ankle when he punished her too severely. Although the father was very angry about being reported, he soon realized that he needed help with this child. The continued support of the home visitor, including her identification of resources to assist the parent with child care, convinced him to continue his participation in the home visiting program. It is noteworthy that this home visitor needed much support from her supervisor and colleagues to see that her reporting of this client was not only mandatory, but resulted in a better situation for everyone.

Although child neglect is more frequently observed than child abuse, it is less frequently reported (Trainor, 1983). There are several reasons for this, the primary one being a lack of clear definition of what constitutes child neglect. We have cautioned home visitors who are concerned about neglect to first check whether what they are seeing is merely a difference in values orientation and cultural beliefs between themselves and their client families. Child-rearing practices common in one culture may seem like neglect to those of another culture. In light of the broad range of cultures that home visitors may encounter, it is important that they remain alert to their own orientation and be scrupulous in not judging clients according to their own system of values. Scrutiny of the real consequences to children of the behavior in question should consider factors critical to health and safety, not style or other peripheral issues.

Every state has laws that address the issues of child abuse and neglect, and home visitors need to know and comply with these laws. Regardless of program intent, a part of every home visitor's training should include a session on local legal procedures to be followed when child abuse is suspected.

In recent years, concern has developed about the potential for infringement on parental rights by professionals in their zeal to protect children. Some experts believe that, too frequently, interpretation of child abuse laws has inappropriately placed the burden of proof on parents to convince courts that they are capable of caring for their children (Davidson, 1984). Yet, the powerlessness of children must remain paramount in the minds of professionals when weighing the balance between the needs of children and the rights of parents. Where uncertainty or ambiguity exists, home visitors should seek consultation from supervisors, child protection agencies, and other appropriate sources to ensure fair treatment of parents as well as the protection of children.

There may be no situation more difficult for home visitors to face than one involving child abuse. Parents who abuse their children almost always generate feelings of anger in those persons who interact with them. Home visitors may ask themselves, "How can I help this mother who has hurt her child, when I find her behavior so detestable?" We suggest an approach that includes three major points.

First, home visitors must consider the entire family as their clients in need of treatment. Conceptualizing the family as the client links the abuser to the same system as the injured child, and serves to help the home visitor see that if she wishes to help the child, she will need to help the parent. The goal, if at all possible, is to strengthen the family so that it can become a more healthily functioning unit, enabling parent and child to remain together. Second, home visitors must try to perceive the abusive parent as someone who needs help. The third point for home visitors to remember is to try to keep feelings separate from actions. By this we mean that although the abusive parent's action is not acceptable, the feelings of frustration, fatigue, or helplessness behind the actions are legitimate feelings that the home visitor can accept. Likewise, home visitors must accept their own negative feelings toward the parent without translating these feelings into destructive or unprofessional behavior of their own.

Accepting people's feelings and recognizing their needs, however, do not inevitably result in ease of communication and productive interaction. There may be a lack of basic trust on the part of the parent that help will be given, especially if the parent has been an abused child. Helfer (1980) describes in detail the developmental experience of children who grow up in abusive homes, and we refer the reader to that chapter of his book as an excellent presentation of the developmental deficits of abused children that may persist through adulthood. A very brief summary of Helfer's analysis can be captured in the following: The upbringing of abused children has taught them "that they are 'no damn good,' unable to help others, have minimal skills for finding and keeping real close friends . . . and are easily discouraged and depressed" (p. 48).

Home visitors will need considerable support from supervisory and collegial staff when working with maltreating parents. We hope that the discussion presented here will help facilitate home visitors' work with these intensely troubled families.

Family Violence

Just as home visitors may see or suspect child abuse in a family, they may visit in homes where other kinds of family violence occur. According to 1984 FBI statistics, 24% of homicides are perpetrated against family members, which is probably an underestimate given that some undiagnosed infant deaths may also be the result of abuse by a family member (Straus & Gelles, 1986). Women in the United States are more likely to be assaulted in their own homes than anywhere else they may be (Straus, Gelles, & Steinmetz, 1980). Unlike child abuse, cases of wife-beating are not required to be reported. Consequently, fewer data exist on its incidence and prevalence. Although some believe that marital abuse may be declining, it has been questioned whether any reliable estimates can be made for comparison over a period of time (Straus & Gelles, 1986). According to one national survey, violence by husbands against wives declined 27% from 1975 to 1985 (Straus & Gelles, 1986). Although this reduction is encouraging, it still leaves an estimated 1.6 million wives who are beaten at least once annually.

Whether marital abuse is increasing or decreasing, home visitors may find themselves from time to time in households where wife-beating is occurring. (We are aware that men can be the victims in spouse abuse, but we will focus on women because of the considerably higher prevalence of women as victims). Learning some basic facts about spouse abuse will help home visitors be better prepared to handle it.

Relevant Theory and Research

In recent decades, much research has been conducted on the subject of spouse abuse. As a result, there is wide agreement about the dynamics involved in violent relationships, how individuals come to hurt those they claim to love, and why others seem to allow and endure it. Bowlby (1984) has conceptualized family violence as a disorder in the attachment and caregiving functions of family systems. His understanding of abusive relationships, based on his own work and those of many researchers, provides a conceptual framework that visitors may find useful, and which we summarize below.

Many of the men who batter their wives or girlfriends were themselves abused as children. Studies have shown that most men who commit violent crimes outside the home were childhood victims of brutality. Likewise, many battered wives were abused as children, and/or grew up in rejecting and violent households. Since children learn to treat others as they themselves have been treated, to some degree it can be accepted that men who batter and women who endure it are repeating what they have learned in childhood. However, the mere repetition of a pattern of behavior does not sufficiently explain how these dynamics are perpetuated in many families. Looking more closely at the interaction between partners in abusive relationships, several patterns emerge. Each partner appears to believe the other needs him or her, while denying his or her own need for the other. Thus, violence may often follow either threats of abandonment or actual abandonment. Each partner seeks the love and care he or she was denied as a child, the man through coercion, the woman through enduring pain. To each individual, the violent relationship seems preferable to the alternative—being alone.

This conceptualization of the psychodynamics in abusive relationships is not the only way to understand family violence. Sociological and economic factors also need to be considered. Although family violence occurs across the socioeconomic spectrum, it appears to be more frequently associated with lower socioeconomic status (Gelles, 1987). Victims of spouse abuse also appear to be isolated from informal and formal sources of support (Fiedler, Briar, & Pierce, 1984). In addition, the patriarchal structure of our society subtly and overtly supports the physical dominance of men over women, which provides a climate of acceptance for men who beat women (Hilberman, 1980; Hofeller, 1982; Walker, 1983).

Past studies have tended to propose theories about the abused woman's personality and past experience as primary in explaining who would be abused and who would not. These studies would often identify the woman as having been maltreated as a child, having low self-esteem and poor relationship skills, lacking education and coping skills, being immature and impulsive, being unable to express herself, and having learned to feel helpless (Roy, 1977; Walker, 1979). Recent research has focused upon the batterer, and reveals that it is not primarily the characteristics of the victim or her life-style that explain the abuse, but the characteristics of the abuser. Hotaling and Sugarman (1986), as well as other researchers, have discovered that in addition to the history of family violence that male batterers have often endured, they are also often poorly adjusted individuals with antisocial behavior, poor self-esteem and sense of personal efficacy, and low levels of assertiveness, and are frequently of a low educational, occupational, and income status. Many studies have also found that abusive husbands are extremely jealous, suspicious, and possessive of their wives (Hilberman, 1980).

The inevitable question arises: Why do women stay? The answers to this question are varied and complex, and may never fully explain this highly personal choice to an outsider. They are helpful, however, in trying to understand abusive situations and especially in trying to find a way to help. In a review of research on battered women, Strube (1988) found that women who stay are those "who lack the economic means to leave an abusive relationship, are willing to tolerate abuse so long as it does not become too severe or involve the children, and who appear to be very committed to making their relationship last" (p. 98). Battered women often lack enough education or work experience to enable them to develop the skills necessary to support themselves and their children independently; these women believe that their alternative to staying with abusive husbands is poverty (Fiedler, Briar, & Pierce, 1984). One study published earlier this decade indicated that increased employment opportunities for women have provided the resources for more women to remove themselves from violent marriages (Kalmuss & Straus, 1982). Other women may choose to stay because they have accepted the notion, internalized perhaps since their own childhoods, that they are deserving of punishment, or that this is simply the way it is. Others may be too frightened of the consequences of leaving, particularly if they have tried to do so in the past and have suffered repercussions from vengeful husbands or boyfriends. Women frequently see themselves as solely responsible for the entire marital relationship, and hence its failure is also their fault, leaving them too ashamed to seek help or to leave (Duncan, 1982; Pahl, 1985).

The social isolation that we mentioned earlier, coupled with economic dependence, can create a deep sense of powerlessness and leave a woman feeling that she has no ability to extricate herself from a violent situation. One study found that most women who stay with abusive mates do so in order to have a relationship with another person, and some stated that they "needed to interpret their spouses' violence as intensity of caring or love because if they left their mates, there would be no one in their lives" (Duncan, 1982, p. 219). Other women may have profound beliefs regarding marriage and commitment, often derived from cultural beliefs or religious convictions, and may therefore accept whatever situation they find within marriage or other cohabitation arrangements, even if this includes pain and danger (Snyder & Scheer, 1981). And, there are those who out of love, dependence, fear, or desperation, always hope that things will change.

Implications for Home Visitors

It is important that home visitors be conscious of their own feelings about spouse abuse and be aware that they will bring their own orientation toward this form of family violence into the home visiting process. It is also important to know the signs and symptoms of spouse abuse, how and why women may endure violent relationships, and helpful approaches to take when working with abused women. Home visitors also need to be aware of safety issues for their abused clients as well as for themselves.

Why is it important for home visitors to examine their feelings about spouse abuse? The primary reason for doing so is that such examination will prepare them for their own reaction when confronted with the reality or potentiality of spouse abuse; it will thereby enable them to moderate their reactions in a way that will be helpful to their clients. Although it may be natural to want to express strong negative feelings toward the perpetrator and steer a course of rescue for the victim, these reactions may not turn out to be helpful to the client. Home visitors who have had the opportunity to discuss domestic violence as part of their training and to share their thoughts and experiences with colleagues and supervisors will be better equipped to handle it.

In order to assist women in violent households, home visitors must be able to recognize the situation when it is present. It is not likely that a woman will disclose an abusive act unless there has been a long-standing, trusting relationship between her and her home visitor. In light of this, home visitors must be sensitive to signs and clues suggesting violence in the home. The following have been identified as particularly significant: (1) signs of violence, such as bruises, cuts, burns, scratches, and blackened eyes; (2) multiple somatic complaints on the part of the victim; (3) children with multiple somatic complaints, behavioral problems, and emotional disturbance; (4) high level of anxiety, fearfulness, apprehension, and depression; (5) self-destructive behavior, including suicidal ideation and threats, self-mutilation, and chronic self-deprecating remarks; and (6) insomnia and/or violent nightmares (Renz, Munson, Wayland, & Fusaro, 1980). None of these signs will invariably be linked to spouse abuse, but, when present, they should alert the home visitor that something is wrong. When home visitors see evidence that arouses their suspicions, they are obliged to pursue the subject with their clients, albeit carefully.

What can a home visitor do when she suspects that the woman she is visiting is being abused? First of all, the home visitor needs to make it clear that she is willing to talk about and deal with the topic. As a part of the trusting relationship that the home visitor and client have established, the client needs to know that the home visitor is aware of the potential for violence in people's lives (not just in this particular situation) and is open to addressing it. This approach is very different from confronting a client with suspicions.

If the abused woman should disclose to a home visitor that she is being harmed, the home visitor should respond with concern and attention, encouraging the client to talk about her situation. After the client has talked about the abuse, the home visitor should address several factors, if the client is willing. These include safety issues, educating the client about resources available to her, and helping her with coping strategies.

To help the client, it is important to obtain information about the type, severity, frequency, and context of the violent episodes (Renz, et al., 1980). For example, is the woman in imminent danger of severe harm? If so, precautions must be taken, if the woman allows, to ensure her and her children's safety. If the violence is predictable, is there any way to avoid it? Are there resources available to help the client? These would include police, shelters, legal assistance, counseling, and financial relief. What plans can the client make for escaping violence once she senses an episode is imminent? How can she deal with violence once it has begun? These are all very practical avenues to explore and can be very helpful, perhaps lifesaving, in emergencies.

Often, a battered woman has become isolated physically, emotionally, and socially. The regular presence of a home visitor can help reduce that sense of isolation. In addition to linking her to community agencies that can provide practical relief, a home visitor may be able to help her client join a support group for battered women. Before referring a client to a support group, however, home visitors should find out about the leadership and composition of the group. Some visitors have found that ethnic minority women are very reluctant to participate in groups in which the leader and most of the participants are white, and vice-versa (J. Crooms, personal communication, July 1989).

Research has found that most battered women are unaware that other women have similar problems (Gelles, 1987). Learning that others have experienced the same things, have had the same feelings, and have dealt with the same realities can be very effective in decreasing a woman's isolation. By hearing about other women's experiences and sharing her own, a woman may also be better able to think about alternatives to her situation. Learning that they are not alone also tends to help battered women become less self-critical and decreases their sense of themselves as mentally unstable (Duncan, 1982). Battered women are often relieved to discover that their reactions are "normal" for their situations, and that others also feel afraid, helpless, angry, guilty, ashamed, and responsible for the violence.

One essential way to offer help is to engage the abused woman in active problem solving in her own behalf. Helping her to say what it is that she really wants, helping her identify her options and resources, and then discussing their consequences can help the client become aware of the strengths and options that she does indeed possess. This problem-solving approach is particularly suitable for battered women because people under extreme stress have difficulty thinking through their concerns and have often lost hope. Increasing an individual's sense of self-control through successful problem solving is an obvious goal for effective home visiting. It is especially appropriate when visiting in households where violence is a problem.

Possibly the most important concept for an abused woman to learn and accept is that she does not deserve to be abused, no matter what circumstances surround the beating. It is critical that the victims do not blame themselves for the brutality they suffer. Popular stereotypes and myths, though changing in the late 1980s, tend to perpetuate the concept that women actually provoke violence and even enjoy it, and thus are not deserving of assistance (Hofeller, 1982). Battered women often come to believe these ideas themselves, which increases their sense of shame and thus makes it more difficult for them to seek help. Home visitors can do much to correct these misconceptions of battered women.

Research has shown that support from outside the family influences the patterns of violence; battered women who receive outside support and encouragement are better able to get help and make changes within their family lives (Giles-Sims, 1983; Pahl, 1985). Home visitors can contribute to the support abused clients will need in order to leave their abusive mates or effect satisfactory improvements within their relationships.

If the home visitor is working with a woman who does not want to talk about the abuse she is receiving, the visitor initially should voice her concern and willingness to listen. She may need to repeat her concern many times. If the client does not respond to this approach, the home visitor must not insist on pursuing the subject, for doing so could very well alienate the client and destroy an existing good relationship. Home visitors have found that most abused women will, in time, want to talk about abusive incidents.

If at any time a home visitor feels that she is in danger when visiting a violent household, she should remove herself as quickly as possible. When threats to the home visitor's personal safety are grave enough, home visiting should be terminated in consultation with program staff until the danger abates. Every home visiting program should have clear policies and procedures for handling dangerous situations, and these should be a part of each home visitor's training. Should home visits be stopped, the program should make strenuous efforts to maintain contact with the abused spouse, possibly visiting her in another, safer environment, or establishing other methods for communicating. It is especially critical in this situation that home visitors leave the lines of communication open and offer the abused woman continued support.

It is not the role of the home visitor to tell the battered woman what she should do. There are several reasons for this. Primary among them is the fact that the woman must bear the consequences of whatever action she chooses to take (or not take); the home visitor does not. The woman knows her husband or boyfriend intimately; the home visitor does not.

Another reason to refrain from giving direct advice is that only the battered woman knows exactly how she feels. In spite of the most sincere and skillful efforts at understanding, the home visitor cannot know her client's actual feelings. An additional reason for not making decisions, even for a client willing to allow it, is that this may reinforce the client's feelings of powerlessness and inability to control her own life (Renz, et al., 1980).

When visiting families that may be overwhelmed with problems of family violence, it is critical that home visitors neither take on the responsibility of this knowledge and its demands for treatment alone nor be overwhelmed themselves by unrealistic expectations about what they can accomplish. With violent families, as with other stressful client situations, home visitors must appraise their own knowledge and skills, and seek substantial assistance from supervisors and colleagues to help them gather the resources and emotional support they need. Furthermore, in dealing with family violence, as with any of the other situations described in this chapter, home visitors need to be very well informed of existing community resources and to help families access such resources.

Substance Abuse

Every home visitor needs to be aware of the possibility of substance abuse among her client population. Although home visitors may be more likely to be aware of such abuse with populations identified as at risk, they should be aware of the possibility that clients of all ages, both male and female, and in all educational and socioeconomic groups are potential abusers of alcohol and other drugs. In some neighborhoods, illegal drug dealing may also be relatively common. Home visitors must be aware of the impact that drug dealing can have on their home visiting procedures and on the lives of clients and their families.

Relevant Theory and Research

Alcoholism and other drug addictions are debilitating illnesses that severely affect the addict and his or her family. It is estimated that there are at least 10 million alcoholics among the adult population in the United States, a number that includes only those individuals who have been identified through treatment programs, drunk driving offenses, and other public records (Kaslow & Mountz, 1985). The current level of illegal drug use in this country is not accurately measurable due to its illegality and the fact that its consequences on the human body are not always as demonstrable as are those of alcohol. Nevertheless, we know that there is a serious national problem with drug use and dealing.

The signs of alcoholism and other drug addictions range from the obvious, such as acute intoxication, to the subtle, such as confusion. Depression also frequently accompanies alcoholism (Madden, 1984). A client who does not remember having set up an appointment may have scheduled it while under the influence of a drug. Inability to function on the job, financial difficulties, and poor social relationships may indicate a problem with substance abuse. Insomnia and consequent daytime somnolence and irritability, inability to concentrate, and expressions of paranoia may also be symptoms of addiction (Senay, 1983). Home visitors have also found that extreme changes in mood from one visit to the next often signal problems with substance abuse (for example, changes from friendliness and cooperation during one visit to blatant hostility at the next). Problems with the legal system, such as an arrest for drunken driving, may be part of the constellation of symptoms. Family relationships may be unstable and unpredictable.

The consequences of maternal substance abuse for children can begin before birth. Women who abuse substances are at increased risk of having premature and low birthweight babies (Bry, 1983). It is widely recognized that heavy alcohol consumption can result in serious birth defects, collectively known as "fetal alcohol syndrome" (Blume, 1985). Children with this disorder usually are of low birthweight and have mental retardation, facial malformations, or other abnormalities. Even moderate amounts of alcohol consumption are believed to have harmful effects on fetal development. Fetal alcohol syndrome is the third leading cause of mental retardation due to birth defects (Blume, 1985).

The incidence of babies born already addicted to drugs in utero is increasing (U.S. House of Representatives, 1986). Infants of addicted mothers may suffer from neonatal withdrawal symptoms, such as tremors, respiratory and feeding difficulties, and decreased muscle tone (Bry, 1983). When cocaine is the addicting substance, infants are at significantly increased risk of Sudden Infant Death Syndrome. Cocaine-addicted mothers have higher rates of spontaneous abortion and onset of labor with ruptured placenta immediately after cocaine injection (Chasnoff, Burns, Schnoll, & Burns, 1985). Marijuana use during pregnancy has also been found to have adverse effects on fetal growth and development (Hingson, Alpert, Day, Dooling, Kayne, Morelock, Oppenheimer, & Zuckerman, 1982).

Another serious risk to infants at birth is the danger that mothers infected with Acquired Immuno-Deficiency Syndrome (AIDS) can transmit the virus to the developing fetus. This danger is relevant to substance abuse because two of the groups at high risk for contracting AIDS are intravenous drug users and their sexual partners (National Institute on Drug Abuse, 1987). Thus, a mother who is injecting herself with cocaine, opiates, or other substances and who shares needles with AIDS-infected users is acutely vulnerable to AIDS. Infected mothers can, in turn, transmit the virus through the placenta to the developing fetus or to the newborn through exposure to infected blood and vaginal fluids during birth; the virus can also be transmitted to the nursing baby through infected breast milk (Rogers, 1987). Although not all babies born to mothers who have AIDS are infected, they are clearly at significant risk.

The effect that parental substance abuse can have on parenting is also of grave concern. Several studies have shown that the quality of parental care usually suffers when substances are abused (Finnegan, 1979; Mello, 1980). Behaviors that are at least in part a result of substance abuse include mothers' increased irritability, depression, anxiety, and aggression, along with decreased ability to learn from experience (Pickens & Heston, 1981). These factors suggest an increased risk for child neglect and abuse among children of addicted parents. Parents who are seriously involved with substances can become so preoccupied with obtaining and maintaining their supply that they could neglect their children. Home visitors have found very young children left alone while their mother leaves to "shoot up". They have also found clients acutely intoxicated or comatose while their infants and young children were present and unsupervised.

Substance abuse is often associated with violent behavior in families. This relationship is not surprising since it is well known that substance abuse impairs judgment and self-control. Many home visitors have worked with clients who will say, "He hits me and the kids only when he's been drinking; otherwise, things are fine." But, "only when he's been drinking" can translate into a potentially dangerous and severely dysfunctional family.

Implications for Home Visitors

The appropriate responses for a home visitor who suspects that her client may be abusing a substance are similar to responses discussed earlier in the sections on child abuse and family violence, including openness to discussing the problem, offering support, and helping the client obtain professional services.

Behaviors associated with substance abuse can have many different causes, and a home visitor should not conclude that her client is having problems with substance abuse on the basis of any one of these factors. However, if she observes such dysfunctional behaviors over a period of time, a home visitor is well advised to investigate the possibility that substance abuse may be involved.

A home visitor who is aware of the risks to infants arising from maternal substance abuse is in a position to share this knowledge with a client who is either considering pregnancy or is already pregnant. She is obliged to inform an unknowing mother about such conditions as Fetal Alcohol Syndrome and AIDS and either to provide (if appropriate) or help her client obtain counseling and medical care. In almost every community, there are programs for the treatment of addiction. These usually include public clinics, both outpatient and inpatient, offered through community mental health centers, and private clinics and counselors. Self-help groups, such as Alcoholics Anonymous, and support groups for family members, such as Alanon and Alateen, are found in most communities, as well as self-help groups for the abusers of other drugs. These groups are free of cost and confidential. Home visitors must realize, however, that clients often deny that they have a substance abuse problem or are very adept at hiding one. Until they accept that they have a problem, they will not be willing to accept help with it.

Although alcoholism and the abuse of other drugs are comparable in symptomatology and consequences, there is one clear difference between them: Alcohol consumption is legal for individuals above the drinking age, while the use of nonprescription drugs is not. The difference that this presents for the home visitor is a question about whether or not to report illegal drug use to the proper authorities.

Unlike child abuse laws, there are no specific laws requiring the reporting of illegal drug use, except for underage alcohol use, as far as we are aware. However, there is an element of moral pressure exerted on members of society to abide by the laws and not to condone those who break them. Our suggestion is that the home visitor first help her client to secure professional treatment for her drug problem. If this fails and if the home visitor believes that her client and/or her children are endangered because of drugs, further action is warranted. Such action may involve notification of child protective services, substance abuse agencies, or law enforcement, depending on local regulations.

As we discussed in an earlier section on safety issues, home visitors need to be aware of their own vulnerability to danger, as well as the vulnerability of their clients. When families are deeply involved in drug addiction or drug dealing, home visitors must assess the potential danger to themselves in continuing to visit in the home. Under no circumstances should home visitors remain in the client's home when drug dealing or illegal drug use is openly occurring. The visitor must make it clear to her client that she cannot condone or participate in illegal activities and that her intention is to leave the home if this happens. This position does not mean that a home visitor must remove herself from a home immediately if she suspects that her client is under the influence of drugs or when she sees drug paraphernalia in the home. There should be evidence of illegal activity before a home visitor feels it necessary to leave.

Visiting families that are heavily involved with substance abuse on a continuing basis can be very stressful. In addition to the support a home visitor needs to visit in such settings, ongoing assessments should be made of the client's ability to benefit from home visiting services. If a client is unwilling to seek help for substance abuse that seriously impairs her ability to function, especially her parental functioning, she may well be unable to benefit from whatever the home visiting program has to offer.

Adolescent Parents

Adolescent parents may present particular challenges to home visitors. Although adolescent parenting in and of itself is not a "problem" in the way that family violence and substance abuse are, it does deserve special consideration here. Home visiting with an adolescent parent requires a level of awareness, sensitivity, and skill idiosyncratic to the situation. Because home visiting programs often address the needs of infants and children, it is likely that home visitors will have adolescent mothers in their caseloads.

Relevant Theory and Research

In 1985, 477,705 infants were born to women younger than twenty, representing 12.7% of all live births in this country (Hughes, Johnson, Rosenbaum, Butler, & Simons, 1988). Eighty-five percent of these teenage parents were unmarried and, of these, more than 80% lived in households headed by their own parents, other relatives, or friends; only 26% of all teen parents maintain their own households (U.S. House of Representatives, 1986).

Although indications are that births to teens are declining somewhat, partly due to the decreasing population in this age group, teenage pregnancy is still increasing (Hughes, et al., 1988). With the possibility that access to abortions for indigent teenagers may become more restricted, adolescent mothers may experience an even higher birth rate in the coming years, and there may also be an increase in dangerous illegal abortions and their attendant health risks.

Given these figures, it is evident that home visitors need to understand the social, psychological, economic, and health status of adolescent parents. We can begin to understand the challenges facing adolescent parents by looking at their offspring. Infants born to teenage mothers are significantly more likely to be of low birthweight than are infants born to older mothers (Hughes, et al., 1988). Low birthweight carries certain risks to the infant, including increased likelihood of developmental delays, serious illnesses, and hospitalizations. Low birthweight infants place a heavier burden of care on parents than normal-weight infants, who typically do not present such an array of problems (Mc-Cormick, 1985).

The health and developmental status of adolescent parents that is relevant to home visiting can be summarized as follows. Teenage mothers are less likely to receive prenatal care than are older mothers (Hughes, et al., 1988). Biological youth is not an independent risk factor in contributing to low birthweight babies and other poor birth outcomes, but factors that are often present with teenage parents such as poor prenatal care, low socioeconomic status, and nutritional status, do clearly contribute to risk (Mc-Cormick, 1984). Adolescent mothers are also at increased risk for toxemia, anemia, prolonged labor, and premature labor (U.S. House of Representatives, 1983).

In addition to the risks of poor health, adolescent mothers face the disruption and perhaps termination of their education, thus compromising their potential wage-earning capacities, just when those capacities acquire new and urgent meaning—a child to support. The social consequences of adolescent parenthood are also great. Although many new mothers feel isolated, for adolescents this sense of isolation may be greatly heightened because just as their interests begin to focus intently on their peer group, they become isolated from those peers. Furthermore, teenaged parents are isolated from the childrearing information networks and those that provide long-term social support (Halpern & Covey, 1983).

Adolescent parents usually have inadequate knowledge of child development. Hence, they often overestimate their children's abilities and underestimate their needs, thereby posing the risk of abuse when the child cannot perform as expected. In addition, adolescent parents, through ignorance, may neglect to provide adequate food, clothing, and medical care. Studies have also found hat adolescent parents, particularly the poor and youngest ones, generally do not provide cognitive stimulation sufficient for normal development; consequently, their children are often deficient in cognitive areas (Halpern & Covey, 1983).

Sadler and Catrone (1983) describe adolescent parents as dealing with a dual developmental crisis—that of adolescence and that of parenting. They provide a conceptual framework for understanding the processes of both developmental stages and how these lie in potential conflict with each other. Adolescence and early parenting are both periods of growth and change, with unique developmental tasks and challenges, and the resulting pressure of these two growth periods on adolescent parents is significant.

The characteristic egocentricity of adolescence stands in direct conflict with the requirement that parents recognize their infants as separate from themselves and in need of intensive care and attention. Often young mothers are not able to differentiate between their own feelings and needs and those of their infants. Consequently, they may project their own thoughts, feelings, and reactions onto their infant, such as preferences for foods or clothing. This lack of perception that their infants' needs are separate and different from their own may have harmful consequences for the infant, with no harmful intent on the part of the mother. One home visitor whose adolescent client's baby was diagnosed as "failure to thrive" found that her client had been trying to feed her 4-month-old those foods she herself most enjoyed: french fries, soft drinks, ice cream, and even pizza!

Another developmental task of adolescence is the diverting of attention from the nuclear family to others in the social environment (Sadler & Catrone, 1983). Teenagers need to develop social relationships in preparation for establishing and maintaining mature adult relationships in the future. This need to intensify social relationships with peers collides head-on with the infant's need for mother's attention. In addition, just when adolescents must and do begin to strive in earnest for independence from their families, having an infant to care for will usually increase the adolescent mother's dependence on her own parents for emotional and economic support, as well as for direct care for the infant. The decision about who cares for the infant may become an area of serious conflict between mother and grandmother and a battlefield on which a home visitor may find herself.

The third developmental task that may create conflict between adolescence and parenting is that of cognitive development. In Piagetian terms, the adolescent is in the process of acquiring the ability to think abstractly. This acquisition is a gradual process and is not accomplished simply because of the demands of reality. Consequently, the adolescent parent may not yet be able to think in the abstract or future-oriented terms that are necessary to problem solve for her infant's care. She may not be able to understand the concepts of child development; therefore, she may have unrealistic expectations of current child needs and developmentally appropriate behavior, with limited ability to plan for the child's future needs.

Implications for Home Visitors

Being aware of the developmental tasks and needs of adolescents can help enable home visitors to accept, without judgment, behavior and attitudes that they might find unacceptable in adult parents. This does not mean that home visitors should be willing to compromise the health and safety of their adolescent clients' children. Rather, it means that home visitors should acknowledge the developmental context of the adolescent and make allowances for adolescent behavior.

It is helpful to remember that adolescents do not comprise a homogeneous group. They vary widely in levels of maturity, cognitive development, personality characteristics, and environmental setting. It is up to the home visitor to assess her individual client, gearing her assistance to the needs and strengths appropriate for that particular client. Most adolescent parents, however, need support, and home visiting provides an excellent procedure for providing this support. In a study of adolescent mothers, Colletta and Gregg (1981) found that the level of stress adolescent mothers experienced depended primarily on three variables. In order of primacy, these were amount of support received, level of self-esteem, and coping style. Social support is widely recognized as an important element in reducing stress (Caplan, 1974; Moroney, 1987), and stress has been shown to interfere with mothers' ability to care for their children due to its role in contributing to maternal depression (Belle, 1982).

Home visitors' roles in supporting adolescent parents are critical, whether adolescent parents remain in their parents' home or establish their own households. Although technically there are resources available to teenage parents in many communities, they are often fragmented and confusing; navigating the bewildering network of bureaucratic procedures can be a formidable obstacle for young parents (Moore & Burt, 1982). Helping her client learn how to make use of available services is a significant responsibility for the home visitor and can have many beneficial effects. Clients learn not only where the services are and how to use them, but through the modeling of the home visitor, they can learn how to be better advocates for themselves and their children.

As we mentioned earlier, one of the fundamental tasks of adolescence is the development of independence from one's parents. This becomes especially problematic for an adolescent mother who depends upon her own parents for child care and other support. Because the home visitor is an objective and reliable adult outside the teenager's family, she is in a unique position to assist the adolescent with learning her new role as mother and to help her continue to develop those skills needed to increase her own independence.

The confusion over parenting roles in a multigenerational household can, however, present home visitors with several challenges as well as opportunities. We have found that home visitors are often unwillingly thrust into the controversy between the adolescent mother and her parents over the issue of who is really responsible for the adolescent's baby. Home visitors in other programs have reported similar difficulties (Olds, 1988). There are no easy answers to this dilemma, but we do have several suggestions we believe are helpful.

Foremost, the home visitor needs to approach the adolescent parent and her family from a family systems perspective. The imbalance that invariably results when an adolescent parent and her child reside with the adolescent's parents must be openly acknowledged, and all family members need assistance in learning to accept this imbalance and restructure family roles and boundaries (Nathanson, Baird, & Jemail, 1986). A home visitor must take care not to contribute to family disequilibrium by aligning herself with any one family member against other family members. Supporting all family members honestly will help to alleviate angry and painful feelings, and help to minimize the possibility that the baby will become the center of a power struggle.

In terms of focusing attention on the child's primary caregiver, it is important to recognize two existing realities; the first being that the infant's grandmother will almost always be significantly involved in the child's care, and her feelings and contributions need to be acknowledged. The second reality is that over the child's lifetime, the mother will most likely assume ultimate responsibility for the child's care. Therefore, although the grandmother must be acknowledged by the home visitor, the mother will usually be the primary caretaker in the long run. The strengths that the home visitor helps her adolescent client develop, such as advocating for her child with community agencies, would serve to benefit both child and mother as the mother learns to generalize these skills to other aspects of her life.

Although we have emphasized in earlier sections the importance of responding to clients' needs when they seem to override program goals, this deserves particular emphasis when working with adolescent parents. These young people are often experiencing high levels of stress, confusion, frustration, and despair, and home visitors' efforts should first be directed to addressing the parents' needs. In the Parent to Parent Program in Vermont (Halpern & Covey, 1983), in which home visitors met with adolescent parents for the purpose of improving their parenting skills, most visitors found that in the early weeks of the program, the greater part of their efforts were focused upon the personal problems of the adolescent mother. Over time, however, the majority of these home visitors found that they could shift their attention more closely to the planned content of the program. Our experience has been similar with most parents, but especially with adolescent parents.

One unintended side effect of any home visiting program, as we have mentioned earlier in this book, is that clients can feel overwhelmed by the expectations of the program and the copious amounts of new information. This may be particularly true for adolescents. Home visitors we know have found that concentrating on only one aspect of parenting at one time is often essential when working with teenaged mothers. Prioritizing children's needs should serve as a guideline in helping home visitors to determine in which order to work on issues with adolescent parents. Home visitors have found that adolescents often respond enthusiastically to their own achievements and are interested in building on these.

Home visiting with adolescent parents can be frustrating and difficult. Yet, as we know from our own and many home visitors' experiences, this can be one of the most rewarding aspects of home visiting for both the young parents and the home visitor. Keeping in mind some of the unique problems and perspectives of adolescent parents should enable home visitors to find ways to provide them with the help they so keenly need.

Summary

This chapter has presented four distinct topics for consideration: child abuse, spouse abuse, substance abuse, and teenage parenting. Although these topics have been treated separately in this chapter, in reality, home visitors may expect to find elements of all of these influencing some of their clients' lives. For example, the abused children we discussed may grow up to abuse their own children, or to be the perpetrators or victims of spouse abuse. Substance abuse is frequently involved in both child abuse and domestic violence. The stresses of adolescent parenting may well increase the vulnerability of these young parents to abusing their children, being abused by their parents and sexual partners, and turning to alcohol or other drugs for relief.

Home visitors are therefore likely to encounter families that are dealing with more than one of the above-mentioned problems. Just as these are not usually found in isolation from one another, home visitors will not find individual family members suffering from a problem that does not affect the whole family. The entire family system is affected by the problems we have presented in this chapter. Our reminder for home visitors is that the family itself, rather than any individual family member, is best seen as the client. Supporting and strengthening the family as a unit is the ultimate and underlying goal for any home visiting intervention.

8

Professional Issues Facing Home Visitors

Although the roles of home visitors vary considerably, concern about human welfare is a common thread within the profession. The path to promoting and supporting that welfare, however, is not always clear. At times, this path brings the home visitor face-to-face with the differences in values, customs, and beliefs inherent in a multicultural nation and in a multidisciplinary helping profession. Making judgments concerning intervention procedures may reveal differences between the values of the client and those of the home visitor, and sometimes between the values of the home visitor and those of her program. Such problems are not unique to home visiting, but they are a part of all helping professions in which one person is in a position to make decisions concerning the services offered to another. Ethical dilemmas evolve into questions in the home visitor's mind, beginning with the basic question, "Should I intervene?" If the home visitor answers "Yes," then other difficult questions, such as these, will arise: "What is the best way to intervene? How do I balance the needs of the different family members? Should I *always* tell the truth? Should I tell the truth in *this* situation? When, if ever, can I share information given to me in confidence?"

Ethical questions such as these are an intrinsic part of many aspects of home visiting already described in this book, such as philosophy, training, and working with families. In each of the previous sections, we have indicated that complex issues are often part of a home visitor's job. We have set aside this chapter on ethical and professional issues so as to provide a more in-depth consideration.

In the first half of this chapter, we will focus on several ethical concerns that can emerge in the relationship between a home visitor and a client. We will also discuss guidelines and a code of ethics that may help the home visitor weigh her obligations when faced with dilemmas. The last half of the chapter will deal with two broader issues that face the profession of home visiting—issues that also involve questions of values—burnout and working in multidisciplinary teams.

Home Visitor/Client Issues

Many different ethical questions are likely to arise during the life of a home visitor's relationship with a client. In this section, we will present two descriptions of the kinds of ethical dilemmas that the practice of home visiting raises. Then we will propose a framework for evaluating such situations, and explore several specific ethical issues, including honesty, confidentiality, and the fair and equitable allotment of a home visitor's time.

One frequently encountered question is how to determine what is in a client's best interest. If a mother has agreed to participate in a home visiting program to acquire parenting skills and to learn specific educational activities to use with her child, the mother is clearly the client. But sometimes grandparents and older siblings become involved, and this is when home visitors may encounter a dilemma. Visiting a client who lives in an extended family can lead to home visitors being drawn into conflicts between different family members, as in, for example, a disagreement between a parent and a grandparent about how best to raise a child. At these times, deciding what is in "the client's best interest" may become more difficult because three or four people, or even the whole family, may be involved as identifiable clients.

A different kind of ethical dilemma is raised when there is a law or policy that seems to conflict with a home visitor's ability to help the family. The decision to report suspected child abuse is a classic example of such a dilemma. Most states require professionals to report cases to state authorities, but sometimes home visitors believe that such reporting would disrupt their relationship with the parent, a relationship they believe is more helpful to the abusing parent than one the state agency is likely to impose.

Regardless of individual family circumstances and no matter how doubtful the outcome of reporting may be, home visitors must follow the law on reporting abuse or neglect. Though the policy and procedure may be clear, that does not alleviate the anxiety or reduce the difficulty faced by the home visitor who is trying to decide on the best course of action regarding an abuse or neglect situation. When has a parent gone over the line from firm discipline to child abuse? How much "neglect" is reportable neglect? Once abuse is reported, how does one continue to be an effective home visitor with the family? Neither science nor research can tell a home visitor exactly what to do in these situations. They involve judgments based on knowledge of each family's circumstances. The following section presents several guidelines that should be of help in making these judgments.

A Framework for Assessing Values Conflicts

In his book, *Ethical Dilemmas in Social Service,* Frederick Reamer (1982) discussed the place of reason and moral principles in social service. Fundamental to any discussion of ethics are two features of the actions involved, specifically whether the actions are voluntary and purposive. If the actions are voluntary, they are under the person's control. If they are purposive, they are to achieve basic goods (food, shelter, life) or additive goods (goods beyond the basic, such as education, self-esteem, income). By evaluating the weights of these various features involved in human service work, Reamer (pp. 76-79, 1982) suggested the following six guidelines to consider when resolving conflicts between values and duties:

1. *Rules against basic harms to the necessary preconditions of action (such as life, health, food, shelter, mental equilibrium) take precedence over rules against harms, such as lying or revealing confidential information, or threats to additive goods, such as recreation, education, and wealth.*[1] This guideline means that the basic well-being of a person is more important than following rules or acquiring secondary

benefits. For example, a person's life or health is more important than a home visitor's absolute honesty. We know of one home visitor who was faced with a dramatic example of such a conflict. She felt compelled to lie to a threatening father concerning the location of his girlfriend and child, even though the home visitor herself had taken them to a women's shelter. In this case, the clients' safety took precedence over telling the truth as to their whereabouts. This guideline also justifies a home visitor's decision to report an abusive or neglectful mother to a protective services agency. In such cases, the child's safety takes precedence over the protection of the mother's confidentiality.

2. *An individual's right to basic well-being (the necessary preconditions of action) takes precedence over another individual's right to freedom.* A client may freely choose to do something that we might consider self-destructive, unless the exercise of that freedom interferes with someone else's basic well-being. A home visitor may consider it a problem when a client continues to take drugs while on probation, even though client and home visitor both know that abstention from drugs is a condition of the woman's parole. The home visitor may counsel and cajole her client, and may urge attendance at a treatment program. The scope of intervention for the drug problem at this point is between home visitor and client. If the woman's behavior is harming children in the household, either through neglect or by placing them in dangerous situations, the need for intervention necessarily changes. The children's basic well-being takes precedence over the mother's freedom of choice to take drugs. The home visitor may need to report what she has seen to the protective services agency.

3. *An individual's right to freedom takes precedence over his or her own right to basic well-being. If an informed client voluntarily chooses to take an action that could threaten himself, his freedom to do so takes precedence over his basic mental and physical well-being.* The key words in this guideline are "informed client." A home visitor may temporarily interfere to determine how informed or how voluntary the client's actions are. Maternal depression is a type of problem that many home visitors may encounter in programs serving mothers and infants. A home visitor may urge the depressed parent to seek therapy, but she can refuse to do so. The mother's condition could worsen to the point where the home visitor believes that the mother is suicidal. The home visitor

should then take responsible action, knowing that seriously depressed individuals are not always able to respond in their own best interest. Other family members (husband or parent) need to be involved so that the visitor can urge them to seek help for the woman. Through her agency or other authority, the home visitor may recommend that her client be evaluated for possible hospitalization. It is then up to a psychiatrist or psychologist, not the home visitor, to determine the voluntariness of the woman's actions.

4. *The obligation to obey laws, rules, and regulations to which one* [the home visitor] *has voluntarily and freely consented ordinarily overrides one's right to engage voluntarily and freely in a manner which conflicts with these laws, rules, and regulations.* This guideline means that home visitors are generally expected to obey the laws of society and the policies of their employer and profession. For example, home visitors may be expected to follow an agency rule that a supervisor must be consulted before any referral is made to an outside agency on behalf of a client. Although a home visitor may believe that this rule inhibits her ability to work effectively, she has voluntarily agreed to the rule by accepting employment with the agency, and she must honor it. Under Rule 5, exceptions to this expectation are discussed.

5. *Individuals' (clients') rights to well-being may override laws, rules, regulations, and arrangements of voluntary associations in cases of conflict.* Following this guideline, a home visitor is obligated to violate a rule if a client's well-being is in clear jeopardy. Assume, for example, that a home visitor arrives for a home visit and observes that the child is in serious respiratory distress. Furthermore, the mother has not understood the seriousness of the child's breathing difficulties. The home visitor may want to call an ambulance immediately or take the mother and child to an emergency room. If she follows her agency's referral rule mentioned in the example above, however, she is supposed to have her supervisor's authorization. What if no supervisor can be reached by phone? What if the family she is visiting has no phone? In this case, the child's right to timely medical care should override the agency's rules for referral, and the home visitor should seek help immediately. Home visitors should be informed in advance of the possibilities for such exceptions and should be given guidelines for making decisions under such circumstances.

6. *The obligation to prevent basic harms such as starvation, and to promote public goods such as housing, education, and public assistance overrides the right to retain one's property.* Reamer presents this guideline as the justification for society to tax its members in order to provide for those in need. Among home visitors, one often sees this guideline in action when home visitors use their own money to buy groceries that will feed a family through the weekend, or give clothes their own children have outgrown to their client families with younger children. These activities are certainly not necessary to be an effective home visitor, but for some clients in some circumstances, we know that home visitors do use their own resources.

Consideration of these six guidelines by Reamer can help home visitors assess their relative obligations toward family members, themselves, and society, and be aware of alternate possibilities for action. However, neither this set nor any other set of ethical principles can be followed rigidly in daily practice. Rules cannot cover every kind of choice that must be made when a home visitor is closely involved with a client. Nevertheless, with knowledge of ethical guidelines applied to difficult choices, decisions will be informed and thoughtful, if not easy.

A Code of Ethics

Most helping professions have an established code of ethics. Psychologists have the "Ethical Principles of Psychologists" (APA, 1981), and social workers have a "Code of Ethics" (National Association of Social Workers, 1980). Because home visiting has no formal professional organization, though it is a part of nursing, social work, and education, it has no formalized professional ethical code of its own. We believe that the National Association of Social Workers' Code of Ethics, with very few changes, could serve very well as a statement of ethical conduct for the home visiting profession.

This code of ethics for social workers covers professional propriety, competence, and integrity, as well as ethical responsibilities to clients, colleagues, employers, and the profession. High standards of personal conduct and professional competency are emphasized. Service to others is considered the primary obligation, but service should be guided by knowledge and research. In providing service to clients, the clients' interests are primary, fostering their independence is most important, and confidentiality is a client right. Respect, fairness, and courtesy are expected in collegial relationships, and commitments to employing organizations are stressed. A section is included on maintaining the ethics and values of the profession and promoting the general welfare of society.

A code such as this can offer guidance in the general principles of ethical conduct underlying home visit practice, but it is not a set of rules describing specific behavior in all situations. While hard decisions still have to be made concerning individual client situations, a code of ethics describes the fundamental values and the overall spirit in which practice decisions can be made.

Many home visitors have some familiarity with the ethical issues that surface within their profession because of their educational or experiential background in one of these other areas, or through a home visitor training program. For example, home visitors with training in child development may be familiar with Kohlberg's conception of six stages of moral development (Kohlberg, 1984) and can relate some of this knowledge to ethical decision-making in home visiting. Other home visitors, however, have had no specific instruction or ethical training. Because of the complexities of these issues in home visiting, we believe that a discussion of ethics should be mandatory in home visitor training programs and should be covered periodically during in-service sessions. Formally addressing ethical issues in preservice or in-service training underscores its importance and provides the support home visitors need in their day-by-day work. Certainly, ethics is a topic that is indirectly addressed every time a home visitor considers or discusses in supervision her obligations and behavior with clients. We now turn to four specific ethical issues that sometimes concern home visitors.

Honesty

Some would agree with Kant that truth is unconditional: A home visitor should always tell the truth. Others believe that under some circumstances, withholding information or telling a lie might avoid harmful consequences to an individual's well-being. Following a rigid always-tell-the-truth rule might be shortsighted and result in harm to the client. We mentioned earlier the situation in which a home visitor lied about the location of a child when an angry, potentially violent, father came looking for the child. In the home visitor's judgment, a lie in this situation protected her client's best interests. While this principle says it is permissible to lie, then certainly the circumstances under which it is justifiable must be carefully considered and relatively extreme. On this issue, caring, competent professionals are certain to have some disagreement. Home visitors need to be aware that they may face dilemmas that call into question their own values and challenge them to make difficult but necessary judgment calls. Honesty, as the saying goes, may not always be the best policy.

Confidentiality

Confidentiality is considered a paramount value because it is presumed to be the basis for a meaningful and effective relationship between home visitor and client. Protecting the confidentiality of information shared by the client is part of the code of ethics of all helping professions and certainly applies to home visiting. Would a family share concerns and goals with a home visitor if they thought their problems or aspirations would be shared with several others? Confidentiality is an ethical obligation for a home visitor; it may be violated only if an individual's well-being is in jeopardy or in the type of professional situations described below.

Home visitors often learn intimate and personal details from some of their families, information some home visitors wish they had not learned. Home visitors are under obligation never to discuss this information in public and to share only necessary information with other professionals who have some direct interest in the case. A home visitor is usually part of a larger team of people, such as physicians, nurses, and school counselors, who are also involved in the delivery of special services to the family. To contribute to the overall program, the home visitor has an obligation to share pertinent family information with these other professionals; however, even in these situations, in order to avoid any undue invasion of the family's privacy, the visitor should carefully consider and balance any information she discloses.

It is in these professional situations that many home visitors have concerns about what and how much to share. Some are reluctant to share any information at all. The key word seems to be "pertinent." Other members of the team may have useful information to share (i.e., about resources) if they know the pertinent facts. They may see the family in other settings (i.e., medical clinics) and, if they knew the pertinent concerns, could help the home visitor monitor the family's needs. In these situations, sharing pertinent information is for the purpose of enhancing the client's well-being, and it is therefore acceptable practice within the team approach to service. Sharing information is particularly important when team members may be making recommendations that another member knows will not work because she is aware of other information not known to the rest of the team.

Because home visitors may occasionally have to breach confidentiality, they should avoid giving the client the impression that absolutely no information will ever be shared with others. For example, families should know that most information will be held in confidence, but that in circumstances involving safety and well-being, the home visitor may disclose information to third parties. If information is routinely shared with a treatment team, then the client should be informed that this is the case. Visitors should think about how to discuss this issue with clients in the initial stages of home visiting. Once a visitor has built bonds of trust and respect with clients, the clients will usually be open with their conversations with visitors, not because they believe there will be absolute confidentiality, but because they trust the visitor's judgment about sharing information.

Limits of Appropriate Intervention

At times, a home visitor may believe that she is the only outside helper who has a good relationship with a family. As a result, she may also assume that she should take the lead in responding to all family problems (for example, by providing in-depth counseling for a client in a crisis situation). Yet, there are prudent limitations upon the practice of all service providers, and home visitors are no exception. Levenstein (1981) called this ethical issue the "skills mismatch" between the home visitor who delivers a program and the services that she undertakes to deliver. The likelihood that a home visitor will have to address this professional issue may be higher than that of other helpers because the home visitor may be the only service provider the family sees and some of her clients may not be willing to seek services from someone else.

It is critical for home visitors to recognize that they cannot be all things to all people. Though we have addressed the needs for extensive training, and have identified many situations wherein home visiting is a desirable service alternative, the visitor cannot be expected to respond to all the difficulties and stresses she will encounter in the families she visits. Though home visitors should be able to recognize family needs that may not be directly related to the scope of services they can provide, their response to family needs must be directly related to their competence to intervene in particular situations.

Terminating Services

Even though the program goals have not been met, are there situations when services to a family can or should be terminated? There are frustrating days when home visitors must surely want to "dismiss" some of their clients. They have been stood up for the tenth time, discovered that the client had missed the hard-to-set-up appointment at the hearing clinic, or observed once again the glassy gaze of a young mother who had vowed to stay off drugs. When can or should home visit services be terminated, and what are the issues that would justify such a decision?

Reamer (1982) states that "a client's failure to cooperate with a treatment plan is, by itself, ordinarily not an acceptable reason for terminating service" (p. 128). Terminating treatment under these conditions would violate the client's basic right to well-being, a right that takes precedence over the home visitor's right to free choice (that is, terminating services to the client). It is permissible to terminate a client, but there are conditions that should be met before doing so.

Usually a consideration to terminate arises because the client is not cooperating with the program's or the home visitor's plan, or at least appears to be uncooperative. In such situations, one must investigate the reasons for the client's lack of cooperation. Did the client have any say in the decision-making about the type or course of intervention being conducted? If not, perhaps a renegotiation of the terms of the visitor-client relationship is in order and would bring about more cooperation. Clients are rarely motivated to follow a plan that has been imposed on them. Is the client freely participating in the program, or was she coerced in some way? If participation was court-ordered, then what are the conditions for the client who is no longer participating in the home visits? What motivation is there to continue? Does the client have the motivation but not the skills necessary to carry through with the program's objectives? If so, how can the home visitor teach or improve those skills?

After examining such issues, a home visitor may determine that a new course of treatment is required, or that the client is lacking in the motivation or skills needed to cooperate with the program in the foreseeable future. She may decide that her services would be better used by another family and that termination of services is appropriate. Under no circumstances is the home visitor under obligation to continue revising treatment endlessly to try to achieve cooperation.

Decisions to terminate are also based on real-world issues of distribution of time. If a program has a waiting list of clients, it is tempting to terminate services for difficult clients and to enroll a new family that may benefit from the program. In such a case, a home visitor and the program director must weigh the needs and resources of one family against those of another. Issues that need to be considered include determining which client is in more dire need, which client may actually benefit from the services, how "thin" can the time of the home visitor be stretched, and can two new families be served by dropping one uncooperative family living far away and taking up excessive travel time? Issues such as these become relevant when considering whether to close a case. Making the decision thoughtfully requires the consideration of the consequences for the families' well-being, as well as weighing the duties of a limited resource—the home visitor.

Summary

The first part of this chapter has described some of the ethical concerns that a home visitor is likely to face in the course of visiting and helping a client or a family. These problems are common to all home visitors working within the field, affecting them at the day-by-day practice level as they make specific decisions concerning individual families or family members. Such issues are of concern to the profession as a whole, but they are basically played out in the individual relationships between a home visitor and her clients.

Issues Concerning the Profession

Among the professional issues related to home visiting, two stand out as particularly important: burnout, a concern of home visitors because of the difficulty involved in the kind of work they perform, and working in multidisciplinary teams, a situation inherent in the settings within which home visitors typically work.

Professional Burnout

As a term, *burnout* has only been in the professional literature since 1974 when Freudenberger wrote about the problem in free clinics and other alternative agencies that depended on volunteer help. It was soon apparent that the concept applied to paid, salaried, or self-employed professionals as well.

Edelwich and Brodsky (1980) defined burnout as a "progressive loss of idealism, energy, and purpose experienced by people in the helping professions as a result of the conditions of their work" (p. 14). Burnout can result from many conditions, including low pay, insufficient training, ungrateful clients, heavy caseloads, and political constraints and realities. Another condition is the unpredictability of work with clients, a situation found to be more stressful to social workers than the actual amount of work (Fineman, 1985). The costs of burnout are high: staff turnover, the expense of training a new person, lowering of project staff morale, and loss of continuity of contact and communication with the client.

Edelwich and Brodsky conclude that preventing burnout among all helping professionals is virtually impossible. The characteristics of people who choose to work in the helping professions (i.e., idealistic, compassionate, dedicated) and the conditions that inevitably exist in most circumstances in those professions (i.e., poverty, heavy caseloads, long hours) combine to create burnout. However, preparing to resist and successfully overcome burnout can be accomplished by better recognizing or anticipating how, when, and why burnout occurs.

Edelwich and Brodsky describe a four-stage progression of burnout: idealistic enthusiasm, stagnation, frustration, and apathy. They also suggest possible interventions that can be used at these four points. Unfortunately, the need for interventions with the professional are often not noticed until the last stage when the symptoms of burnout are really obvious.

At the very beginning of a job, idealistic enthusiasm may actually be a sign of impending burnout. A home visitor may be too unrealistic in her expectations of the clients and the progress they might make, and in expectations for herself: how much she might accomplish and how she might be received. At this stage, an appropriate intervention is a dose of realism. A supervisor, trainer, or an experienced colleague can be the voice of reason, making it clear that not all goals can be met and not all clients will welcome their visitor. Home visitors need to tell themselves that being realistic is not the same as backing down, and setting realistic goals is one way to prevent burnout.

The second stage toward potential burnout is stagnation, when the initial burst of enthusiasm ebbs and the home visitor may feel stalled in her work. Time away from her own family may begin to take its toll. The job is getting done, but the visitor's personal needs are not being met. At this point, the intervention is movement—to get something happening again for the visitor as well as the client. Perhaps a supervisor can help the visitor look at her clients a little differently and renew the meaning of the work for her. Focusing, or re-focusing, on the process of home visiting may be one way to recharge the energy of the home visitor. If realistic goals have been forgotten, perhaps goals can be revised with plans put in effect for moving toward those goals. A supervisor can spend time evaluating how much has been accomplished by the home visitor, and this less pessimistic view often infuses a sense of purpose again. Small victories are part of the overall success of the work.

The stagnation phase of burnout is followed by the frustration phase, or what Edelwich and Brodsky call the "core of burnout." Not only is the visitor unhappy about the job, but she is no longer *doing* the job. The quality of service to the client is reduced. Perhaps physical symptoms appear, such as headaches, backaches, or nervousness. If something doesn't help the home visitor find satisfaction in her work, the fourth stage of burnout, apathy, is reached. In this stage, one might see an obvious turning away from others and a sense of detachment and distance from clients and coworkers, which is often perceived as boredom and indifference.

Setting realistic expectations, focusing on the process, and celebrating the small successes are interventions for burnout mentioned thus far that involve a rethinking or cognitive reappraisal on the part of the home visitor, perhaps with the help of a supervisor. Reappraisal can help a home visitor keep her work in perspective and focused on the positive. In addition to cognitive reappraisal, possible actions that can be taken are additional education, setting a different routine or schedule, making an on-the-job adjustment (such as changing some job activities), or, ultimately, leaving the field. Sometimes attending a workshop can rejuvenate enthusiasm and can be a useful tool for learning. However, the "workshop high" is only temporary, and other changes need to be made in the job's routine or in the definition of the job.

Also important in burnout prevention is support from colleagues and supervisors, preferably support opportunities that are built into the program, such as regular individualized supervision. In some home visiting programs, visitors themselves organize regular, though informal, after-work or lunch get-togethers where they can meet. In one home visiting project, the Infant Health and Development Program (1989), annual meetings were conducted for home visitors from eight cities because these workshops were important for in-service training and skills improvement. However, these annual meetings were also of immeasurable value in providing contact with the network of other home visitors, informal contacts that provided home visitors with knowledge and support from one another. These informal benefits may have been as important and useful as the formal content of the workshops. These experiences emphasized to us the importance of providing such preventive opportunities to home visiting program staff. Though regular travel to out-of-state meetings will not be possible in many service programs, other arrangements can be made to bring together home visitors (for example, districtwide meetings).

Working to become a better helper has been suggested as one way to counteract burnout. When a home visitor improves her own skills, the rewards accrue for the home visitor and potentially for the client. Even when some of her clients do not seem to make progress, the home visitor should be able to see herself making progress and therefore feel some accomplishment in her work. Many of the skills mentioned in Chapter 5 (i.e., listening, questioning, problem solving) help a home visitor interact well with clients, and they can also help insulate against burnout. Through conscious action on the part of the home visitor and supervisor to improve and fine-tune these skills, the process of home visiting and the development of oneself through this job can be made a focus. The visitor can then measure her own progress, as well as that of her clients, and find successes in her own work even at times when it may be hard to see successes in the clients' lives.

The Multidisciplinary Team Approach

Many home visitors will find themselves operating within a team with other professionals who approach child and family problems from differing backgrounds. The advantage of a multidisciplinary team approach is that several individuals are able to work together to communicate, collaborate, and consolidate specialized knowledge, and then to develop a well-informed plan of action with a client and carry it out. Many problems are so complex (for example, child abuse) that treating them adequately requires several different areas of expertise. Recent federal laws, such as PL 99-457, have anticipated such complexities and mandate a multidisciplinary team approach to developing programs (Gallagher, Trohanis, & Clifford, 1989).

While the advantages of the team model are numerous, there can be disadvantages or frustrations, especially for the team member—often the home visitor—who is in the field and in most frequent contact with the family. Frequent contacts may lead the home visitor to feel that she is shouldering a disproportionately large share of the work involved with the family, especially if she does not feel supported by the team or if she doesn't agree with all aspects of the intervention approach. Some team members may be perceived as having more status or influence than others. In working with teams of physicians, nurses, and social workers, home visitors report that more credence is sometimes given to the opinions of those with a medical background, regardless of whether the problem is a medical, educational, social, or psychological one. Even among the different medical members of a team, there is frequently a tendency for the physician to take the lead in decision-making regardless of his or her programmatic role. This problem of group hierarchy seems especially prevalent within teams whose members have worked solely within one professional area and who do not have previous multidisciplinary team experience. Some home visitors often feel they are at the bottom of the professional totem pole, and perceive that their opinions are not as valued as those with higher degrees or higher administrative rank. This situation is potentially nonproductive and divisive.

There are two key people involved in the solutions to these problems, the home visitor herself and the program director. First, the home visitor must learn to speak up and not defer automatically to those who think they are more knowledgeable. She should try to be confident in her knowledge of the clients, their concerns, and the most likely ways to help them. Second, the program director must set the tone. If the director has delegated team leadership to another person, then this person must set the tone. It is the responsibility of program leadership to promote an atmosphere of collegiality, respect for each person's contribution, and recognition of the need for varying competencies.

The leader can more easily accomplish these goals if all the professionals participating in the team—educators, social workers, nurses, physical therapists—are members of the same unit or same project because there are more opportunities for team members to interact and more advantage gained by the project as a result of good teamwork. However, home visitors may sometimes participate in community-based teams, where each member represents a different agency and the team leader has limited authority over individual team participants. In such teams, home visitors may have to work a little harder to be heard or to promote collegiality.

Teams have many different roles, including selecting cases, sharing information, planning services, and monitoring community-wide needs. In the process of carrying out these activities, a team will be involved in many aspects of problem solving, such as discussing family needs, resources, and possible treatment plans. In all these activities, it is important that each team member be assumed to carry equal weight in the decision-making, though each may defer at times to those with the most pertinent knowledge about a particular situation. Equally important, the team should provide emotional support and encouragement to the team member most directly responsible for carrying out the treatment plan. This approach not only boosts staff morale, but it also provides the client with the best services possible.

A leader can also improve the team's effectiveness by providing frequent opportunities for communication. Within team meetings, discussion should be facilitated. All relevant information should be exchanged, including the need for additional information and sources for obtaining it. This is another area in which some teams have difficulties. A member who doesn't value the expertise of another team member may be less willing to share all relevant information about the family or to give careful consideration to each discipline's perspective.

A team member's professional attitude can change after spending some time "walking in the other person's shoes." When a home visitor spends a day in the hospital pediatric clinic, or when the pediatrician accompanies the home visitor on a few visits, each may come to a better understanding of the other's position. Experiencing the family or the job from the other's point of view is, for some, a totally new discovery, one that develops a greater understanding of the client as seen from the other profession's point of view. It also can result in greater future collegial support.

Sometimes a leadership change can help improve team communication, something as easy as rotating the group facilitator. Outside consultation, such as hiring a psychologist to conduct sessions on professional communication and values, can help the team recognize the value of information from many sources. Although it specifically focuses on teams dealing with child abuse, *The New Child Protection Team Handbook* (Bross, Krugman, Lenherr, Rosenberg, & Schmitt, 1988) is an excellent source of useful information about types of multidisciplinary teams, including a chapter on conducting effective team meetings (Grosz & Denson, 1988).

Summary

In this chapter, we have described the need to assure training and discussion of ethical areas before sending home visitors into the field to participate in relationships that will often raise thorny issues of conscience. The framework for ethical decision making described by Reamer and the Code of Ethics of the National Association of Social Workers were useful to us in considering this area, but there are others. However, no framework or set of guidelines will make decision making easy. Visiting people in their homes to potentially influence and affect their lives will inevitably lead to ethical dilemmas. This will occur regardless of the main intent of the visiting program (medical, educational, or social support) or the main clients of the program (teenagers, parents of prematures, or abusive parents). Responding thoughtfully, acting competently, and referring where appropriate are the actions of an accountable home visitor, one who is best able to promote the welfare of the client.

Note

1. The six guidelines are quoted directly from Reamer (1982), pages 76-79. The examples are our own.

9

Assessment and Documentation in Home Visiting

Two major types of record-keeping are typically required by a home visiting program: client assessment and program documentation. Client assessments are generally conducted to determine client needs, the program's effectiveness for clients, and client satisfaction with the program. Documentation procedures that are often used in home visiting programs include daily monitoring of the delivery of the home visit program to ensure its delivery and quality, and obtaining data sufficient to replicate the program. Both client assessment and program documentation provide information that is useful for research purposes and interagency collaboration, and both types of data are sometimes needed to meet legal, reimbursement, or certification requirements. Because assessments and documentation are often a part of a home visitor's job responsibilities, it is helpful to be familiar with different types of assessment measures and documentation procedures.

In this chapter, we will discuss different reasons for assessment of clients and several strategies for measurement. We will also describe various types of program documentation that are useful in home visiting, including some illustrative forms that have been utilized by one home visiting program. The advantages and disadvantages associated with each kind of record-keeping will be discussed, as well as those associated with the process of data collection in general. Because anyone choosing a measure for use in a home visit program should take into account certain basic issues concerning the characteristics of assessments, these issues will be briefly summarized. Finally, we will conclude with a discussion of the benefits of using assessment and documentation information as a part of program evaluation, looking at evaluation from the standpoint of the client, the visitor, the supervisor, the program director, and the public policymaker.

The overall importance of record-keeping for home visitors is indicated by its inclusion as one of the competency goals in the Child Development Associate National Credentialing Program goals for home visitors: "The competent (home visitor) candidate develops and uses observation skills and evaluation instruments to record relevant information about children and their families in a nonjudgmental manner" (National Credentialing Program, 1987, p. 38). Assessment is a collaborative process between the home visitor and the family; in the best of circumstances, it is a vital and ongoing part of intervention. Information gathered through observation, interview, or assessment instrument can be used by the home visitor and family to shape the course of intervention to meet family needs.

We have divided the following discussion of record-keeping into three sections, basically distinguished by the time period during which the assessments or documentation procedures are typically used: initial data collection, outcome data collection, and ongoing program documentation. Initial data collection is often part of an intake process conducted by a home visit program. Information about the client is gathered, ranging from demographic, descriptive information to client attitudes, problems, and needs. Outcome data collection typically takes place at or near the end of a program or on an infrequent basis (i.e., yearly). Information about client attitudes, characteristics, and/or behaviors is gathered in order to determine the effectiveness of the program. This type of data collection is often associated with home visiting research projects, although many primarily service delivery projects also collect outcome data on their clients. Ongoing program documentation is the kind of record-keeping that is done throughout the course of home visiting to describe or summarize the procedures and content of the program delivered to the client.

TABLE 9.1: Assessment and Documentation Overview

| | Client Assessments | | Ongoing Program Documentation |
	Initial Data	Outcome Data	
Types	Intake Demographic Client needs	Client functioning Attitude, Behavior Home environment Client satisfaction	Home visit procedures Program content Referral contacts Client behavior
When	Early visits	Typically yearly, biannually, or end of program	Daily or weekly
Examples	Interviews Checklists	Questionnaires Observations	Home visit reports Case notes
Goals	Document client needs. Individualize program.	Show client progress and program effectiveness.	Monitor program delivery and client progress. Replicate successful programs.

Table 9.1 provides an overview of the three types of record-keeping that will be covered in this chapter.

A common consideration relevant to each type of data collection is that specific and valid reasons should exist for including assessments and documentation as part of routine home visiting procedures. Assessments of clients, whether individuals or families, can be time-consuming and sometimes intrusive, and documentation of home visiting can take a visitor's time away from other potentially more constructive activities. Thus, the advantages to be gained by the assessment or documentation information should outweigh the potential disadvantages. The following sections discuss in more detail several of the specific reasons for making record-keeping a part of the responsibility of home visitors.

Initial Data Collection

Two kinds of initial data collection will be discussed here: gathering basic facts about clients and about their needs. Both kinds are typically part of a program's intake process and may be gathered by the home visitor or another staff member. If the home visitor does not gather the information directly, she should have access to all relevant initial records concerning the client in order to make good decisions with the client about potential services.

Demographic Data Collection

If basic demographic information has not already been collected by the program, the home visitor will want to find out a few facts in the earliest stages of visiting, probably during the first visit or two. Obtaining such information during the initial intake process is usually easy because people typically expect to answer certain kinds of questions when they enroll in new programs.

Learning about the constellation of household members and their roles helps the home visitor know the supports available to her client and what problems may be faced by the client or family. If a parent-child pair is the focus of the home visits, the home visitor should know something about how they spend their days. Is the child in day care? If the mother is a teenager, does she attend school? Who cares for the child when the mother is out? What is her phone number at work, and would it be alright to phone her there to schedule visits? Many of these facts are easy to discover in the course of the first visit or two through friendly conversation with the mother. Completion of a basic questionnaire that lists some of this information is useful, especially if the home visitor's caseload is extensive. Examples of such forms are included in *The Head Start Home Visitor Handbook* (Wolfe & Herwig, 1986) and *Working Together: A Guide to Parent Involvement* (Coletta, 1977).

Determining Clients' Needs

Another type of early assessment involved in some home visiting programs is an assessment of an individual client's needs or the needs of the family. Needs assessment is consistent with the first principle of home visiting presented in Chapter 2, namely that family support should enhance the ability of families to work toward *their own* goals. A home visitor should not presume to know the needs of the client. It is too easy for her biases and beliefs to be projected onto the client. Identifying needs *for* the family can reinforce their view of themselves as ineffective problem-solvers and begins the home visitor-client relationship with a built-in inequity ("I know what's best for you") rather than a joint sharing or working together.

An informative assessment of client needs can be conducted just by listening well during the first few visits and letting the parent verbalize his or her worries, joys, and hopes. Good interviewing skills will help a home visitor elicit parent needs, even during early visits before the visitor and client get to know each other very well.

Another way to conduct needs assessment is through the use of a checklist of client needs, concerns, skills, and strengths. The checklist can be answered in writing by the client on a rating form, or it can be completed with the visitor reading the items and explaining them, if necessary. The process of completing a checklist may act as a mechanism for a family to state verbally a concern they had been harboring for some time. Completion of the checklist provides an opportunity for the concern to be discussed openly.

Whatever method is used, an interview or a checklist, a good assessment of needs identifies client or family strengths and goals as well as weaknesses and problems. As the Head Start home visiting program concludes, a needs assessment accomplishes the following three steps: identifies strengths and needs, sets priorities for goals, and begins to plan ways to meet the goals (Wolfe & Herwig, 1986).

We include here two measures to illustrate the kind of assessment data that can be gathered early in the program and that can be of functional use to the home visitor and program planners, as well as to the family. The Family Needs Survey (Bailey & Simeonsson, 1988) is an example of an assessment that measures the parents' needs for information about their child, for family and friend support, for information about resources, and for other needs that may be present in a family of a child with a disability. The first section of this 35-question scale, entitled "Needs for Information," is displayed in Table 9.2. Although the survey was specifically written for families of handicapped children, most of it is general enough that it could be used with many different types of families. It is presented here as an example of a relatively direct and nonthreatening approach to the assessment of client needs

TABLE 9.2: Family Needs Survey (excerpt)

Donald Bailey
Rune Simeonsson

Frank Porter Graham Child Development Center
The University of North Carolina at Chapel Hill
© All Rights Reserved 1985

FORM H

Family Name/ID _____   Relationship to child _____

Date _____

INSTRUCTIONS: Listed below are some of the needs expressed by parents of special children. Please read each statement and decide if you need help in this area. Then circle the number (1, 2, or 3) that represents your response to the need.

	Definitely do not need help with this	Not sure	Definitely need help with this
NEEDS FOR INFORMATION			
1. I need more information about my child's condition or disability.	1	2	3
2. I need more information about how to handle my child's behavior.	1	2	3
3. I need more information about how to teach my child.	1	2	3
4. I need more information on how to play with or talk to my child.	1	2	3
5. I need more information about the services that my child might receive in the future.	1	2	3
6. I need more information on the services that are presently available for my child.	1	2	3
7. I need more information about how children grow and develop.	1	2	3

and one that has immediate implications for the interventionist. Areas that are scored high on the measure are areas to be addressed in the program, if possible. After completing the paper-and-pencil part of the needs assessment, it is important to discuss with the family their priorities for addressing these needs. Although an answer on the survey may indicate the family's awareness of a need, the family may not necessarily be ready to address it.

A measure that takes into account the ways in which families would like to receive information or help is the Family Information Preference Inventory (Turnbull & Turnbull, 1986). Similar to the Family Needs Survey, parents are asked to indicate which of several listed topics are of interest to them. Then they are asked about the format in which they would like to receive help or information about topics of interest (for example, written information, parent groups, or home visits). The checklist includes an open-ended section to let parents indicate any additional needs they might have. No summary scores are calculated from this particular measure, but answers to individual items are used by the service provider to plan intervention content and procedures. The alternative delivery methods used in the inventory can be particular to the services that could be offered by the specific intervention program. Any home visiting program could adopt the format of this measure, tailoring the list of needs to their client population and the alternative ways of meeting needs to their own service alternatives.

The authors of the Family Information Preference Inventory have recently raised a concern over the use of paper-and-pencil assessments such as the two just described (Summers, Dell'Oliver, Turnbull, Benson, Santelli, Campbell, & Siegel-Causey, 1989). These kinds of assessments, as well as structured interviews, are often used to gather information needed for the Individualized Family Service Plan (IFSP) required by PL 99-457. However, data from over 100 parents and professionals involved in IFSPs indicate that they overwhelmingly prefer informal approaches and open-ended conversations as the most family-sensitive way of developing the IFSP. Although validated instruments are often required for objectivity or accountability, a more informal process is clearly preferred by families and should be given consideration.

This preference highlights the need for a home visit program to ensure that those assessments that *are* used provide functionally useful information to the home visitor. Many programs spend much time and effort collecting information about topics that may not enlighten the home visitor or help plan the course of the visits. For example, family stress is a frequently assessed characteristic that, while interesting from a theoretical point of view, may do little to guide the home visitor or program. Measuring stress also tends to emphasize the negative, focusing on problems and worries, many of which may not be directly addressable by the specific program. A measure of stress has limited usefulness in the day-to-day practices involved in home visiting.

To summarize the major purpose of initial data collection, information obtained from a needs assessment and from initial demographic information should help a home visitor individualize the particular home visit program to best meet the client's needs. To the extent that this information can be gathered in an informal and unstructured way, family preferences will be better met.

Outcome Data Collection

Most home visitors have an impression or a feeling about the effectiveness of their services to, or support for, a family or client. They see parents making progress towards self-sufficiency, and they see children learning and playing more appropriately. They can tell when a client needs extra encouragement to continue making progress toward a goal. These clinical impressions are valuable and often very accurate. However, impressionistic data tend to be imprecise and subjective, and positive changes in behavior may not be noted by a home visitor expecting to see something else. As a result, many home visit programs require the collection of systematic outcome data.

From an ethical standpoint, a professional will always want to know whether the intervention provided to the client accomplished what it was intended to do. Not only is this information part of good practice, but accountability is increasingly required as part of program funding or certification. For a home visiting program, outcome questions might address whether the support provided by the home visitor was useful to the client, whether the information delivered was acted upon, or whether the family seemed to make any progress toward the goals that they identified. Measuring the program's effectiveness for the client may show positive or negative results. If positive, the interventions can be repeated with other similar clients; if negative, interventions can be modified or discontinued.

Many different kinds of outcome assessment have been used in home visit programs. The domains of measurement frequently tapped are the home environment, client or family functioning, the client's physical or mental health, and client satisfaction. If a child is part of the home visit program, especially if the program is focused on children, outcome measures might include assessments of cognitive, social, or self-help skills; parent knowledge or attitudes about childrearing; or parent-child interaction. Because entire books have been written about each of these types of assessment, this section will only briefly mention some of the instruments that have been used frequently by home visiting programs.

Home and Family Environment

The Home Observation for the Measurement of the Environment, or HOME (Caldwell & Bradley, 1984), is probably the best known measure used to document the physical and social environment of infants and young children. The HOME can be scored after a 30- to 60-minute visit with a parent in the family's residence. It uses a yes/no format for scoring items based on observation by the assessor and through parental report. Higher scores indicate more optimal, stimulating environments for young children. Major subscores include the physical organization of the environment, maternal involvement with the child, and opportunities for variety.

The HOME was used as an outcome measure in a year-long home visit intervention with parents of preterm infants (Barrera, Rosenbaum, & Cunningham, 1986). Groups with a developmental intervention focused on learning activities and a parent-infant intervention focused on parents' observation and interaction skills were compared to preterm and full-term control groups that received no intervention. At the end of the study, the HOME scores of the parent-infant interaction group and the full-term control group were the highest and were significantly better than the scores of the preterm control group. The HOME scores of the developmental intervention group were only somewhat higher than those of the preterm control group. Improvements in the Bayley developmental scores of the infants in the intervention groups were small and nonsignificant. In this study the effectiveness of the parent-infant home visit intervention was best demonstrated by improvements in the HOME scores.

A measure of the broader family environment, the Family Environment Scale, was developed by Moos (1974) and has been used in a wide variety of programs serving different types of clients. This scale focuses on the psychological climate of the family and is frequently used in research to determine different categories or types of families. This 90-question scale measures nine dimensions, including independence, conflict, expression, and achievement, and also provides a profile of a family using these dimensions. Such information would be useful to a home visiting program if different kinds of intervention were expected to be more acceptable to, or helpful for, particular types of families as profiled by this measure.

Client or Family Functioning

The goal of many home visit programs is to help clients better understand some aspect of family living, such as how to raise children without being abusive, or to cope better with a particular problem, such as learning to provide home care for a chronically ill child. Client outcome measures in this area include problem solving or coping scales, such as the Wasik Problem Solving Rating Scale (Wasik, et al., 1988) and the Folkman-Lazarus Ways of Coping Checklist (Folkman & Lazarus, 1980). These measures assess whether a client has the cognitive or behavioral skills that are deemed important for handling a particular short-term or long-term problem. The objective of home visiting in these cases is to help the client obtain coping skills sufficient to handle the particular situation.

Because home visiting is usually conducted in a family environment, even if one specific person is the main participant in the home visit program, family functioning is often of interest as an outcome variable. Based upon different theories of family functioning, many different measures are available. Olson, McCubbin,

Patterson, and their colleagues have developed several measures of family functioning that are generally easy to score. Data from various comparison samples are also available on these measures. The Family Adaptability and Cohesion Evaluation Scales (FACES III), a 30-question rating scale measuring family cohesion and adaptability, is useful in measuring perceived and ideal functioning (Olson, Portner, & Lavee, 1985). A family's coping ability is measured by the Family Crisis Oriented Personal Evaluation Scales, or F-COPES (McCubbin, Olson, & Larson, 1981). The F-COPES is a 30-item inventory measuring problem solving, support seeking, family mobilization, and other relevant family characteristics.

As mentioned earlier, many home visit programs include a measure of stress as one kind of family functioning measure. In fact, measures of stress and coping are often included together in an assessment package under the presumption that they are tapping similar client or family constructs (Krauss, 1988). Stress measures include checklists of recent life events, such as the Schedule of Recent Events (Holmes & Rahe, 1967), a measure that has been used to show that the number of recent life events is related to the number of illnesses within the next year. Another measure is the Life Experiences Survey (Sarason, Johnson, & Siegel, 1978), which yields separate indices of undesirable and desirable life changes that have occurred recently, as well as a rating of the extent to which those changes influenced the individual. Scores are related to measures of anxiety, depression, and lack of coping.

For a program to choose these particular measures of client and family functioning as outcome assessments, there should be some presumption that the home visit intervention could reasonably be expected to have an effect on these complex and sometimes pervasive problems. Because many of these measures overlap considerably in concepts of family roles, support, and problem solving, selection of the measures should be guided by the philosophy and techniques of the particular home visiting program.

Parent-Child Interactions

Because many home visiting programs are designed for parents and their children, parent-child interaction is an outcome that's often measured. The goal of many parent-child home visiting programs is to improve some aspect of the parent's knowledge of her child, information on child development, or behavior with her child or children. The purpose of a parent-child assessment in these programs would be to find out whether the parent's behavior with the child changed as a result of the home visit intervention. Does the parent respond more often to the child's cues? Is her language with her children less directive and more informative? How and when does the parent try to exercise control over the child?

Attempts have been made to answer these and other questions in the area of parent-child interaction, but there is no standard assessment instrument or procedure. It is possible to ask parents to report on how they interact with their children, but many parents are not accurate reporters (Yarrow, Campbell, & Burton, 1968). Some programs have observed mothers and children playing together in their homes or in clinic settings. The observations are usually coded in ways that are specific to the behaviors that were targeted for change in the home visit program. For example, in the Family-Oriented Home Visiting Program, teaching style was measured. Mothers who had received nine months of weekly home visits had more positive teaching styles than mothers who had not received home visits (Gray & Ruttle, 1980).

Other programs have developed rating scales for visitors or other staff to describe the general tone of the interaction between mother and child, and/or the pacing, language exchanges, or reinforcement seen during the home visit or clinic sessions. In a program conducted with low-income teen mothers in Washington, D.C., visits occurred in a mobile van that went around to parents' homes and apartments. Home visitors were public health nurses who delivered well-baby health care and discussed infant stimulation. They also brought an educational toy on almost every visit, talked with the mother about learning and development, and placed major emphasis on language stimulation. Using a rating scale to judge the frequency with which mothers vocalized to their children, this study showed that intervention mothers vocalized more often than nonintervention mothers. The groups did not differ in the extent to which the mothers permitted their children's exploratory behavior nor in how they handled unacceptable behavior (Gutelius, Kirsch, MacDonald, Brooks, & McErlean, 1977).

Still other home visiting programs have set up problem-solving situations to see how the mother helps the child with a pre-scribed or semi-structured task. In the Mother-Child Home Pro-gram (MCHP), a program of home visits for low-income mothers of two to four year-old children, a visitor delivered toys and then modeled how to use them, encouraging the mother to participate. At the end of the program, mothers and children were left alone in a room to play with a toy train and a form board. From video-tapes of these sessions, ten categories of behavior were tallied, such as labeling, verbalization of actions, and verbal praise. The mean frequencies of these desirable behaviors ranged from 33% to 51% higher in the intervention groups (Madden, O'Hara, & Leven-stein, 1984).

Howrigan (1988) has recently written a thorough review of parent-child interaction measures in family-oriented programs, noting several methodological considerations and describing the research on many different kinds of parent-child assessment. In particular, she notes, we must be aware of the wide diversity in parent-child interaction styles and seriously question our assump-tions about which styles or how much of certain behaviors are "better." Slaughter (1988) has recommended that methods used to establish normative data include racially and ethnically diverse populations. Data should also be gathered by people of the same race or ethnic group. In addition to considering the issues men-tioned by Howrigan and Slaughter, special weight should be given to the match between program goals and what the parent-child assessment actually measures. Given the time and effort usually involved in collecting parent-child interaction assessments, a home visit program should choose instruments carefully.

Client Satisfaction

Determining satisfaction is important because clients are more likely to follow through with the goals or procedures of programs that they like. If the program is ongoing, the client's self-report can lead to changes that could be made in an undesirable aspect of the program that might help the client become more responsive or involved. Even if program changes were not possible for the current client, the information could be used by a home visitor to modify her approach with the next, similar client, or it could be used by a program to revise overall program goals or content.

Because each program is different, a client satisfaction measure may need to be tailored for a specific home visit program. The Client Satisfaction Questionnaire (Larsen, Attkisson, Hargreaves, & Nguyen, 1979), seen in Table 9.3, is an example of a relatively short questionnaire that is very broad in content. One of the difficulties in determining client satisfaction is that it may be impossible to disentangle this measure from client progress. Another difficulty is that the clients may not recognize their satisfaction until after the program ends. Even so, it is certainly advisable to obtain some measure of clients' ratings of the services they received.

Regular Assessment of Client Progress

Most of the examples of outcome assessments mentioned so far in this section are given relatively infrequently to clients, perhaps every six months or yearly, because they require time to administer, sometimes require special expertise to administer, and many are not sensitive to changes in behavior over a short period of time.

Bloom and Fischer (1982) list several reasons why it is important to use some kind of *regular* measurement of client progress. Such measurement enhances intervention planning, focuses on specific targets, allows progress or regression to be noted quickly (even small changes), serves as a motivator for the client and practitioner, and provides clear evidence about the effectiveness of specific practices. Although written for social workers, many of the points made by these authors are relevant for all home visitors and home visiting programs.

Whereas many programs have no regular assessments and others rely on routine but infrequent (semiannual or annual) assessments, regular recording of progress toward goals can be a very informative practice. For example, if the goal of a specific home visiting program is to ensure that a medically fragile newborn receives appropriate medical care, then visits to a follow-up clinic would be an appropriate and measurable behavior. If the home visitor and mother could see that an increasingly higher percentage of appointments were being kept, then this positive change would indicate program success and would be rewarding to both

TABLE 9.3: The Client Satisfaction Questionnaire (CSQ)

Please help us improve our program by answering some questions about the services you have received at the _____ . We are interested in your honest opinions, whether they are positive or negative. <u>Please answer all of the questions</u>. We also welcome your comments and suggestions. Thank you very much, we appreciate your help.

Circle Your Answer

1. How would you rate the quality of service you received?

4	3	2	1
Excellent	Good	Fair	Poor

2. Did you get the kind of service you wanted?

1	2	3	4
No, definitely not	No, not really	Yes, generally	Yes, definitely

*3. To what extent has our program met your needs?

4	3	2	1
Almost all of my needs have been met.	Most of my needs have been met.	Only a few of my needs have been met.	None of my needs have been met.

4. If a friend were in need of similar help, would you recommend our program to him/her?

1	2	3	4
No, definitely not	No, I don't think so.	Yes, I think so.	Yes, definitely

5. How satisfied are you with the amount of help you received?

1	2	3	4
Quite dissatisfied	Indifferent or mildly dissatisfied	Mostly satisfied	Very satisfied

6. Have the services you received helped you to deal more effectively with your problems?

4	3	2	1
Yes, they helped a great deal.	Yes, they helped somewhat.	No, they really didn't help.	No, they seemed to to make things worse

*7. In an overall, general sense, how satisfied are you with the service you received?

4	3	2	1
Very satisfied	Mostly satisfied	Indifferent or mildly dissatisfied	Quite dissatisfied

8. If you were to seek help again, would you come back to our program?

1	2	3	4
No, definitely not	No, I don't think so.	Yes, I think so.	Yes, definitely

Write Comments Below

*Can be used as a shorter scale

Reprinted with permission from *Evaluation and Program Planning, 2.* D. Larsen, C. Attkisson, W. Hargreaves, & T. Nguyen, Assessment of client patient satisfaction: Development of a general scale. Copyright © 1979, Pergamon Journals Ltd.

visitor and mother. Ultimately, the expected outcome of better child health might also be documented, but since it is a characteristic less reliably and less frequently measured, it should not be the only measure of program success.

Another example of the advantage of regular recording of progress toward outcome goals is one that is applicable to many home visiting programs with families of young children. In many such programs, children's cognitive and language progress is measured to document the success of the intervention being delivered (for example, the delivery and use of a specific curriculum for children). These assessments include the Bayley Scales of Infant Development, the Stanford-Binet Intelligence Test, the Wechsler Intelligence Scale for Children, the Sequenced Inventory of Communicative Development, and the Peabody Picture Vocabulary Test. These tests are widely used in research but must be administered by a qualified person, usually in an office setting rather than in the home. The measures are time-consuming and are not designed to be given frequently. Thus, these measures provide an overall assessment of one type of outcome, but are not given regularly enough to measure incremental progress or to indicate when to modify an existing approach with a particular family.

Measuring specific targeted behaviors on a regular basis can also indicate program outcome, and it is relatively easy to accomplish. For example, the goal of many programs is to have parents participate in learning activities with their child. As the home visitor introduces each new activity, the parents can add it to their list of activities to be used with the child. If each time the parent plays with the child using the various activities, they make a check mark beside the activity, then both parents and home visitor have a visual record of progress in interacting with the child with different activities.

Most readers will recognize these simple recording procedures as the hallmark of behavioral assessment. In the context of home visiting, such behaviors as keeping clinic appointments and using learning activities with a child can be systematically recorded, just as better child health and improved cognitive development can be measured. The progress measures of behavior are more easily and frequently recorded, and provide more immediate and useful information to both the home visitor and the parents than outcome measures recorded only once at the end of a program. Most importantly, by choosing such behaviors to record, the home visitor can regularly monitor the effectiveness of her approach with each family. The home visiting program can document the array of different interventions being used and the ongoing progress of individual clients, in addition to the overall effectiveness of the program for the clients, which is typically substantiated by standardized outcomes.

Ongoing Program Documentation

Obtaining information on program implementation is another basic purpose of some documentation often requested of home visitors. Documentation of program delivery requires procedures that allow the home visitor to describe the frequency, content, and quality of her interactions with the parent, and to describe the parent's receipt of or use of any other services that may be offered by the program. Program documentation is the area in which home visit interventions have reported the least amount of information. This may be in part attributable to the uniqueness of programs—they deliver many different services in different ways. In addition, although standardized measures are available to document program outcome, such as language or cognitive development, such standardized measures are not available to document the process of home visiting.

To document program implementation, some home visit projects or supervisors require detailed case notes about each visit; other programs require little more than a weekly log sheet of contacts. Striking a balance between over- and under-documentation is important. Reporting too little about what was actually done by the home visitor makes it difficult to know whether the intervention as described was really delivered. On the other hand, reporting extensively on the program delivery (for example, preparing case notes on every visit or contact) is time-consuming for the visitor and whoever eventually reads such notes. Extensive recording may also lead to careless documentation by home visitors who feel overburdened with paperwork. In addition, case notes are subject to many possible deficiencies, such as the lack of concrete examples supporting causal hypotheses, no guidance as to the appropriate intervention, and infrequent recording

(Gambrill & Stein, 1983). As valuable as thorough documentation may be in some cases, program directors should realize that excessive paperwork is often cited as a reason for burnout in the social services field. Program directors or supervisors must make choices about what kinds of documentation will be required, considering their own program's needs and weighing the advantages and disadvantages.

In the research programs we have conducted, we have probably erred on the side of over-reporting. In these research programs, we needed to know that the home visit intervention was actually delivered to the families as intended in order to draw conclusions about the effects of the program. Detailed information on the process and content of home visiting also helped us more easily tell others how to replicate the programs.

Two documentation forms from the Infant Health and Development Program (IHDP, 1989) are included in the Appendix as examples of program documentation: the Home Visit Report Form and the Record of Family Contact Form. For the IHDP, our research group at the Frank Porter Graham Child Development Center received private foundation funds to develop, implement, monitor, and document the intervention.

The IHDP Home Visit Report Form was completed by home visitors after each home visit and turned in to the supervisor weekly. Information contained on this form documented the participants in the visit, the location and length of the visit, the main content of the visit (problem solving and curriculum activities), and the general tone of the visit. (The technical information at the top of the first page—form number, version—was required for data management procedures.) The last page of this form was available for written notes about events not captured by the multiple-choice questions on the form. This form is a more elaborate version of the home visit report form used in Project CARE in North Carolina, which was itself a modification of the home visit report form used by the Parent Educational Program in Florida (Gordon & Guinagh, 1978). As the content and nature of our visit programs have evolved, so have the forms used to document them, which illustrates again why there are no standardized program documentation measures in use.

In the IHDP, home visitors completed the Home Visit Report Form as soon as possible after a visit, often in their cars if the neighborhood was safe, in a nearby coffee shop on a break between visits, or back at the office after the visit. Immediate completion of visit documentation is important for accuracy. The home visitors' supervisors used these same forms as the basis for their supervisory sessions with the visitors, and researchers used them to study the process of home visiting.

Responses to the questions on the Home Visit Report Form were entered weekly into a computerized data base by staff at the sites. Data were summarized monthly for each individual visitor for each of the eight IHDP sites, and for all participating families in the intervention group. In this way, visitors could check their own progress, and we could monitor the progress of individual sites to see that the program was consistently delivered from site to site, as planned. On a bimonthly basis we were also able to use the data from these forms to summarize each individual family's participation in the program. We are aware that research programs inherently document more than service programs and that most home visit programs do not have support for frequent and careful documentation activities. Nevertheless, we found the documentation we obtained to be very helpful for many nonresearch purposes—for home visitors, their supervisors, and ourselves—and consequently suggest that programs consider the routine use of a home visit report form.

The Record of Family Contact form (also in the Appendix) was developed to document the many interactions that the home visitors had with the families other than home visits, such as telephone calls or conversations with another family member when the mother was not at home. It was also used to document the contacts that home visitors had with other agencies on behalf of families, such as with social services staff, clinic staff, or food and nutrition programs. Information from these forms, added to the data from the Home Visit Report Form, provided a fuller picture of the actual work of a visitor during the course of the week. For example, one visitor spent most of two days making contacts with various social workers and community service agencies on behalf of, and with, a mother who needed temporary shelter for herself and two children. Although these activities were not part of a home visit, they were important support for the mother, provided because of her participation in IHDP, and would not have been documented if only the Home Visit Report Form had been used.

A review of such activities provides data that program directors and supervisors can use in planning work loads, making decisions on training activities, supervising home visitors, and evaluating their program's relationships with other community agencies.

In IHDP, home visitors reported yearly on the amount of time they spent engaged in various project activities, such as direct interaction with families, attending meetings, travel to and from home visits, and completing paperwork such as the two forms presented here. Their estimates of the amount of time spent on record-keeping averaged 15%, or about 6 hours per week, a little more than an hour a day. To some of them, that seemed like a long time, but at the end of the program, home visitors reported that the required documentation had helped them consolidate their thoughts about families and plan for future visits. When asked to suggest changes in the Home Visit Report Form, few visitors suggested shortening the form. In fact, many even suggested additional questions that they felt should have been regularly included. Their reaction suggests that when documentation procedures are relevant to the specific program and useful to the home visitors, record-keeping is not likely to be considered a burden.

We are currently conducting analyses to better understand which IHDP home visiting variables are most related to outcome and to family characteristics. In this way, future documentation procedures may be simplified by focusing questions more specifically on those home visit events or processes that research determines to be most predictive of outcomes.

Basic Characteristics of Assessment Measures

If a home visit program chooses to use an assessment measure, there are several characteristics that should be considered, including the utility of the measure, its reliability and validity, the time it takes to administer or collect, and how directly it measures a person's behavior or feelings. This section is intended as a brief overview of the major features home visitors or program directors need to consider when choosing assessment instruments. (For more information on these characteristics, the reader is referred to

Bloom & Fischer, 1982; Brinkerhoff, Brethower, Hluchyj, and Nowakowski, 1983).

Usefulness of a Measure

Before administering needless questionnaires to clients, the first consideration should be whether to use one at all. What will be gained by using an assessment measure, and of what value is the particular one under consideration? Does it provide information that will help plan the most appropriate intervention? Does it help ascertain the client's needs or the factors influencing the client? Choosing a measure because it "looks interesting" or measures a currently "hot" topic are not valid reasons for assessment. Other questions relate to resources. Who is available to administer the measure? How much time or money will it take to collect the information? Who will process and summarize the information? Good assessment measures are often given, but the data from them is never used because these questions are not sufficiently contemplated in choosing a measurement approach.

Reliability

Reliability refers to the consistency and stability of the measure. Reliability indicates whether a measure produces the same results when used with the same person over time, with two different versions of the measure, or by two different administrators of the measure. If information from these conditions is highly similar or consistent, then the measure is said to have high (good) reliability and is therefore more useful.

Reliability is important because it indicates that differences that one might see from one test occasion to another are likely due to behavioral changes or attitude changes, not to problems with the measure itself. For example, one goal of a home visit program for teenaged mothers might be to increase the supports available to, and used by, the young mothers. If the support level is rated higher after one year in the program than at the beginning, then the program might conclude that it was having a positive effect. If the reliability of the instrument had not yet been determined, however, the higher ratings could have been due to measurement error.

Validity

The validity of an assessment means that the instrument actually measures what it is supposed to measure. If it is a measure of mother-child interactions, then it should actually measure mother-child interactions, not mother judgment or attitudes. There are several types of validity, some involving statistical procedures and others involving judgments about the properties of the measure. Face validity is a subjective judgment based on whether the questions actually do measure the characteristic or behavior of interest. Criterion-related validity refers to whether the measure compares well with other possible measures of the same characteristic or behavior whose validity has already been established. There are other types of validity not mentioned here, but ultimately they all provide information on how well the assessment measures what it is intended to measure.

When choosing assessments, a home visit program must consider the validity of the assessment. In the example used above (the program to increase supports to teen mothers), suppose the program's measure of maternal support was really a measure of perceived social support rather than actual social support. It could well be a measure of high reliability and might well show increases for many mothers over the course of a year of home visiting. However, before concluding that the program had helped the mothers find and use more social supports, the validity of the measure should be determined. Otherwise, the wrong conclusions might be drawn.

Directness

Directness is another characteristic of measures that should be considered when selecting measures for use in a home visit program. Direct measures of how a person actually behaves or thinks are more useful than indirect measures that require inferences or interpretations (Hersen & Barlow, 1976). Direct measures usually have higher predictive validity than indirect measures and are also easier to relate to the specific intervention being considered or delivered. For example, the very purpose of the home visitor may be to see that more clinic appointments are kept by the mother for her newborn baby. Measuring clinic attendance is a direct measure of that intervention goal. Measuring why clinic visits are made or not made would involve indirect information. While interesting and potentially useful, this information would involve an interpretation on the part of the mother in answering the "why" questions and an interpretation on the part of the home visitor in figuring out what her answers mean. In most cases, a direct measure is better.

To summarize some of the major characteristics of assessments or documentation procedures that should be considered, a home visit program should use valid and reliable measures that are easy to implement. The measures should supply useful information, as directly as possible, about the client or the potential intervention strategy.

Assessment and Documentation from Different Perspectives

Many of the client assessment measures or program documentation procedures mentioned in this chapter were used in research studies of home visiting, many of which were summarized in Chapter 1. Most of these studies used classical experimental design with procedures such as random assignment of families to treatment and control groups or case-control matching, and many other procedures typical of a well-designed research study of home visiting. Assessment and documentation have provided the research knowledge base of home visiting.

Client assessment measures and program documentation procedures are also an integral part of program evaluation. Determining the extent to which a program's goals have been met and providing information for decision-making are the major goals of program evaluation. With increasing demands for program accountability from federal, state, and private agencies, more home visiting programs that have been exclusively service delivery projects will be required to gather evaluation data—information that will document service delivery and/or effectiveness. In that sense, they will become more research oriented, too. That should not pose too much difficulty for home visitors because, in fact, we believe that home visitors are engaged daily in a type of research with each of their clients.

Whether or not she consciously labels it as research, an effective home visitor regularly follows these research procedures: making a preliminary assessment of the situation (called baseline data collection in research); stating goals with the client (operationalizing the variables); noting progress or regression based on her observation of the client (recording data); and summarizing the situation for her supervisor (data analysis and discussion). To the extent that the visitor is already incorporating research strategies into her own daily work, participating in an evaluation or research process will not be much different from her current practice. We mention this similarity between a home visitor's clinical work and a researcher's scientific work to point out that the line between effective practice and clinical research is sometimes quite thin, and sometimes the two overlap. Home visitors and their program directors should realize that they may already be routinely collecting data that could contribute to a better understanding of home visiting processes and outcomes.

In this chapter, we have described different types of measures and recording procedures that might be used in a home visit program. These procedures should have benefits for the client, the home visitor, her supervisor, the program administrator, and the public policymaker. The last section of this chapter will look at the advantages of evaluation from these different points of view.

From the Client's Perspective

The ultimate beneficiary of the evaluation process should be the client. In return for the time spent completing forms, answering questions (sometimes very personal), or being observed or videotaped, the individual should expect to receive better services because the program staff should be better informed. If self-monitoring is part of the assessment procedures, the client may also increase in self-awareness and may learn a skill (self-monitoring) useful in handling other situations. Information obtained from assessments or regular documentation may also provide the client with more objective information about progress made during the program. She may, for example, be able to see her handicapped child master a list of basic self-care skills. Information of this type should ensure better decision-making by the client about the course of treatment.

From the Home Visitor's Perspective

From the home visitor's point of view, assessment measures should help her be more aware of the client's needs and goals, of alternative strategies to use to help the client, and of progress made toward the selected goals. With good assessment or monitoring data, the home visitor's decision-making with the client will be based on objective data as well as subjective feelings about the situation. Tracking of the client's movement toward independence and subsequent reinforcement of such progress will be made easier for the home visitor. In short, assessment benefits the home visitor by making her a better helper and a more knowledgeable professional.

Record-keeping may also increase the visitor's awareness or consciousness of personal and professional growth and development. This potential benefit of assessment and documentation would be more likely if some of the results of the record-keeping were summarized on a regular basis and presented to the home visitor and if such feedback were interpreted with the help of a supervisor. It is not necessary for home visitors to have formal coursework or training in specific evaluation skills in order to use an evaluation of client progress in the case planning for the clients.

From the Supervisor's Perspective

From the point of view of a supervisor of home visitors, assessment information can help in the supervision of home visitors, the evaluation of client progress, and in making decisions about intervention procedures. A supervisor must be aware of the many different assessment decisions made by the home visiting staff in the course of helping each of their families. Unless a program requires the use of specific assessment procedures, a supervisor of home visitors must be familiar with many different assessments and documentation procedures used by the field staff. She also needs to be familiar with each home visitor's ability to use these different assessment strategies. Some home visitors might prefer observational measures, but they may be more effective with interviewing methods. A wide variety of experiences with, and knowledge of, assessments will allow the supervisor to more effectively guide home visiting staff in the selection, use, and interpretation of measures.

To a supervisor, having any relevant substantive information is preferable to having none or to having only the home visitor's clinical impression. Thus, while the supervisor is challenged by the breadth of assessments used by her staff, the use of relevant and valid assessments by the home visitors provides the supervisor with information with which to more effectively supervise. She can ask about decisions made with clients that might have been influenced by the visitor's personal preference rather than by empirical information. She can help the visitor use assessments to compare two sources of information rather than just rely on the primary reporter (i.e., comparing father's and mother's responses to a needs assessment).

As mentioned in Chapter 4, we also believe that a supervisor should periodically obtain direct information about a home visitor and client by accompanying the home visitor into the home. These clinical observations can be supplemented with information from formal assessments. Of course, all supervision relies somewhat on clinical judgment, just as the home visitors' helping of the families relies a great deal on clinical judgment. However, with both home visitor and supervisor supplementing their clinical judgments with assessment information gathered from clients, services to the client will be enhanced (Gambrill & Stein, 1983).

From the Program Director's Perspective

From the point of view of a home visit program director, program evaluation is becoming an increasingly expected activity, and both client assessments and program documentation are integral to this process. The pressure to evaluate service programs increased in the 1960s when the federal government began requiring written program evaluation plans as conditions for receipt of funds for such programs (Linder, 1983). As the demands for evaluation of service programs have increased, however, they have not been accompanied by clear statements regarding the purposes for conducting evaluations (Hupp & Kaiser, 1986). In this chapter, we have described at least three valid reasons for conducting evaluations of home visiting programs: to determine whether the activities of the program were delivered; to determine whether the program met the clients' needs; and to provide feedback to staff members so that they might improve the services they deliver. An administrator who can show routinely collected information related to each of these topics is in a better position to maintain the support of the agency that is funding the program. Information obtained from assessments and documentation can be used to ensure that the services provided by the program are of high quality. Information gathered can provide the mechanism for changing procedures or caseloads when progress is not being made, either in individual cases or overall.

For the administrator considering evaluation, seven questions identified by Wolery and Bailey (1984) provide excellent guidance (see Table 9.4). The strategies that are associated with each question are necessary to develop a comprehensive evaluation plan. Some of these strategies deal with monitoring the program, and others with monitoring the clients; some strategies call for ongoing evaluation, while others are used only at initial or outcome phases. Question 2, for example, relates to the program's ability to demonstrate that the planned intervention was delivered. The program documentation methods discussed in this chapter would be part of the strategy to address this question. Likewise, assessing client attitudes or behaviors would be part of the strategy necessary to address question 4.

In addition to the resources referenced above, there are two additional resources that would be helpful for program directors interested in evaluating their program. *Working Effectively* is a short, but well-organized and nontechnical, guide to evaluation describing ways in which evaluation can become part of the normal work of an organization (Feek, 1988). *Evaluating Family Programs* is an excellent resource book containing several chapters on ways to measure families, parents, and children (Weiss & Jacobs, 1988). An appendix lists about 100 different measures, with information on the developer of the measure and sources of information about the measure.

From the Policymaker's Perspective

Home visit programs exist within the context of local, state, and national debates about how best to support families. Ultimately, effective use of evaluation in home visit programs should provide

TABLE 9.4: Questions and Strategies in Evaluation of Early Intervention

Questions	Strategies
1. Can the program demonstrate that the methods, materials, and overall service delivery represent the best educational practice?	Describe program and philosophy. Develop rationale for program components. Document best practice. Offer professional validation.
2. Can the program demonstrate that the methods espoused in the overall philosophy are implemented accurately and consistently?	Generate record of services. Generate record of implementation of services. Provide evidence of replicability.
3. Can the program demonstrate that it attempts to verify empirically the effectiveness of interventions or other individual program components for which the best educational practice has yet to be verified?	Analyze individual components of intervention program.
4. Can the program demonstrate that it carefully monitors client progress and is sensitive to points at which changes in services need to be made?	Collect and monitor data to document provision of services and to facilitate decision-making.
5. Can the program demonstrate that a system is in place for determining the relative adequacy of client progress and service delivery?	Compare child progress with reference group. Calculate gain relative to time in intervention. Interpret gain relative to criteria. Interpret gain relative to expectation.
6. Can the program demonstrate that it is moving toward the accomplishment of program goals and objectives?	Specify program objectives in measurable terms. Generate questions about program achievement of objectives. Identify data sources; collect data. Prepare report.
7. Can the program demonstrate that the goals, methods and materials, and overall service delivery system are in accordance with the needs and values of the community and clients it serves?	Review needs assessment. Subjectively evaluate program activities and child and family progress.

SOURCE: Bailey, D. B., & Simeonsson, R. J. (1989). *Family assessment in early intervention* Columbus, OH: Charles E. Merrill.

information with which to inform public policymakers as to the need for home visiting, the best approaches to use, and the likely effectiveness of different types of home visiting programs. It will be up to program directors and researchers studying home visiting to choose measures wisely, collect data appropriately, interpret the results cautiously, and not overclaim effectiveness. In this way, policymakers can make informed decisions based on a sound body of information.

Public policymakers are also often influenced by the cost of a method or program. Although there are difficulties involved in using a cost-benefit or cost-effectiveness analysis of home visiting, White (1988) described how such approaches should be viewed by program directors and policymakers in order to make the results of the analysis useful. MacRae (1989) described examples of national programs that initially survived based on legal and moral arguments (Medicare and PL 94-142), but that began to be evaluated from a cost-effectiveness standpoint as time went on and as costs escalated. A parallel could be drawn for policies on home visiting. More data are needed to support cost-effectiveness arguments, and home visiting advocates should be prepared to provide them (Zigler & Black, 1989).

Summary

This chapter has stressed the importance and purposes of different types of client assessment and program documentation that could be used in a home visiting program. Initial assessments should provide information about the client's needs and strengths, and outcome assessments should help both client and visitor determine progress. Regular recording of specific behaviors targeted by the home visit program may help determine progress more immediately and validly. Ongoing program documentation is important for accountability and replication. Some types of assessment are time-consuming and intrusive, and may be met with resistance by clients and home visitors. However, information from well-chosen instruments can be obtained with cooperation from staff and clients and can benefit the client, home visitor, and program. Awareness of families' preference for informal and unstructured information-gathering should prompt con-

sideration of these procedures as a way of obtaining useful family
data. Ultimately, assessment data can add empirical support to the
base of already existing philosophical support for home visit
programs, and program documentation data can guide the development of new programs that follow the best approaches. Together, both types of data should enhance the willingness of public
policymakers to fund effective programs for clients and families.

10

Future Directions in Home Visiting

In *Home Visiting*, we have presented historical information, reviewed philosophical issues, and discussed many topics related to the practice of home visiting. We have taken on this task because we believe that home visiting is one of the most humane, family-centered services of our society. Home visiting is a service uniquely supportive of family life because its home setting can continually remind both the family and the helper that the needs and desires of the family should be paramount.

Although home visiting has a long history and many advocates, its implementation has been handicapped by a fragmentation in the discussions of issues and concerns, with few writers proposing models for integrating the components of home visiting. As a result, little consideration has been given to the interrelationships that exist among the component parts of home visiting programs, such as program goals, resources, and staff, and how these components are affected by and affect each other. For example, one topic of debate in the field has concerned the educational credentials of home visitors. These debates about credentials seem to imply that home visiting is a one-dimensional activity best performed by one type of individual. When we relate credentials to specific program goals, however, it becomes clear that many different educational backgrounds can be appropriate since home visiting programs have different goals.

249

To guide our view of future directions in home visiting, we present in Figure 10.1 a model illustrating major relationships among different program processes and factors that influence these processes. This model can help policymakers, program directors, and home visitors understand the influences that can bear on a particular program component at any point in time, and can help promote policies and decisions that take into account existing relationships among important program variables.

The major program processes we have defined in the model include (1) setting program goals, (2) assessing program resources, (3) hiring staff, (4) implementing the program, and (5) evaluating the program. In this chapter, we will look at the ways these processes influence one another. We will also consider the major influences on these processes, namely family characteristics; credentials, training, and supervision of home visitors; community; and research.

Program Processes

In considering the interrelationships among program processes, we will first consider the relationship of program goals to other program activities. Program goals set the tone and define the limits of a program's operations. Programs typically begin with a guiding philosophy that identifies specific goals to be accomplished. These goals generally determine the resources that will be necessary, though the goals themselves can be influenced by the available resources. If resources are expensive or unavailable, goals may have to be curtailed. If more financial support is available than a program anticipated, it might expand its mission by providing additional services or by adding to the number of clients who are served.

Program resources include fiscal, personnel, physical, and environmental. Any of these four basic resources can have a major effect on the potential accomplishments of a given program. Yet, we know little about the effects of each of these variables on program outcome, and we know even less about how these resources interact with one another to influence program outcomes. Do better-funded programs that pay visitors high salaries have different outcomes than programs that rely on volunteers, though

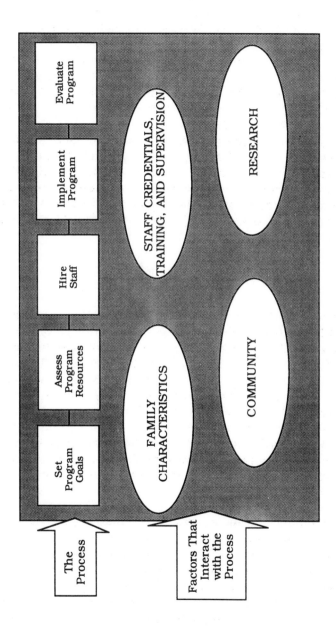

The Process

| Set Program Goals | Assess Program Resources | Hire Staff | Implement Program | Evaluate Program |

FAMILY CHARACTERISTICS

STAFF CREDENTIALS, TRAINING, AND SUPERVISION

COMMUNITY

RESEARCH

Factors That Interact with the Process

Figure 10.1. A Model Illustrating Major Relationships Among Different Program Processes and Factors that Influence These Processes

251

the goals of the programs may be the same? Do programs that provide for extensive supervision of home visitors have greater influence with families or a lower turnover rate among visitors?

Another issue related to resources is how best to allocate resources to maximize services. Should one spread resources to reach the maximum number of families, or should one work more intensely with a few most needy families? Though Richmond raised this issue of resource allocation many years ago, we still have little empirical support to guide practice, and the issue continues to be debated. A program that visits families once every two weeks or once a month can provide services to many more families than a program that provides weekly visits, but in doing so it may sacrifice program effects that could occur as a result of more frequent visits (e.g., Powell & Grantham-McGregor, 1989).

Programs typically consider several variables when making decisions on employment of staff, especially program goals and resources. A program must consider whether or not it needs to employ individuals who already have had professional training in a particular area, such as nursing or teaching, or whether the program can provide the staff with the necessary training to carry out the program's goals. Financial resources will influence how many home visitors can be employed and what salaries they will be paid. Credentials of the staff influence the ability of programs to meet their objectives. It is possible that program objectives cannot be carried out by some home visitors because there is a poor match between their knowledge and skills and the program goals.

Program implementation is the process of actively providing the intended services. It requires interaction between program staff and families and the possible use of specific intervention materials or procedures. The ability to implement a program as designed clearly depends upon the reality of its goals, resources, and staff. Changes in any of these three components can result in potentially significant changes in how the program is implemented.

Evaluation has a role in every service program. Program evaluation information can be obtained from both staff and clients to obtain input on their perceptions of program procedures and effects. Outside consultants can provide an unbiased judgment of a program's procedures and outcomes. Through evaluation, a program can determine whether its own goals and objectives are being met. Such efforts help programs determine when procedures need to be changed, objectives modified, or resources increased.

With the appropriate design procedures, evaluation efforts can add to our empirical data base typically obtained through systematic research studies, as well as provide information for decision-making purposes. Several research designs are appropriate for both program evaluation and research purposes. One such design is the single subject design, in which one or more clients' behaviors are studied intensely over a period of time to determine whether the procedures being implemented are effective or need to be modified. Service programs can also be designed in such a way as to offer planned variations of their program, making possible a comparison of the effectiveness of different procedures.

Factors that Influence Program Processes

Programs do not function independently of a number of important influences. These influences can be described under six headings: family characteristics; staff credentials; staff training; staff supervision; community; and research. The potential influence of each factor is discussed below.

Family Characteristics

Family characteristics obviously have a profound influence on any program. Many home visiting programs are often initiated to provide services based upon a particular set of demographic characteristics of the family, or of the conditions of one individual in the family. We know, though, that considerable diversity exists among families, even among those of similar sociocultural backgrounds. The recognition of this diversity has led to an emphasis on assessing each family's needs and priorities. Such assessments have been a considerable step forward over assuming that all families that are poor, have a chronically ill child, or are experiencing a drug abuse problem all have the same needs.

Yet considerably more effort needs to be expended to study family characteristics as they relate to family needs, family acceptance of services, and family responsiveness to intervention procedures. Understanding that many variables can influence family functioning—social, emotional, cognitive, physical, and educational, among others—should lead program developers to consider the complexity of each family and each individual in the family in the design of services. Obviously, every characteristic cannot be assessed or responded to, but we do need to learn more about the most relevant characteristics in relation to intervention effects. For example, maternal care offered to women pregnant for the first time appears to have more positive outcomes than the same services offered to pregnant women who have previously had children. Parent training is more successful with some families than others. We are just beginning to understand how family strengths contribute to participation and outcome effects. We need, however, considerably more knowledge about many areas, especially family beliefs, values and coping strategies, and how these relate to family functioning. To assess such family characteristics, we need a refinement in measures, an emphasis upon careful interviewing, and an increased ability to use actual observations of family functioning to understand what might be helpful for each family. We also need carefully designed research to address these questions.

Home Visitor Credentials

In Chapter 4, we identified the major categories of home visitor credentials (education, experience, and interpersonal skills), as well as characteristics of age, gender, and ethnicity. Program directors have often stressed the importance of one or more credential, such as maturity, being a parent, or being a nurse. Some believe that a CDA credential is sufficient background for home visitors; others expect visitors to have a bachelor's degree in child development or related areas.

More agreement exists about the interpersonal characteristics of home visitors, with programs almost universally calling for individuals with good interpersonal and communication skills, warmth, judgment, and maturity. Procedures for selecting individuals with such credentials, however, are not well developed and, within the home visiting field, these characteristics have not been systematically evaluated in relation to program outcomes or to other home visitor credentials.

We cannot recommend too strongly the need to consider home visitor credentials in relation to other program components because they are inextricably related to every other major aspect of home visiting. Furthermore, we recommend that future research be directed toward generating knowledge about the importance of various home visitor credentials. Such research will have to be conducted in many programs with differing goals and family characteristics in order to begin to build the data base for future decision-making.

Staff Training

One of the most pressing issues facing home visiting concerns the availability of appropriate and high-quality training. Even in many professional training programs, the knowledge and skills needed by home visitors is not sufficiently covered. The current availability of training can be grouped under five categories: (1) in-service training provided by individual problems; (2) individualized competency training under the national competency credentialing program for CDA; (3) professional training in fields such as social work and nursing; (4) national training efforts, such as Head Start; and (5) statewide training (for example, Missouri's training for the Parents as Teachers Program). Given the widespread interest in home visiting services and the likelihood of increases in home visiting as a function of the implementation of PL 99-457, it is essential to consider the preservice and in-service training needs of home visitors in a more systematic and thorough manner.

Several conditions have contributed to this need for training. First is the practice of employing individuals based upon interpersonal and ethnic characteristics rather than professional training. A result of this practice is that many programs must provide essential training before home visitors can assume their responsibilities. Second, very few written or audiovisual materials exist for the training of home visitors, and those that do exist are not readily known or accessible to others. It takes considerable effort to develop materials, and programs that prepare such materials rarely have the resources to disseminate them. Many programs develop their own materials, but these materials do not become a part of the public domain. The use of training materials is too important and their development too time-consuming to continue this practice. Some summaries of training materials have been prepared (Missouri Department of Elementary and Secondary Education, 1986; Boyd & Herwig, 1980), but additional work needs to be done on summarizing and cataloging materials so that programs can build on the work of one another, rather than repeat similar efforts.

Several efforts need to be initiated in the immediate future. First, formal educational agencies at the community college, four-year college, and graduate educational levels need to rethink the program being provided for students who may be future home visitors, asking very seriously the question, "Are we preparing them for the work they will be engaged in when they provide family-support services in the home?" Such an analysis would most likely lead to an enhancement of the content and experiences that are provided to students to prepare them for future positions.

With the current and future expansion of home visiting programs, it becomes more important for each program to consider coordinating and consolidating training activities within communities. Such community efforts could provide the added advantage of serving as a bridge for interaction among different home visiting programs, as well as to provide home visitors with a broader and more in-depth training than they may have been able to obtain otherwise. Such community activities may be particularly appropriate for periodic professional development activities. A coordinated process would help ensure the opportunity for sharing information among home visitors and the opportunity for newly developed programs to have their visitors learn from experienced home visitors. It is important to note, however, that programs with different philosophical orientations may have difficulty combining training efforts, and efforts would have to be made to avoid confusing home visitors by presenting differing philosophical orientations.

Staff Supervision

In Chapter 4, we stressed our belief in the critical role supervision plays in the practice of home visiting, noting the necessity for support, education, and evaluation of home visitors. We do not believe that most home visiting programs can provide quality services without the provision of supervision for those whose work takes them into clients' homes on a continuing basis. We recommend that professional training programs begin to prepare individuals to assume supervisory roles in home visiting programs. Such preparation could be a part of graduate programs in social work, nursing, or education. Though the available information on procedures for the supervision of home visitors is limited, extensive information or supervision exists in several fields and could be adapted for home visiting (e.g., Gambrill & Stein, 1983).

Two concerns especially need attention in the supervision of home visitors. The first concern is the amount and type of supervision in relation to home visitor credentials, characteristics, and program goals. Second is the need to evaluate the benefits of individual, group, and on-site supervision. Because we have emphasized the importance of supervision in this book, we believe it is important to reiterate a point we made earlier on: Because home visiting is a front-line, stressful, and, at times, lonely position, it calls for more supervision than many other positions (e.g., Gambrill & Stein, 1983).

Community

In our conceptual model of home visiting, all program components should be considered within the larger framework of the community since home visiting is uniquely a community service. It takes place within the community and is inextricably linked with the life of that community.

Community issues are often a concern when hiring home visitors because of the belief that home visitors need to be sensitive to and knowledgeable about those who live in the community. Many programs require that their home visitors be from the same socioeconomic or ethnic group as the population that is served. This requirement can help reduce psychological distance between the program and its clients.

Other community issues, however, need to be considered in the development of future programs, especially the coordination among family agencies. In the same way that the family is considered a system, with each member influencing the total family's functioning, so do the different parts of a community influence the total community's functioning. How different agencies and groups plan and act together toward mutually agreed upon goals can significantly influence the quality of life for all in the community. Many home visiting programs are already closely coordinated with different parts of the community. Most notable are those programs that are either a part of school systems or that have developed close relationships with the school systems. Other notable programs are coordinated with medical agencies. Such programs may be a part of a hospital's routine follow-up procedures for low birthweight, premature infants, or for families not likely to seek routine pediatric care. In some communities, all major education, health, and social services are already coordinating services for families with a handicapped infant or young child.

Home visiting programs can become a part of larger community efforts directed toward the resolution of problem situations that might be adversely affecting many elements of the community. Severely inadequate day-care facilities, for example, could be contributing to child neglect, family stress, family economic status, and the lack of social and cognitive development of large numbers of children. Rather than help each individual family cope with this situation, agencies could collectively help improve the community's day-care resources. This does not mean that a home visiting program will divert all its resources to the resolution of community concerns, but it does mean that any given program should not act in isolation from other community resources, and home visiting programs should take responsibility for calling attention to problematic community situations and work for their resolution.

We are aware that this broader role moves beyond serving only the needs of individual clients to focusing on changes that might more appropriately and effectively meet the needs of a community of clients. The collective experience of home visitors in any one program, however, can be a considerable asset for initiating potential community changes that may have widespread positive effects. This advocacy role was associated with home visitors at the beginning of the twentieth century (Levine & Levine, 1970) and we recognize it again as an important service need as we approach the end of the twentieth century.

There are a number of ways that home visiting programs could become involved in community efforts. We do not propose that the program staff divert all their energies to solving community problems; we do believe, however, that program staff and home visitors are often in a unique role to observe problems in the community that could be addressed on a systems level rather than by many individual community members dealing separately with the problems. Those who work with many families over time come to have an understanding of community barriers to individual well-being. Such knowledge needs to find its way into our communities in ways that can facilitate change. Balancing the need to respond to individuals and families in stress versus the need to change adverse environmental conditions will remain a tension in programs that recognize the importance of both activities.

Research

Research provides the empirical basis for determining the effectiveness of intervention programs. Research on home visiting can provide information on those characteristics of program implementation that are effective, under what conditions, and with which populations. Research findings have already provided a foundation for justifying the provision of certain kinds of home visiting services for certain family and child outcomes. Though this foundation is built upon a small set of research studies and at this point can only minimally inform practice, two examples illustrate how critical empirical knowledge about problem variables can be. In investigating the effects of the frequency of home visits on child and family outcomes, Powell and Grantham-McGregor (1989) provided home visits weekly, biweekly, or monthly. Using child cognitive performance as an outcome measure, they concluded that at least weekly home visits were essential to bring about program effects. In another study using a planned variation, Larson (1980) found that program effects were obtained only when the program was initiated prenatally and not when the program was initiated six weeks postpartum. Though the findings of these two studies clearly cannot be extended across all populations, they provide a serious note of caution in drawing general and possibly erroneous conclusions about the effectiveness of home visiting in general rather than recognizing the conditions under which it may or may not be effective. These studies are also excellent examples of the types of issues that need to be explored in future research to help ensure that services are offered under those conditions most likely to bring about change.

General Recommendations

Based on our experiences, both in the research and practice of home visiting, we have a number of recommendations to make. First, new home visiting initiatives should begin with an awareness of the historical context of home visiting and should build upon the existing knowledge and research in the field. The accumulated evidence provides a foundation that can ensure that new and existing programs are able to benefit from the work of others.

Second, because only a small number of research studies serve as the empirical base for home visiting, the 1990s should be characterized by an extensive series of studies designed to address many issues on the practice of home visiting. We need to explore process and outcome in much more depth, and to study the actual interactions of home visitors and families. Specifically, we recommend that research be conducted to identify those family needs that are best met through home visiting services, including considerations of family characteristics, community, and home visitor qualifications, as part of the design. We strongly recommend that research be conducted on the process of home visiting because so little empirical support or documentation is available. Process variables range from identifying quantitative issues, such as the frequency of home visiting and its duration, to an analysis of the content of the visit, the roles played by the visitor, and the nature of the home visiting curriculum.

We need to conduct research on the relationship between the sociocultural characteristics of the home visitor and both process and outcome variables. We know that some families prefer visitors to share the same ethnic characteristics, and this is clearly an important preference to consider. But does this assure a higher quality service? How do home visitor qualifications interact with family's preference for visitors from similar backgrounds? We need to increase our knowledge in this area so that we can make better matches between families and visitors.

The availability of research instruments to measure process and products has generally lagged behind the needs in the field, though there are several noteworthy instruments, as described in Chapter 9. Because accurate measurement is essential for the advancement of any science, we recommend that additional attention be devoted to the development of measures that are sensitive to the goals of home visiting services. Areas needing attention include family coping and problem solving, and child social and emotional behavior.

We especially recommend that future measurement efforts incorporate the unique opportunities for assessment that are afforded by home visits. Traditionally, many assessment procedures are developed because the client cannot be observed in his or her natural environment. Home visiting makes possible alternative assessment procedures. Both observation and interviewing procedures should be studied for the possibilities each has for providing systematic information on the process of home visiting and the outcome. Both procedures are particularly appropriate for home visiting but have not been fully developed for use in the home.

But we also cannot wait for all the important research to be completed in order to provide services for those in need. The empirical support that does exist provides a basis for continuing services to many populations. Consequently, our second recommendation is to extend home visiting services more broadly, especially to populations for which positive benefits have been demonstrated. We can integrate these two recommendations for both research and service by stressing the need for funding so that appropriate research designs can be implemented within service programs.

We further recommend that all community agencies include a family focus to their goals, and consider providing home visiting services as a way of meeting family needs. Whenever a parent comes for services or whenever services are offered for a child, one should ask, "Does the family also need help to cope with the situation?" Parents should also be included in all major aspects of programs, from the delineation of goals and needs to identifying the components for evaluation.

We also suggest that it is timely to consider the formation of a national association of home visitors. Such an association could serve a number of functions that are not well served presently, especially the coordination of training efforts, helping to ensure that programs do not continually repeat the development activities that others have already done and that they have access to existing resources. The association could provide written communication to keep home visitors informed of the different types of programs around the country, current legislation influencing the practice of home visiting, different approaches to home visiting, and the results of research studies.

Summary

As we begin the last decade of the twentieth century, it is clear that new ways of thinking about home visiting will be needed. The schema presented in this chapter showing the interrelations of program components and influencing factors serves as a guide for considering future needs. As many programs evolve toward a broader scope for intervention, program resources have to be rethought. We must also begin to evaluate more intensely what can be accomplished through home visiting and what cannot, and plan programs accordingly.

One of the most significant changes during the 1980s, that will influence changes in the 1990s, has been the shift in many intervention programs from an individual focus to a family focus. This shift cannot be taken lightly. Providing family support services is considerably more complex than providing an educational curriculum for a young child. It demands a rethinking of the basic credentials and characteristics of home visitors and calls for increasing supports for their professional training and supervision.

We must begin to distinguish different kinds of home visiting programs for certain purposes, recognizing that programs across the country serve families with every possible characteristic, and these differences in family characteristics call for variety and flexibility in services. We must also be cautious not to let adherence to current philosophies interfere with good practice. If family needs are truly best met by services for an individual child, we must not assume that the family would have been better served with broader services.

For the future, we should recognize that home visiting, long recognized as an important process for helping families, will most likely become a more prevalent service, reach more families, serve broader needs, and become a more acceptable, and possibly expected, service. We need to be prepared by beginning now to increase the empirical support and financial resources, and to ensure the availability of well-qualified individuals.

References

Addams, J. (1935). *Forty years at Hull House*. New York: MacMillan.

American Psychological Association. (1981). Ethical principles of psychologists. *American Psychologist, 36*(6), 633-638.

Azar, S. T., Robinson, D. R., Hekimian, E., & Twentyman, M. T. (1984). Unrealistic expectations and problem solving ability in maltreating and comparison mothers. *Journal of Consulting and Clinical Psychology, 52*(4), 687-691.

Bailey, D. B. (1988). Considerations in developing family goals. In D. B. Bailey & R. J. Simeonsson (Eds.), *Family assessment in early intervention* (pp. 229-249). Columbus, OH: Charles E. Merrill.

Bailey, D. B., & Simeonsson, R. J. (1988). *Family assessment in early intervention*. Columbus, OH: Charles E. Merrill.

Bandura, A. (1969). *Principles of behavior modification*. New York: Holt, Rinehart & Winston.

Bandura, A. (1977). *Social learning theory*. Englewood Cliffs, NJ: Prentice-Hall.

Bandura, A., & Walters, R. H. (1963). *Social learning and personality development*. New York: Holt, Rinehart & Winston.

Barnard, K. E., Magyary, D., Sumner, G., Booth, C. L., Mitchell, S. K., & Spieker, S. (1988). Prevention of parenting alterations for women with low social support. *Psychiatry, 51*(3), 248-253.

Barrera, M. E., Rosenbaum, P. L., & Cunningham, C. E. (1986). Early home intervention with low-birth-weight infants and their parents. *Child Development, 57*, 20-33.

Bartky, J. A. (1953). *Supervision as human relations*. Lexington: D. C. Heath.

Bateson, G. (1972). *Steps to an ecology of mind*. New York: Ballantine.

Bateson, G. (1979). *Mind and nature*. New York: E. P. Dutton.

Beck, D. F., & Jones, M. A. (1973). *Progress on family problems: A nationwide study of clients' and counselors' views on family agency services*. New York: Family Service Association of America.

265

Bell, R. Q. (1971). Stimulus control of parent or caregiver behavior by offspring. *Developmental Psychology*, 4, 63-72.

Bell, R. Q. (1974). Contribution of human infants to caregiving and social interactions. In M. Lewis & L. A. Rosenblum (Eds.), *The effects of the infant on its caregiver*(pp. 1–19). New York: John Wiley.

Belle, D. (Ed.). (1982). *Lives in stress: Women and depression*. Beverly Hills, CA: Sage.

Benjamin, A. (1975). *The helping interview*. Boston: Houghton Mifflin.

Berg, C. L., & Helgeson, D. (1984). That first home visit. *Journal of Community Health Nursing*, 1(3), 207-215.

Berkeley Planning Associates. (1982). *The exploration of client characteristics, services and outcomes*. Washington, DC: Department of Health, Education and Welfare, Contract #105-78-1108.

Bijou, S. W. (1984). Parent training: Actualizing the critical conditions of early childhood development. In R. F. Dangel & R. A. Polster (Eds.), *Parent training* (pp. 15-26). New York: Guilford Press.

Blechman, E. A. (1974). The family contact game: A tool to teach interpersonal problem solving. *Family Coordinator*, 23, 269-281.

Blechman, E. A. (1980). Family problem-solving training. *American Journal of Family Therapy*, 8, 3-22.

Bloom, M., & Fischer, J. (1982). *Evaluating practice: Guidelines for the accountable professional*. Englewood Cliffs, NJ: Prentice-Hall.

Blume, S. (1985). Women and alcohol. In T. E. Bratter & G. G. Forrest (Eds.), *Alcoholism and substance abuse* (pp. 623-638). New York: Free Press.

Bowlby, J. (1952). *Maternal care and mental health*. Geneva: World Health Organization.

Bowlby, J. (1969). *Attachment and loss: Vol. 1. Attachment*. New York: Basic Books.

Bowlby, J. (1984). Violence in the family as a disorder of the attachment and caregiving systems. *American Journal of Psychoanalysis*, 44(1), 9-27.

Boyd, J. (1978). *Counselor supervision: Approaches, preparation, practices*. Muncie, IN: Accelerated Development.

Boyd, R. D., & Herwig, J. (1980). *Serving handicapped children in home-based Head Start*. Portage, WI: The Portage Project.

Brammer, L. M., & Shostrom, E. L. (1982). *Therapeutic psychology: Fundamentals of counseling and psychotherapy* (4th ed.). Englewood Cliffs, NJ: Prentice-Hall.

Bremner, R. H. (1971). *Children and youth in America: A documentary history: Vol. II. 1986-1932*. Cambridge, MA: Harvard University Press.

Brickman, P., Rabinowitz, V., Karuza, J., Coates, D., Cohn, E., & Kidder, L. (1982). Models of helping and coping. *American Psychologist*, 37, 368-384.

Brinkerhoff, R. O., Brethower, D. M., Hluchyj, T., & Nowakowski, J. R. (1983). *Program evaluation: A practitioner's guide for trainers and educators*. Boston: Kluwer-Nijhoff.

Bristol, M. M., & Gallagher, J. J. (1982). A family focus for intervention. In C. T. Ramey & P. L. Trohanis (Eds.), *Finding and educating high-risk and handicapped infants* (pp. 137-161). Baltimore, MD: University Park Press.

Bronfenbrenner, U. (1974). *Is early intervention effective? A report on longitudinal evaluation of preschool programs* (Vol. 2). Washington, DC: Department of Health, Education, and Welfare, Office of Child Development.

Bronfenbrenner, U. (1979). *The ecology of human development*. Cambridge, MA: Harvard University Press.

Bronfenbrenner, U. (1987). Family support: The quiet revolution. In S. L. Kagan, D. Powell, B. Weissbourd, & E. Zigler (Eds.), *America's family support programs* (Foreword, pp. xi-xvii). New Haven, CT: Yale University Press.

Bronfenbrenner, U. (1989). Ecological systems theory. *Annals of Child Development*, 6, 185-246.

Bronfenbrenner, U., & Crouter, A. C. (1983). The evolution of environmental models in developmental research. In P. H. Mussen (Ed.), *Handbook of child psychology: Vol. I. History, theory and methods* (W. Kessen, Vol. Ed.), pp. 357-414. New York: John Wiley.

Bross, D. C., Krugman, R. D., Lenherr, M. R., Rosenberg, D. A., & Schmitt, B. D. (Eds.). (1988). *The new child protection team handbook*. New York: Garland.

Bry, B. H. (1983). Substance abuse in women: Etiology and prevention. *Issues in Mental Health Nursing*, 5, 253-272.

Buhler-Wilkerson, K. (1985). Public health nursing: In sickness or in health. *American Journal of Public Health*, 75, 1155-1167.

Cabot, R. C. (1919). *Social work*. Boston: Hougton Mifflin.

Caldwell, B., & Bradley, R. (1984). *Home observation for measurement of the environment*. Little Rock, AR: University of Arkansas, Center for Research on Teaching and Learning.

Cameron, R. J. (1984). Portage in the U.K.: 1984. *Journal of Community Education*, 3(3), 24-33.

Cansler, D. P., Martin, G. H., & Valand, M. C. (1982). *Working with families: A manual for early childhood programs serving the handicapped*. Winston-Salem, NC: Kaplan.

Caplan, G. (1974). *Support systems and community mental health*. New York: Behavioral Publications.

Carkhuff, R. R. (1969). *Helping and human relations. Vol. 1: Selection and training*. New York: Holt, Rinehart & Winston.

Carkhuff, R. R. (1984). *Helping and human relations, Vol. II*. Amherst, MA: Human Resource Development.

Carkhuff, R. R., & Anthony, W. (1979). *The skills of helping: An introduction to counseling*. Amherst, MA: Human Resource Development Press.

Carkhuff, R. R., & Truax, C. B. (1965). Lay mental health counseling. *Journal of Consulting Psychology*, 29, 426-431.

Cauthen, D. B. (1981). The house call in current medical practice. *The Journal of Family Practice*, 13, 209-213.

Chamberlin, R. W. (Ed.). (1980). *Conference exploring the use of home visitors to improve the delivery of preventive services to mothers with young children*. Washington, DC: American Academy of Pediatrics.

Chapman, J., Siegal, E., & Cross, A. (in press). A review and analysis of home visitors and child health. *Pediatrics*.

Chasnoff, I. J., Burns, W. J., Schnoll, S. H., & Burns, K. A. (1985). Cocaine use in pregnancy. *New England Journal of Medicine*, 313, 666-669.

Coletta, A. J. (1977). *Working together: A guide to parent involvement*. Atlanta, GA: Humanics.

Colletta, N. D., & Gregg, C. H. (1981). Adolescent mothers' vulnerability to stress. *The Journal of Nervous and Mental Disease*, 169(1), 50-54.

Combs, A. W., & Avila, D. L. (1985). *Helping relationships*. Boston: Allyn & Bacon.

Cormier, L. S., Cormier, W. H., & Weisser, R. J., Jr. (1984). *Interviewing and helping skills for health professionals*. Monterey, CA: Wadsworth.

Council for Early Childhood Professional Recognition. (1987). *Home visitor: Child development associate assessment system and competency standards*. Washington, DC: Author.

Cyster, R., Clift, P. S., & Battle, S. (1980). *Parental involvement in primary school*. Berkshire, England: National Foundation for Educational Research.

D'Zurilla, T. J., & Goldfried, M. R. (1971). Problem solving and behavior modification. *Journal of Abnormal Psychology, 78*, 107-126.

D'Zurilla, T. J., & Nezu, A. (1982). Social problem solving in adults. In P. C. Kendall (Ed.), *Advances in cognitive-behavioral research and therapy*, (Vol. 1). New York: Academic Press.

Dangel, R. F., & Polster, R. A. (Eds.). (1984). *Parent training*. New York: Guilford Press.

Datta, L. E., & Wasik, B. H. (1988). *"Good morning, Mrs. Swanson": The historical context of home support programs*. Paper presented at the 1988 Family Support in the Home: Policy, Practice, and Research Conference, Honolulu, Hawaii.

Davidson, H. W. (1984). The revolution in family law: Confronting child abuse. In *Perspectives on child maltreatment in the mid '80s* (pp. 35-38). National Center on Child Abuse and Neglect, (DHHS Publication No. OHDS 84-30338). Washington, DC: U.S. Government Printing Office.

Dawson, P. (1980). Home visiting in Europe. In R. W. Chamberlin (Ed.), *Conference exploring the use of home visitors to improve the delivery of preventive services to mothers with young children* (pp. 272-274). Washington, DC: American Academy of Pediatrics.

Dewey, J., & Dewey, J. (1915). *Schools of tomorrow*. New York: E. P. Dutton.

Dorn, F. J. (1986). The social influence model: An overview. In F. J. Dorn (Ed.), *The social influence process in counseling and psychotherapy* (pp. 3-15). Springfield, IL: Charles C. Thomas.

Duncan, D. C. (1982). Cognitive perceptions of battered women (Doctoral dissertation, University of Southern California). *Dissertation Abstracts International, 43*, 01B.

Dunst, C. J., & Trivette, C. M. (1987). Enabling and empowering families: Conceptual and intervention issues. *School Psychology Review, 16*, 443-456.

Dunst, C. J., Trivette, C., & Deal, A. (1988). *Enabling and empowering families: Principles and guidelines for practice*. Cambridge, MA: Brookline Books.

Durlak, J. (1979). Comparative effectiveness of professional and paraprofessional helpers. *Psychological Bulletin, 86*, 80-92.

Edelwich, J., & Brodsky, A. (1980). *Burn-out*. New York: Human Sciences Press.

Egan, G. (1975). *The skilled helper: A model for systematic helping and interpersonal relating*. Belmont, CA: Wadsworth.

Egan, G. (1982). *The skilled helper: Model, skills, and methods for effective helping* (2nd ed.). Monterey, CA: Brooks/Cole.

Ekstein, R. (1972). Supervision of psychotherapy. Is it teaching? Is it administration? Or is it therapy? In D. E. Hendrickson & F. H. Krause (Eds.), *Counseling and psychotherapy: Training and supervision* (pp. 153-156). Columbus, OH: Charles E. Merrill.

Elstein, A. S., Shulman, L. S., & Spratka, S. A. (1978). *Medical problem solving: An analysis of clinical reasoning*. Cambridge, MA: Harvard University Press.

Embry, L. H. (1984). What to do? Matching client characteristics and intervention techniques through a prescriptive taxonomic key. In R. F. Dangel & R. A. Polster (Eds.), *Parent training* (pp. 443-473). New York: Guilford Press.

Feek, W. (1988). *Working effectively: A guide to evaluation techniques*. London: Bedford Square Press.

Felner, R. D., Jason, L. A., Moritsugu, J. N., & Farber, S. S. (1983). Preventive psychology: Evolution and current status. In R. D. Felner, L. A. Jason, J. N. Moritsugu, & S. S. Farber (Eds.) *Preventive psychology: Theory research and practice* (pp. 3-10). Elmsford,NY: Pergamon.

Fiedler, D., Briar, K. H., & Pierce, M. (1984). Services for battered women. *Journal of Sociology and Social Welfare, 11*, 540-557.

Field, T. M., Widmayer, S., Greenberg, R., & Stoller, S. (1982). Effects of parent training on teenage mothers and their daughters. *Pediatrics, 69*, 703-707.

Field, T. M., Widmayer, S. M., Stringer, S., & Ignatoff, E. (1980). Teenage lower-class, black mothers and their preterm infants: An intervention and developmental follow-up. *Child Development, 51*, 426-436.

Fineman, S. (1985). *Social work stress and intervention*. Brookfield, VT: Gower.

Fink, A. E., Wilson, E. E., & Conover, M. B. (1963). *The field of social work*. New York: Holt, Rinehart & Winston.

Finkelhor, D., & Baron, L. (1986). Risk factors for child sexual abuse. *Journal of Interpersonal Violence, 1*(1), 43-71.

Finkelhor, D., Hotaling, G. T., & Yllo, K. (1988). *Stopping family violence*. Newbury Park, CA: Sage.

Finnegan, L. P. (Ed.). (1979). *Drug dependence in pregnancy: Clinical management of mother and child*. National Institute on Drug Abuse Services Monograph Series.

Folkman, S., & Lazarus, R. S. (1980). An analysis of coping in a middle-aged community sample. *Journal of Health and Social Behavior, 21*, 219-239.

Forehand, R. L., & McMahon, R. J. (1981). *Helping the noncompliant child: A clinician's guide to parent training*. New York: Guilford Press.

Forgatch, M. & Patterson, G. R. (1989). *Parents and adolescents living together. Part 2: Family problem solving*. Eugene, OR: Castalia.

Fortune, A. E. (1987). Grief only? Client and social worker reactions to termination. *Clinical Social Work Journal, 15*(2), 159-171.

Fraley, Y. L. (1983, January-February). The Family Support Center: Early intervention for high-risk parents and children. *Children Today, 12*(1), 13-17.

Freudenberger, J. (1974). Staff burn-out. *Journal of Social Issues, 30*(1), 159-165.

Gallagher, J. J., Trohanis, P., & Clifford, R. (1989). *Policy implementation and 99-457*. Baltimore, MD: Paul H. Brookes.

Gambrill, E. (1983). *Casework: A competency based approach*. Englewood Cliffs, NJ: Prentice-Hall.

Gambrill, E. D., & Stein, T. J. (1978). *Supervision in child welfare: A training manual*. Berkeley: University of California, Extension Publication.

Gambrill, E., & Stein, T. J. (1983). *Supervision: A decision-making approach*. Beverly Hills, CA: Sage.

270   HOME VISITING

Garbarino, J. (1987). Family support and the prevention of child maltreatment. In
    S. L. Kagan, D. R. Powell, B. Weissbourd, & E. F. Zigler (Eds.), *America's family
    support programs* (pp. 99-114). New Haven, CT: Yale University Press.
Gelles, R. J. (1987). *Family violence* (2nd ed.). Newbury Parks, CA: Sage.
Giles-Sims, J. (1983). *Wife battering: A systems theory approach*. New York: Guilford
    Press.
Glendinning, C. (1986). *A single door: Social work with the families of disabled children*
    London, England: Allen & Unwin.
Goldfried, M. R., & Davison, G. C. (1976). *Clinical behavior therapy*. New York: Holt
    Rinehart & Winston.
Gordon, R. L. (1975). *Interviewing: Strategy, techniques and tactics*. Homewood, IL
    Dorsey Press.
Gordon, I. J., & Guinagh, B. J. (1978). A home learning center approach to early
    stimulation. *JSAS Catalog of Selected Documents in Psychology, 8*, 6(Ms. No. 1634)
Gordon, I. J., & Guinagh, B. J. (1978, March). *Middle school performance as a function
    of early stimulation*. (Final report to the Administration for Children, Youth and
    Families, Project No. NIH-HEW-OCD-90-C-908). Gainesville: University of Flor
    ida, Institute for Development of Human Resources; and Chapel Hill: University
    of North Carolina, School of Education.
Gray, S. W., & Klaus, R. A. (1970). The early training project: A seventh year report
    Child Development, 41, 909-924.
Gray, S. W., & Ruttle, K. (1980). The Family-Oriented Home Visiting Program: A
    longitudinal study. *Genetic Psychology Monographs, 102*, 299-316.
Gray, S. W., & Wandersman, L. P. (1980). The methodology of home-based interven
    tion studies: Problems and promising strategies. *Child Development, 51*, 993-1009
Grosz, C. A., & Denson, D. B. (1988). Conducting effective team meetings. In D. C
    Bross, R. D. Krugman, M. R. Lenherr, D. A. Rosenberg, & B. D. Schmitt (Eds.)
    The new child protection team handbook (pp. 287-298). New York: Garland.
Gutelius, M. F., Kirsch, A. D., MacDonald, S., Brooks, M. R., & McErlean, T. (1977)
    Controlled study of child health supervision: Behavioral results. *Pediatrics, 60*
    294-304.
Gutelius, M. F., Kirsch, A. D., MacDonald, S., Brooks, M. R., McErlean, T., &
    Newcomb, C. (1972). Promising results from a cognitive stimulation program in
    infancy. *Clinical Pediatrics, 11*, 585-593.
Hackney, H., & Cormier, L. S. (1979). *Counseling strategies and objectives* (2nd ed.)
    Englewood Cliffs, NJ: Prentice-Hall.
Haley, J. (1976). *Problem solving therapy*. New York: Harper & Row.
Haley, J. (1987). *Problem solving therapy*. San Francisco: Jossey-Bass.
Halpern, R. (1984). Lack of effects for home-based early intervention? Some possi
    ble explanations. *American Journal of Orthopsychiatry, 54*(1), 33-42.
Halpern, R. (1986). Home-based early intervention: Dimensions of current practice
    Child Welfare, 65, 387.
Halpern, R. (1987). Key social and demographic trends affecting young families
    Implications for early childhood care and education. *Young Children, 42*, 34-40.
Halpern, R., & Covey, L. (1983). Community support for adolescent parents and
    their children: The Parent-to-Parent Program in Vermont. *Journal of Primary
    Prevention, 3*(3), 160-173.

Halpern, R., & Larner, M. (1988). The design of family support programs in high-risk communities: Lessons from the Child Survival/Fair Start initiative. In D. R. Powell (Ed.), *Parent education as early childhood intervention: Emerging directions in theory, research, and practice.* Norwood, NJ: Ablex.

Hannon, P., & Jackson, A. (1987). Educational home visiting and the teaching of reading. *Educational Research, 29*(3), 183-191.

Hardy-Brown, K., Miller, B., Dean, J., Carrasco, C., & Thompson, S. (1987). Home based intervention: Catalyst and challenge to the therapeutic relationship. *Zero to Three, 8*(1), 8-12.

Hausman, B., & Weiss, H. (1987). *State-sponsored family support and education: The rationale for school-based services.* Unpublished manuscript. Boston, Harvard Family Research Project.

Heins, H. C., Nance, N. W., & Ferguson, J. E. (1987). Social support in improving perinatal outcome: The Resource Mothers Program. *Pregnancy and Social Support, 70,* 263-266.

Helfer, R. E. (1980). Developmental deficits which limit interpersonal skills. In C. H. Kempe & R. E. Helfer (Eds.), *The battered child* (3rd ed.) (pp. 36-48). Chicago: University of Chicago Press.

Herrenkohl, E. C., Herrenkohl, R. C., Toedter, L., & Yanushefski, A. M. (1984). Parent-child interactions in abusive and non-abusive families. *Journal of the American Academy of Child Psychiatry, 23,* 641-648.

Hersen, M., & Barlow, D. H. (1976). *Single case experimental designs.* Elmsford, NY: Pergamon.

Hess, R. D. (1970). Social class and ethnic influences upon socialization. In P. H. Mussen (Ed.), *Carmichael's manual of child psychology* (Vol. 2, 3rd ed.). Hawthorne, NY: Aldine.

Heywood, J. S. (1959). *Children in care: The development of the service for the deprived child.* London: Ruthledge & Kegan Paul.

Hilberman, E. (1980). Overview: The "wife-beater's wife" reconsidered. *American Journal of Psychiatry, 137,* 1336-47.

Hingson, R., Alpert, J. J., Day, N., Dooling, E., Kayne, H., Morelock, S., Oppenheimer, E., & Zuckerman, B. (1982). Effects of maternal drinking and marijuana use on fetal growth and development. *Pediatrics, 70,* 539-546.

Hirst, K., & Hannon, P. (1989). An evaluation of a pre-school home-teaching program. *Educational Research, 31*(3).

Hofeller, K. H. (1982). *Social, psychological and situational factors in wife abuse.* Palo Alto: R&E Research Associates, Inc.

Holbrook, T. (1983). Going among them: The evolution of the home visit. *Journal of Sociology and Social Welfare, 10*(1), 112-135.

Hollis, F., & Wood, M. E. (1981). *Casework: A psychosocial therapy* (3rd ed.). New York: Random House.

Hollister, W. G., & Miller, F. T. (1977). Problem solving strategies in consultation. *American Journal of Orthopsychiatry, 47,* 445-450.

Holmes, T. H., & Rahe, R. H. (1967). The social readjustment rating scale. *Journal of Psychosomatic Research, 11,* 213-218.

Hotaling, G. T., & Sugarman, D. (1986). An analysis of risk markers in husband to wife violence: The current state of knowledge. *Violence and victims, 1*(2), 101-124.

Howrigan, G. A. (1988). Evaluating parent-child interaction outcomes of family support and education programs. In H. B. Weiss & F. H. Jacobs (Eds.), *Evaluating family programs* (pp. 95-130). New York: Aldine de Gruyter.

Hughes, D., Johnson, K., Rosenbaum, S., Butler, E., & Simons, J. (1988). *The health of America's children: Maternal and child health data book*. Washington, DC: Children's Defense Fund.

Hunt, J. M. (1961). *Intelligence and experience*. New York: Ronald Press.

Hupp, S. C., & Kaiser, A. P. (1986). Evaluating education programs for severely handicapped preschoolers. In L. Bickman & D. L. Weatherford (Eds.), *Evaluating early intervention programs for severely handicapped children and their families* (pp. 233-261). Austin, TX: Pro-ed.

Infant Health and Development Program. (1989). *Enhancing the outcomes of low birth weight, premature infants: A multisite randomized trial*. Manuscript submitted for publication.

Intagliata, J., & Doyle, N. (1984). Enhancing social support for parents of developmentally disabled children: Training in interpersonal problem solving skills. *Mental Retardation, 22*(1), 4-11.

Jackson, A. M. (1984). Child neglect: An overview. In *Perspectives on child maltreatment in the mid-1980's* (pp. 15-17). National Center on Child Abuse and Neglect (DHHS Publication No. OHDS 84-30338). Washington, DC: U.S. Government Printing Office.

Jackson, A., & Hannon, P. (1987, June). Home visiting in primary education. *Education*, 3-13.

Jackson, D. D. (1957). The question of family homeostasis. *Psychiatric Quarterly Supplement, 31*, 79-90.

Jahoda, M. (1958). *Current concepts of positive mental health*. New York: Basic Books.

James, W. (1899). *Talk to teachers*. New York: Holt.

Jenkins, S. (1981). *The ethnic dilemma in social services*. New York: Free Press.

Jenkins, S. (1987). Ethnicity and family support. In S. L. Kagan, D. R. Powell, B. Weissbourd, & E. F. Zigler (Eds.), *America's family support programs* (pp. 282-294). New Haven, CT: Yale University Press.

Johnson, B. H., McGonigel, M. J., & Kaufmann, R. K. (Eds.). (1989). *Guidelines and recommended practices and the individualized service plan*. National Early Childhood Technical Assistance System. Washington, DC: Association for the Care of Children's Health.

Kadushin, A. (1976). *Supervision in social work*. New York: Columbia University Press.

Kagan, S. L., Powell, D. R., Weissbourd, B., & Zigler, E. F. (Eds.). (1987). *America's family support programs* (pp. 21-37). New Haven, CT: Yale University Press.

Kalmuss, D. S., & Straus, M. A. (1982). Wife's marital dependency and wife abuse. *Journal of Marriage and the Family, 44*, 227-286.

Kaslow, F. W., & Mountz, T. (1985). Ethical and legal issues in the treatment of alcoholics and substance abusers. In T. E. Bratter & G. G. Forrest (Eds.), *Alcoholism and substance abuse* (pp. 577-593). New York: Free Press.

Kelley, M. L., Embry, L. H., & Baer, D. M. (1979). Skills for child management and family support. *Behavior Modification, 3*, 383-396.

Kempe, H. (1976). Approaches to preventing child abuse: The health visitor concept. *American Journal of Diseases of Children, 130*, 941-947.

Kohlberg, L. (1984). *Essays in moral development. Volume II: The psychology of moral development.* San Francisco: Harper & Row.

Koop, C. E. (1987). *Surgeon general's report: Children with special health care needs.* Washington, DC: Department of Health and Human Services.

Krauss, M. W. (1988). Measures of stress and coping in families. In H. B. Weiss & F. H. Jacobs (Eds.), *Evaluating family programs* (pp. 177-194). New York: Aldine de Gruyter.

Kubany, E. S., Roberts, R. N., Furuno, S., Hosaka, C., & Matsuda, K. (1989). *A community based model of home visiting.* Manuscript submitted for publication.

Langholm, M. (1961). *Family and child welfare in Norway.* Oslo, Norway: Norwegian Joint Committee on International Social Policy.

Larner, M., & Halpern, R. (1987). Lay home visiting programs: Strengths, tensions, and challenges. *Zero to Three. 8*(1), 1-7.

Larsen, D., Attkisson, C., Hargreaves, W., & Nguyen, T. (1979). Assessment of client patient satisfaction: Development of a general scale. *Evaluation and Program Planning, 2*(3), 197-207.

Larson, C. (1980). Efficacy of prenatal and postpartum home visits on child health and development. *Pediatrics, 66,* 191-197.

Lazar, I., Darlington, R., Murray, H., Royce, J., & Snipper, A. (1982). Lasting effects of early education: A report from the consortium for longitudinal studies. *Monographs of the Society for Research in Child Development, 47*(Serial No. 195), 2-3.

Leahy, K. M., Cobb, M. M., & Jones, M. C. (1982). *Community Health Nursing* (4th ed.). New York: McGraw-Hill.

Levenstein, P. (1981). Ethical considerations in home-based programs. In M. Bryce & J. C. Lloyd (Eds.), *Treating families in the home: An alternative to placement* (pp. 222-236). Springfield, IL: Charles C. Thomas.

Levenstein, P. (1988). *Messages from home: The mother-child home program and the prevention of social disadvantage.* Columbus: Ohio State University Press.

Levine, M., & Levine, A. (1970). *A social history of the helping services: Clinic, court, school, and community.* New York: Appleton-Century-Crofts.

Levinson, H. L. (1977). Termination of psychotherapy: Some salient issues. *Social Casework, 58,* 480-489.

Linder, T. (1983). *Early childhood special education: Program development and administration.* Baltimore, MD: Paul H. Brookes.

Long, L., Paradise, L. V., & Long, T. J. (1981). *Questioning: Skills for the helping process.* Monterey, CA: Brooks/Cole.

Love, J. M., Nauta, M. J., Coelen, C. G., Hewett, K., & Ruopp, R. R. (1976). *National Home Start evaluation: Final report, findings, and implications.* Ypsilanti, MI: High Scope Educational Research Foundation.

Lutzker, J. R. (1984). Project 12-ways: Treating child abuse and neglect from an ecobehavioral perspective. In R. F. Dangel & R. A. Polster (Eds.), *Parent training: Foundation of research and practice* (pp. 260-297). New York: Guilford Press.

Lutzker, J. R., & Rice, J. M. (1984). Project 12-ways: Measuring outcome of a large in-home service for treatment and prevention of child abuse and neglect. *Child Abuse and Neglect, 8,* 519-524.

MacRae, D. (1989). The use of outcome measures in implementing policies for handicapped children. In J. J. Gallagher, P. L. Trohanis, & R. M. Clifford (Eds.), *Policy implementation and PL 99-457* (pp. 183-198). Baltimore, MD: Paul H. Brookes.

Madden, J. S. (1984). *A guide to alcohol and drug dependence.* Bristol, England: John Wright.

Madden, J., O'Hara, J., & Levenstein, P. (1984). Home again: Effects of the Mother-Child Home Program on mother and child. *Child Development, 55,* 636-647.

Mager, R. F. (1962). *Preparing instructional objectives.* Belmont, CA: Fearson.

Mager, R. F. (1972). *Goal analysis.* Belmont, CA: Fearson.

Mager, R. F., & Pipe, P. (1970). *Analyzing performance problems.* Belmont, CA: Fearson.

Margolin, G. (1982). Ethical and legal considerations in marital and family therapy. *American Psychologist, 37,* 788-801.

McCormick, M. (1984). High-risk young mothers: Infant mortality and morbidity in four areas in the United States, 1973-1978. *American Journal of Public Health, 74*(1), 18-23.

McCormick, M. (1985). The contribution of low birth weight to infant mortality and childhood morbidity. *The New England Journal of Medicine, 312,* 82-90.

McCubbin, H. I., Olson, D., & Larsen, A. (1981). Family crisis oriented personal scales. In H. I. McCubbin & J. Patterson, *Family stress, resources, and coping: Tools for research, education and clinical intervention.* St. Paul: Family Stress Project, University of Minnesota.

McGuire, C. H, & Babbott, D. (1967). Simulations technique in the measurement of problem-solving skills. *Journal of Educational Measurement, 4,* 1-10.

Mello, N. K. (1980). Some behavioral and biological aspects of alcohol problems in women. In O. J. Kalant (Ed.), *Alcohol and drug problems in women* (pp. 263-298). New York: Plenum.

Miles, M. S. (1986). Counseling strategies. In S. H. Johnson (Ed.), *Nursing assessment and strategies for the family at risk: High risk parenting* (2nd ed.) (pp. 343-360). Philadelphia: J. B. Lippincott.

Miller, C. A. (1987). *Maternal health and infant survival.* Washington, DC: National Center for Clinical Infant Programs.

Minuchin, P. (1985). Families and individual development: Provocations from the field of family therapy. *Child Development, 56,* 289-302.

Minuchin, S. (1974). *Families and family therapy.* Cambridge, MA: Harvard University Press.

Missouri Department of Elementary and Secondary Education. (1986). *Parents as Teachers Program planning and implementation guide and curriculum materials* (rev. ed.). Jefferson City, MO.

Monteiro, L. A. (1985). Florence Nightingale on public health nursing. *American Journal of Public Health, 75,* 181-186.

Moore, K. A., & Burt, M. R. (1982). *Private crisis, public cost: Policy perspectives on teenage childbearing.* Washington, DC: The Urban Institute.

Moos, R. H. (1974). *Family Environment Scale.* Palo Alto, CA: Consulting Psychologists Press.

Moroney, R. (1987). Social support systems: Families and social policy. In S. L. Kagan, D. Powell, B. Weissbourd, & E. Ziegler (Eds.), *America's family support programs* (pp. 21-37). New Haven, CT: Yale University Press.

Moynihan, D. P. (1986). *Family and nation.* New York: Harcourt Brace Jovanovich.

Muller, M., & Leviton, A. (1986). In-home versus clinic-based services for the developmentally disabled child: Who is the primary client - parent or child? *Social Work in Health Care, 11*(3), 75-88.

Mulvey, L. A. (1988, February). *Training*. Paper presented at the Family Support in the Home: Policy, Practice, and Research Conference, Honolulu, Hawaii.

Nathanson, M., Baird, A., & Jemail, J. (1986). Family functioning and the adolescent mother: A systems approach. *Adolescence, 21*, 827-841.

National Association of Social Workers, Inc. (1980). *Code of Ethics of the National Association of Social Workers*. Silver Spring, MD: Author.

National Commission on Infant Mortality. (1989). *Home visiting: Opening doors for America's pregnant women and children*. Washington, DC: Author

National Credentialing Program. (1987). *Home Visitor, Child Development Associate Assessment System and Competency Standards*. (Available from the Council for Early Childhood Professional Recognition, 1718 Connecticut Avenue, N.W., Suite 500, Washington, DC 20009).

National Institute on Drug Abuse. (1987). *Drug abuse and drug abuse research* (DHHS Publication No. ADM 87-1486). Rockville, MD: U.S. Government Printing Office.

Nightingale, F. (1894). *Health teaching in towns and villages, rural hygiene*. London, England: Spottiswoode and Co.

Norris-Shortle, C., & Cohen, R. R. (1987, January). Home visits revisited. *Social Casework: The Journal of Contemporary Social Work*, 54-58.

Nuckolls, K., Cassell, J., & Kaplan, B. (1972). Psychosocial aspects, life crisis, and prognosis of pregnancy. *American Journal of Epidemiology, 95*, 431-441.

O'Keefe, A. (1978). *What Head Start means to families - Executive summary*. Washington, DC: Administration for Children, Youth, and Families (Department of Health, Education, and Welfare).

Olds, D. L. (1988a). Common design and methodological problems encountered in evaluating family support services: Illustrations from the Prenatal/Early Infancy Project. In H. Weiss & F. Jacobs (Eds.), *Evaluating family programs.* (pp. 239-261). Chicago: Aldine Press.

Olds, D. L. (1988b). The Prenatal/Early Infancy Project. In R. H. Price, E. L. Cohen, R. P. Lorion, & J. Ramos-McKay (Eds.), *14 ounces of prevention: A casebook for practitioners* (pp. 9-23). Washington, DC: American Psychological Association.

Olds, D., Henderson, C., Chamberlin, R., & Tatelbaum, R. (1986). Preventing child abuse and neglect: A randomized trial of nurse home visitation. *Pediatrics, 78*, 65-78.

Olds, D. L., Henderson, C. R., Jr., Tatelbaum, R., & Chamberlin, R. (1985). Improving the delivery of prenatal care and outcomes of pregnancy: A randomized trial of nurse home visitation. *Pediatrics, 77*, 16-28.

Olds, D. L., Henderson, C. R., Jr., Tatelbaum, R., & Chamberlin, R. (1988). Improving the life-course development of socially disadvantaged mothers: A randomized trial of nurse home visitation. *American Journal of Public Health, 78*, 1436-1445.

Olson, D. H., Portner, J., & Lavee, Y. (1985). FACES III. In D. H. Olson, H. I. McCubbin, H. Barnes, A. Larsen, M. Muxen, & M. Wilson (Eds.), *Family inventories: Inventories in a national survey of families across the family life cycle*. St. Paul: University of Minnesota, Family Social Science.

Pahl, J. (1985). Implications for policy and practice. In J. Pahl (Ed.), *Private violence and public policy* (pp. 181-192). Boston: Rutledge & Kegan Paul.

Patterson, G. R. (1975). *Families: Applications of social learning to family life* (rev. ed.). Champaign, IL: Research Press.

Patterson, G. R. (1976). The aggressive child: Victim and architect of a coercive system. In E. J. Mash, L. A. Hamerlynick, & L. C. Handy (Eds.), *Behavior modification and families: Vol. 1, Theory and research.* New York: Brunner/Mazel.

Patterson, G. R., & Forgatch, M. (1987). *Parents and adolescents living together. Part 1: The basics.* Eugene, OR: Castalia.

Patterson, G. R., Weiss, R. L., & Hops, H. (1976). Training of marital skills: Some problems and concepts. In H. Leitenberg (Ed.), *Handbook of operant techniques* (pp. 493-523). Englewood Cliffs, NJ: Prentice-Hall.

Pearl, A., & Riessman, F. (1965). *New careers for the poor: The nonprofessional in human services.* New York: Free Press.

Pedersen, P. P. (1981). The cultural inclusiveness of counseling. In P. P. Pedersen, J. G. Draguns, W. J. Lonner, & J. E. Trimble (Eds.), *Counseling across cultures* (pp. 22-58). Honolulu: The University Press of Hawaii.

Perlman, H. H. (1957). *Social casework: A problem solving process.* Chicago: University of Chicago Press.

Peterson, D. (1968). *The clinical study of social behavior.* New York: Appleton-Century-Crofts.

Pfannenstiel, J. C., & Seltzer, D. A. (1985). *Evaluation report: New Parents as Teachers Project.* Jefferson City: Missouri Department of Elementary & Secondary Education.

Phillips, E. L., Wolf, M. M., Fixsen, D. L., & Bailey, J. S. (1970). The Achievement Place Model: A community-based, family-style, behavior modification program for pre-delinquents. In J. L. Khanna (Ed.), *New treatment approaches to juvenile delinquency* (pp. 34-86). Springfield, IL: Charles C. Thomas.

Piaget, J. (1952). *The origins of intelligence in children.* New York: International Universities Press.

Pickens, R. W., & Heston, L. L. (1981). Personality factors in human drug self-administration. In T. Thompson & C. E. Johansen (Eds.), *Behavioral pharmacology of human drug dependence* (pp. 45-74). (Research Monograph 37). Rockville, MD: National Institute on Drug Abuse.

Pinker, R. (1973). *Social theory and social policy.* London: Heinemann.

Polansky, N. A., Ammons, P. W., & Gaudin, J. M., Jr. (1984). Loneliness and isolation in child neglect. *Social Casework, 65*(5), 279-285.

Poulton, G. (1983). Origin and development of preschool home visiting. In G. Aplin & G. Pugh (Eds.), *Perspectives for preschool home visiting.* London-Conventry: National Children's Bureau/Community Education Development Centre.

Powell, C., & Grantham-McGregor, S. (1989). Home visiting of varying frequency and child development. *Pediatrics, 84,* 157-164.

Price, H. R., Cowen, E. L., Lorion, R. P., & Ramos-McKay, J. (Eds.). (1988). *14 Ounces of prevention: A casebook for practitioners.* Washington, DC: American Psychological Association.

Pugh, G. (1981). *Parents as partners: Intervention schemes and group work with parents of handicapped children.* London: National Children's Bureau.

Ramey, C. T., Bryant, D. M., Campbell, F. G., Sparling, J. J., & Wasik, B. H. (1988). Early intervention for high-risk children: The Carolina Early Intervention Program. In R. H. Price, E. L. Cowen, R. P. Lorion, & J. Ramos-McKay (Eds.), *14 ounces of prevention: A casebook for practitioners* (pp. 32-43). Washington, DC: American Psychological Association.

Ramey, C. T., Bryant, D. M., Sparling, J. J., & Wasik, B. H. (1984). A biosocial systems perspective on environmental interventions for low birthweight infants. *Clinical Obstetrics and Gynecology, 27*, 672-692.

Ramey, C. T., Bryant, D. M., Sparling, J. J., & Wasik, B. H. (1985). Educational interventions to enhance intellectual development: Comprehensive daycare vs family education. In S. Harel & N. Anastasiow (Eds.), *The "at-risk" infant: Psychological, social and medical aspects* (pp. 75-85). Baltimore, MD: Paul H. Brookes.

Ramey, C. T., Bryant, D., Wasik, B. H., Sparling, J. J., Fendt, K. H., & LaVange, L. (1989). *The Infant Health and Development Program for low birthweight premature infants: Program elements, family participation, and child intelligence.* Manuscript submitted for publication.

Ramey, C. T., Bryant, D. M., & Suarez, T. M. (1985). Preschool compensatory education and the modifiability of intelligence: A critical review. In D. Detterman (Ed.), *Current topics in human intelligence* (pp. 247-296). Norwood, NJ: Ablex.

Ramey, C. T., & Smith, B. J. (1977). Assessing the intellectual consequences of early intervention with high-risk infants. *American Journal of Mental Deficiency, 8*, 318-324.

Ramey, C. T., Sparling, J. J., & Wasik, B. H. (1981). Creating social environments to facilitate language development. In R. Schiefelbusch & D. Bricker (Eds.), *Early language intervention.* Baltimore, MD: University Park Press.

Ramey, C. T., Trohanis, P. L., & Hostler, S. (1982). Issues in finding and educating high-risk and handicapped infants. In C. T. Ramey & P. L. Trohanis (Eds.), *Finding and educating high-risk and handicapped infants* (pp. 1-17). Baltimore, MD: University Park Press.

Rauh, V. A., Achenbach, T. M., Nurcombe, B., Howell, C. T., & Teti, D. M. (1988). Minimizing adverse effects of low birthweight: Four-year results of an early intervention program. *Child Development, 59*, 544-553.

Rausch, H., & Bordin, E. (1957). Warmth in personality development. *Psychiatry, 20*, 351-363.

Raven, J. (1980). Parents, teachers and children - A study of an educational home-visiting scheme. Kent, England: Hodder and Stoughton for SCRE.

Reamer, F. G. (1982). *Ethical dilemmas in social service.* New York: Columbia University Press.

Rees, S. J. (1983). Families' perceptions of services for handicapped children. *International Journal of Rehabilitation Research, 6*, 475-476.

Renz, C., Munson, K., Wayland, K., & Fusaro, B. (1980). *Training manual for battered women advocates.* Durham, NC: Orange/Durham Coalition for Battered Women.

Reschly, B. (1979). *Supporting the changing family: A guide to the Parent-to-Parent Model.* Ypsilanti, MI: High/Scope Educational Research Foundation.

Resnick, M. B., Eyler, F. E., Nelson, M. D., Eitzman, D. V., & Buccizrelli, R. L. (1987). Developmental intervention for low birthweight infants: Improved early developmental outcome. *Pediatrics, 80*, 68-74.

Richmond, M. (1917). *Social diagnosis.* New York: Russell Sage.

Richmond, M. E. (1899). *Friendly visiting among the poor.* New York: MacMillan.

Roberts, D. E., & Heinrich, J. (1985). Public health nursing comes of age. *American Journal of Public Health, 75*, 1162-1172.

Roberts, R. N. (1988). *Family support in the home: Home visiting programs and P.L. 99-457.* Washington, DC: Association for the Care of Children's Health.

Roberts, R. N. (1988). Welcoming our baby: An early intervention program for Hawaiian families. *Children Today, 17,* 6-10.

Roberts, R. N., & Wasik, B. H. (1989). *National home visiting survey: Agency affiliation, family characteristics, purposes, and services provided.* Submitted for publication.

Robin, A. L. (1979). Problem-solving communication training: A behavior approach to the treatment of parent-adolescent conflict. *The American Journal of Family Therapy, 7,* 69-82.

Robin, A. L., & Foster, S. L. (1989). *Negotiating parent-adolescent conflict: A behavioral family systems approach.* New York: Guilford Press.

Rogers, C. (1951). *Client-centered therapy.* Boston: Houghton Mifflin.

Rogers, C. (1957). The necessary and sufficient conditions of therapeutic personality change. *Journal of Consulting Psychology, 21,* 95-103.

Rogers, M. F. (1987). Transmission of human immuniodeficiency virus infection in the United States. *Report of the Surgeon General's workshop on children with HIV infection and their families* (DHHS Publication No. HRS-D-MC87-1). Washington, DC: U.S. Department of Health and Human Services.

Rosenfield-Schlichter, M. D., Sarber, R. E., Bueno, G., Greene, B. F., & Lutzker, J. R. (1983). Maintaining accountability for an ecobehavioral treatment of one aspect of child neglect: Personal cleanliness. *Education and Treatment of Children, 6*(2), 153-164.

Roy, M. (Ed.). (1977). *Battered women: A psychosociological study of domestic violence.* New York: Van Nostrand Reinhold.

Sadler, L. S. & Catrone, C. (1983). The adolescent parent: A dual developmental crisis. *Journal of Adolescent Health Care, 4*(2), 100-105.

Sameroff, A. J. (1983). Developmental systems: Contexts and evolution. In W. Kessen (Ed.), *Handbook of child psychology: Vol. 2. History, theory, and methods* (pp. 237-294). New York: John Wiley.

Sameroff, A. J., & Chandler, M. J. (1975). Reproductive risk and the continuum of caretaking causality. In F. D. Horowitz (Ed.), *Review of child development research: Vol. 4* (pp. 187-244). Chicago: University of Chicago Press.

Sarason, I. G., Johnson, J. H., & Siegel, J. M. (1978). Assessing the impact of life changes: Development of the life experiences survey. *Journal of Consulting and Clinical Psychology, 46,* 932-946.

Scarr, S., & McCartney, K. (1988). Far from home: An experimental evaluation of the Mother-Child Home Program in Bermuda. *Child Development, 59,* 531-543.

Schaefer, E. S., & Aaronson, M. (1977). Infant education project: Implementation and implications of the home-tutoring program. In R. K. Parker (Ed.), *The preschool in action* (2nd ed.). Boston: Allyn & Bacon.

Schectman, F. (1986). Time and the practice of psychotherapy. *Psychotherapy, 23,* 521-525.

Schweinhart, L. J., & Weikart, D. B. (1980). *Young children grow up: The effects of the Perry Preschool Program on youth through age 15.* Ypsilanti, MI: High/Scope Education Research Foundation.

Seay, T., & Altkreuse, M. (1979). Verbal and nonverbal behavior in judgments of facilitative conditions. *Journal of Counseling Psychology, 26,* 108-119.

Senay, E. C. (1983). *Substance abuse disorders in clinical practice.* Boston: John Wright.

Shure, M. B., & Spivack, G. (1972). Means-ends thinking, adjustment and social class almong elementary school-aged children. *Journal of Consulting and Clinical Psychology*, *38*, 348-353.

Shure, M. B., & Spivack, G. (1978). *Problem-solving techniques in childrearing*. San Francisco, CA: Jossey-Bass.

Sia, C. J., & Breakey, G. F. (1985). The role of the medical home in child abuse prevention and positive child development. *Hawaii Medical Journal*, *44*(7), 242-243.

Slaughter, D. T. (1983). Early intervention and its effects on maternal and child development. *Monographs of the Society for Research in Child Development*, *48*(4, Serial No. 202).

Slaughter, D. T. (1988). Programs for racially and ethnically diverse American families: Some critical issues. In H. B. Weiss & F. H. Jacobs (Eds.), *Evaluating family programs* (pp. 461-476). New York: Aldine de Gruyter.

Smith, G. (Ed.). (1975). *Educational priority: Vol. 4. The West Riding Project*. London, England: HMSO.

Snyder, D. K., & Scheer, N. S. (1981). Predicting disposition following brief residence at a shelter for battered women. *American Journal of Community Psychology*, *9*, 559-566.

Solomon, B. B. (1976). *Black empowerment: Social work in oppressed communities*. New York: Columbia University Press.

Soloman, B. B. (1985). How do we really empower families? New strategies for social work practitioners. *Family Resource Coalition Report*, *3*, 2-3.

Sparling, J., & Lewis, I. (1979). *Learning games for the first three years: A guide to parent-child play*. New York: Walker and Company. (Paperback edition by Berkley Publishing Corp., NY, 1981).

Sparling, J., & Lewis, I. (1984). *Learning games for threes and fours: A guide to adult and child play*. New York: Walker and Company.

Sparling, J., & Lewis, I. (1985a). *Learning games for the first three years: A program for parent/center partnership*. New York: Walker and Company. (Paperback edition by Berkley Publishing Corp., NY).

Sparling, J., & Lewis, I. (1985b). *Partners for learning*. Lewisville, NC: Kaplan Press.

Sparling, J. J., Lewis, I., & Neuwirth, S. (in press). *Early partners*. Lewisville, NC: Kaplan Press.

Spivack, G., & Shure, M. B. (1974). *Social adjustment of young children*. San Francisco: Jossey-Bass.

Statistical Abstract of the United States (109th ed.). (1989). Bureau of the Census. Washington, DC: U.S. Government Printing Office.

Steele, B. F. (1980). Psychodynamic factors in child abuse. In C. H. Kempe & R. E. Helfer (Eds.), *The battered child* (3rd ed.) (pp. 49-85). Chicago: University of Chicago Press.

Straus, M. A., & Gelles, R. (1986). Societal change and change in family violence from 1975-1985 as revealed by two national surveys. *Journal of Marriage and the Family,*'*48*, 465-479.

Straus, M. A., Gelles, R., & Steinmetz, S. (1980). *Behind closed doors: Violence in the American family*. Garden City, NY: Doubleday.

.

Strube, M. J. (1988). The decision to leave an abusive relationship. In G. T. Hotaling, D. Finkelhor, J. T. Kirkpatrick, & M. A. Straus (Eds.), *Coping with family violence: Research and policy perspectives* (pp. 93-106). Newbury Park, CA: Sage.

Summers, J. A., Dell'Oliver, C., Turnbull, A. P., Benson, H. A., Santelli, G., Campbell, M., & Siegel-Causey, E. (in press). Focusing in on the IFSP process: What are family and practitioner preferences? *Topics in Early Childhood Special Education*.

Tertinger, D. A., Greene, B. F., & Lutzker, J. R. (1984). Home safety: Development and validation of one component of an ecobehavioral treatment program for abused and neglected children. *Journal of Applied Behavior Analysis, 17*, 159-174.

Trainor, C. M. (Ed.). (1983). *The dilemma of child neglect: Identification and treatment.* Denver, CO: The American Humane Association.

Truax, C., & Carkhuff, R. (1967). *Toward effective counseling and psychotherapy.* Chicago, IL: Aldine.

Turnbull, A. P., & Turnbull, H. R. (1986). *Families, professionals, and exceptionality: A special partnership.* Columbus, OH: Charles E. Merrill.

U. S. House of Representatives. (1983). *Teen parents and their children: Issues and programs.* A report of the Select Committee on Children, Youth and Families, July 20, 1983. Washington, DC: U.S. Government Printing Office.

U. S. House of Representatives. (1984). *Violence and abuse in American families.* Testimony presented on June 14, 1984. Hearing before the Select Committee on Children, Youth and Families. Washington, DC: U.S. Government Printing Office.

U. S. House of Representatives. (1986a). *Placing infants at risk: Parental addiction and disease testimony.* Presented at the Hearing before the Select Committee on Children, Youth and Families, May 10, 1986. Washington, DC: U.S. Government Printing Office.

U. S. House of Representatives. (1986b). *Teen pregnancy: What is being done?* A report of the Select Committee on Children, Youth and Families, December 1985. Washington, DC: U.S. Government Printing Office.

Wagner, M., & Wagner, M. (1976). *The Danish National Child Care System.* Boulder, CO: Westview.

Wahler, R. G. (1980). The insular mother: Her problems in parent-child treatment. *Journal of Applied Behavior Analysis, 13*, 207-219.

Wahler, R. G., & Dumas, J. E. (1984). Changing the observational coding styles of insular and noninsular mothers: A step toward maintenance of parent training effects. In R. F. Dangel & R. A. Polster (Eds.), *Parent training* (pp. 379-416). New York: Guilford Press.

Walker, L. (1983). Victimology and the psychological perspectives of battered women. *Victimology, 8*(1-2), 82-104.

Walker, L. C. (1979). *The battered woman.* New York: Harper & Row.

Warnock, M. (1978). *Special education needs.* Report of the Committee of Enquiry into the Education of Handicapped Children and Young People. England; HMSO.

Warren, D. I. (1980). Support systems in different types of neighborhoods. In J. Garbarino & S. H. Stocking (Eds.), *Protecting children from abuse and neglect* (pp. 61-93). San Francisco: Jossey-Bass.

Wasik, B. H. (1983, August). *Teaching parents to solve problems: A behavioral - ecological perspective.* Presented at the American Psychological Association meeting, Anaheim, CA.

Wasik, B. H. (1984). *Coping with parenting through effective problem solving: A Handbook for professionals.* Unpublished manuscript. Frank Porter Graham Child Development Center, University of North Carolina at Chapel Hill.

Wasik, B. H., Bryant, D. M., Kent, M. E., Powell, J. W., Vatz, C., & Ecklund, K. (1988, August). *Reliability and validity of two social problem solving instruments.* Paper presented at the American Psychological Association, Atlanta, GA.

Wasik, B. H., & Fishbein, J. E. (1982). Problem solving: A model for supervision in professional psychology. *Professional Psychology, 13,* 559-564.

Wasik, B. H., & Lyons, C. (1984). *A handbook on home visiting.* Unpublished manuscript. Chapel Hill: Frank Porter Graham Child Development Center, University of North Carolina.

Wasik, B. H., & Ramey, C. T. (Eds.). (1982). *Manual of home visiting in Project CARE.* Chapel Hill: Frank Porter Graham Child Development Center, University of North Carolina.

Wasik, B. H., Ramey, C. T., Bryant, D. M., & Sparling, J. J. (in press). A longitudinal study of two early intervention strategies: Project CARE. *Child Development.*

Wasik, B. H., & Roberts, R. N. (1989a). Home visiting with low income families. *Family Resource Coalition Report, 9,* 8-9.

Wasik, B. H., & Roberts, R. N. (1989b). *National home visiting survey: Hiring, training, and supervision.* Manuscript submitted for publication.

Weikart, D. P., Bond, J. T., & McNeil, J. T. (1978). The Ypsilanti Preschool Project: Preschool years and longitudinal results. *Monographs of the High Scope Educational Research Foundation,* No. 3. Ypsilanti, MI: High Scope.

Weiss, H. B. (1989). State family support and educational programs: Lessons from the pioneers. *American Journal of Orthopsychiatry, 59,* 32-48.

Weiss, H. B., & Jacobs, F. H. (Eds.). (1988). *Evaluating family programs.* New York: Aldine de Gruyter.

Weissbourd, B. (1983). The family support movement: Greater than the sum of its parts. *Zero to Three, 4*(1), 8-10.

Weissbourd, B. (1987). Design, staffing, and funding of family support programs. In S. L. Kagan, D. R. Powell, B. Weissbourd, & E. F. Zigler (Eds.), *America's family support programs* (pp. 245-268). New Haven, CT: Yale University Press.

Weissbourd, B., & Kagan, S. L. (1989). Family support programs: Catalysts for change. *American Journal of Orthopsychiatry, 59*(1), 20-31.

Wells, K. B., Benson, M. C., Hoff, P., & Stuber, M. (1987). A home-visit program for first-year medical students as perceived by participating families. *Family Medicine, 19,* 364-367.

Whall, A. L. (1986). The family as the unit of care in nursing: A historical review. *Public Health Nursing, 3,* 240-249.

White, B. L. (1975). *The first three years of life.* Englewood Cliffs, NJ: Prentice-Hall.

White, K. R. (1988). Cost analyses in family support programs. In H. B. Weiss & F. H. Jacobs (Eds.), *Evaluating family programs* (pp. 429-444). New York: Aldine de Gruyter.

Wolery, M., & Bailey, D. B. (1984). Alternatives to impact evaluation: Suggestions for program evaluation in early intervention. *Journal of the Division for Early Childhood*, *9*, 27-37.

Wolfe, B. & Herwig, J. (Eds.). (1986). *The Head Start home visitor handbook*. Portage, WI: The Portage Project.

Yarrow, M. R., Campbell, J. D., & Burton, R. V. (1968). *Child rearing: An inquiry into research and methods*. San Francisco: Jossey-Bass.

Zigler, E., & Black, K. B. (1989). America's family support movement: Strengths and limitations. *American Journal of Orthopsychiatry*, *59*(1), 6-19.

Zigler, E., & Freedman, J. (1987a). Early experience, malleability, and Head Start. In J. J. Gallagher & C. T. Ramey (Eds.), *The malleability of children* (pp. 85-95). Baltimore, MD: Paul H. Brooks.

Zigler, E. F., & Freedman, J. (1987b). Head Start: A pioneer of family support. In S. L. Kagan, D. R. Powell, B. Weissbourd, & E. F. Zigler (Eds.), *America's family support programs, perspectives, and prospects* (pp. 576-76). New Haven, CT: Yale University Press.

Appendix: Home Visit Report Forms Used in the Infant Health and Development Program

Child Name: _____ Date: _____ / _____ / _____ Visitor Name: _____

HOME VISIT REPORT
Identification Information

Form #		IHDP #	
Form Date 3/9/86	Version: M 0 1 / 0 5	Visitor #	
Site Name (1st 3 letters)	___ ___ ___	Week of (Sunday's date)	___ ___ ___ ___ ___ ___
Site #	___	Visit Date (if completed)	m m d d y y
			___ ___ ___ ___ ___ ___
		Time of Day (to nearest hour)	m m d d y y
			___ ___ am pm
			h h

Part I. General Procedure of the Visit

Y N O   1. Was a visit made this week? (O = A visit was not planned this week)

___ ___   2. How many times this week did you or the caregiver call or send a message or did you stop by the home in order to schedule this or future visits? (If this visit was scheduled at the previous visit, enter 0)

(a) ___ ___   3. If a visit was *not* made, the reason was: (Record 1 or 2 responses)
(b) ___ ___   1) Visitor unable to reach the caregiver to schedule a visit (ex: unable to locate family)
                   2) Caregiver was not home at the scheduled time, refused, left the home when you arrived, or did not answer the door
                   3) Caregiver canceled the visit
                   4) Parent was ill or out of town
                   5) Child was ill
                   6) Child was hospitalized
                   7) Home visitor was unable to visit (ex: scheduling or transportation problems, out of town, illness, bad weather)
                   8) Vacation or holiday
                   9) Parent attended group meeting or other IHDP function in lieu of *home* visit (only if child < 1 yr.)
                   10) Other: _____

Additional comments about **scheduling:**

IF A VISIT WAS *NOT* MADE THIS WEEK, STOP HERE AND SEND THE ABOVE INFORMATION TO FPG.
IF A VISIT WAS MADE, CONTINUE.

___   4. The visit occurred in:
       1) Parent's home 2) Relative or friend's home 3) Daycare center 4) Hospital or clinic 5) Other: _____
       6) Parent-Teacher-Home Visitor Conference

___   5. The visit lasted:
       1) less than 15 minutes   2) 16–30 minutes   3) 31–45 minutes   4) 46–60 minutes   5) more than 1 hour

___   6. During most of the visit the child was:
       1) awake and involved   2) awake but not involved   3) asleep   4) absent from home

___   7. During the visit, other children living in the household were:
       1) awake and involved   2) awake but not involved   3) absent or asleep   4) no other children

(a) ___   8. The home visit was mainly with: (Record 1 or 2 responses)
(b) ___   1) mother 2) father 3) grandmother 4) grandfather 5) sitter 6) another adult: _____

___   9. During the visit, the relationship between the parent (or main person being visited) and the home visitor could be characterized as:
       1) a cooperative, trusting partnership; parent shared concerns about child and self; reciprocal interaction
       2) a working, functional partnership mainly focused on and limited to the curriculum
       3) an uncertain partnership; issues of trust and cooperation in implementing the program
       4) cannot tell

___   10. During the visit, other caregiving adult(s):
        0) were not present   2) did not affect the visit either positively or negatively
        1) contributed positively to the visit 3) adversely affected the visit

___   11. Who accompanied the home visitor on this visit?
        0) No one   2) Another home visitor   4) Daycare teacher
        1) Education director   3) Other: _____

       11a. What was the major reason for other person accompanying the visitor?

Additional comments about **general procedure** of visit:

Child Name: _____ Date: _____ / _____ / _____ Visitor Name: _____

IHDP # _ _ __ __ __ Version 5 Visit Date (if completed) __ __ __ __ __ __
                                                              m m d d y y

Part II. Problem Solving

___ 12. If *Problem Solving* was part of the **last visit,** was there evidence of parent follow through?
(Enter 0 if Problem Solving was not part of the last visit.)
1) Parent successfully took action
2) Parent took action, but not successful yet
3) Parent understood and thought about the problem
4) Parent did not understand or use the ideas or procedures
5) Parent did not want to use problem solving
6) No opportunity to evaluate

Additional comments about **previous Problem Solving** activities:

13. If problems were discussed on **this visit,** what were the **major** areas of concern? (Record 1, 2 or 3 responses)

Child functioning
11) Child health
12) Diet and feeding
13) Developmental progress
14) Problem behaviors
15) Other: _ _____ _

(a) ___

(b)

(c)

Family functioning
21) Parent or family worries due to
special needs of LBW infant
22) Family inter-relationships
23) Parent health or emotional
problems (anxiety, depression)
24) Health or emotional needs
of other family members
25) Other: _____

Environmental needs/community services
31) Housing or food
32) Financial
33) Employment
34) Transportation
35) Legal matters
36) Medical equipment for infant
37) Finding childcare/daycare
38) Other: _____

Administrative
41) Scheduling a visit
42) Helping with forms
43) Introduction to Problem Solving
44) IHDP Child Development Center
45) Other: _____

Additional comments about these or other concerns:

14. If *Problem Solving* was part of **this visit,** complete the following:

14a. Problem Solving was part of this visit because:
(Enter 0 if Problem Solving was not part of this visit and proceed to Question 15.)
1) visitor had planned to cover problem-solving today
2) visitor saw a need and introduced the topic appropriately
3) parent began a discussion of problems or problem-solving

14b. What was the main topic of the Problem Solving discussion?
(Use codes from Question 13 above.)

14c. Which, if any, of these stages of Problem Solving were discussed?
Y N 1) Problem identification
Y N 2) Goal selection
Y N 3) Generation of alternatives
Y N 4) Consideration of consequences
Y N 5) Decision making
Y N 6) Implementation
Y N 7) Evaluation

14d. The parent's reaction to this Problem-Solving discussion was:
1) positive (asked questions, attentive, participated)
2) neutral (listened, but showed little response)
3) negative (inattentive, did not want to participate)

Additional comments about **Problem Solving** discussion:

Child Name: _____ Date: ____ / ____ / ____ Visitor Name: _____

IHDP # ___ ___ ___ ___   Version 5   Visit Date (if completed) ___ ___ ___ ___ ___ ___
                                                                            m   m   d   d   y   y

Part III. Partners for Learning

Remember to ask about and see the activities of the last 4 visits.

15. List the activities or toys that were reviewed on this visit.

1) ___ ___ ___   3) ___ ___ ___   5) ___ ___ ___   7) ___ ___ ___

2) ___ ___ ___   4) ___ ___ ___   6) ___ ___ ___   8) ___ ___ ___

16. If this visit introduced a new **Partners** activity or toy, complete the following:

16a. The name and code of this week's activity(ies) or toy was (were):
(Enter 000 for Act. 1 if no activities were introduced and proceed to Question 17.)

Act. 1 ___ ___ ___   1. _____
Act. 2 ___ ___ ___   2. _____
Act. 3 ___ ___ ___   3. _____

(Remember to record these activities and today's date on the Cumulative Record.)

16b. The parent's reaction to the activity(ies) or toy was:
Act. 1 ___   1) highly interested (asked questions, attentive, participated)
Act. 2 ___   2) interested (listened, but showed little response)
Act. 3 ___   3) not interested (inattentive, critical of activity, would not participate)

16c. After the demonstration or explanation (if no demonstration), the parent:
Act. 1 ___   1) wanted to try activity and was able to do it
               2) wanted to try activity but needed some help
Act. 2 ___   3) was hesitant but tried the activity after encouragement from visitor
               4) showed little interest in trying the activity but finally did with encouragement
Act. 3 ___   5) did not try the activity (or child asleep)
               6) the activity is not the type that could be tried at the time

16d. How did the child respond to the parent or home visitor's demonstration of the activity or toy?
Act. 1 ___   0) activity not demonstrated   4) fussy and/or would not participate
               1) alert and participated with success   5) activity did not require child's participation
Act. 2 ___   2) alert and participated, but not yet successful   6) child not present or child asleep
Act. 3 ___   3) somewhat attentive, responded partially

17. Which of the following *Adult Skills* were emphasized in this visit?
Y N   1) prepare   Y N   5) support
Y N   2) attend   Y N   6) rescue
Y N   3) prompt   Y N   7) build
Y N   4) model

Y N   **18.** Did the parent contribute any original or creative ideas to the Partners activities or suggest a new activity?
If so, describe:

Additional comments about this week's **Partners** activity(ies):

Part IV. Summary Evaluation of Visit

____   **19.** The general tone of the visitor-caregiver interaction was:
       1) positive, supportive, receptive, reciprocal
       2) cooperative, but not enthusiastic   3) uncertain, unenthusiastic
                                                      4) strained

____   **20.** The general tone of the caregiver-child interaction was:
       1) positive, supportive, concerned, and reciprocal
       2) more supportive than nonsupportive   4) nonsupportive
       3) more nonsupportive than supportive   5) not observed

____   **21.** The caregiver's *positive* feedback to her child was:
       1) frequent   2) occasional   3) seldom or never   4) not observed

____   **22.** The caregiver responded to the child's vocalizations (other than crying):
       1) frequently   2) occasionally   3) seldom or never   4) child rarely vocalized   5) not observed

Y N   **23.** Since the last home visit, have there been any family changes or family events that might help or hinder the caregiver
       in the delivery of the intervention program?
       If yes, describe:

Y N   **24.** Were any supplemental materials used on this visit? If so, what were they?

Y N   **25.** Did this visit involve more than one IHDP family? If so, attach a joint visit form.

Child Name: _____ Date of Contact: ___/___/___ Visitor Name: _____

Record of Family Contact

Form Number — M 0 2 (1-3)
Form Date 10/15/86 — Version: 0 3 (4-5)
Site Name (1st 3 letters) — ___ ___ ___ (6-8)
Site # — ___ (9)
IHDP # — ___ ___ ___ ___ (10-13)
Visitor # — ___ ___ ___ (14-16)

1. a. Date of contact: (mm/dd/yy) — ___ ___/___ ___/___ ___ (17-22)
   b. Time of Contact: (to nearest hour) — ___ ___ A P (23-25)

2. Who initiated the contact? — ___ (26)
   1) You 3) Father 5) Foster parent
   2) Mother 4) Grandparent 6) Community agency: _____
   7) Other: _____

3. Who received the contact? — ___ (27)
   1) You 3) Father 5) Foster parent
   2) Mother 4) Grandparent 6) Community agency: _____
   7) Other: _____

4. Type of contact: — ___ (28)
   1) Phone call 3) Contact in home 5) Daycare center contact
   2) Clinic visit 4) In person contact not in home 6) Community agency: _____
   7) Other: _____

5. How long was the contact? (approximately, in minutes) — ___ ___ (29-30)

6. Code the major reason for this contact in columns 28-29: — ___ ___ (31-32)

   If secondary topics were covered, code in columns 30-31, 32-33: — ___ ___ (33-34)
   ___ ___ (35-36)

Child functioning
11) Child health
12) Diet and feeding
13) Developmental progress
14) Problem behaviors
15) Other: _____

Family functioning
21) Parent or family worries due to
    special needs of LBW infant
22) Family inter-relationships
23) Parent health or emotional
    problems (anxiety, depression)
24) Health or emotional needs
    of other family members
25) Other _____

Environmental needs/community services
31) Housing or food
32) Financial
33) Employment
34) Transportation
35) Legal matters
36) Medical equipment for infant
37) Other _____

Administrative
41) Scheduling a future visit
42) Getting information for IHDP purposes
43) Helping with forms
44) Other: _____
45) IHDP Child Development Center

7. Written summary or comments about the contact:

Author Index

Aaronson, M., 30, 31
Achenbach, T. M., 38
Addams, J., 20, 21
Alpert, J. J., 190
Altkreuse, M., 123
American Psychological Association, 69, 206
Ammons, P. W., 176
Anthony, W., 49
Attkisson, C., 232, 233
Avila, D. L., 149, 159
Azar, S. T., 176

Babbott, D., 66
Baer, D. M., 64
Bailey, D. B., 50, 223-224, 245
Bailey, J. S., 30
Baird, A., 197
Bandura, A., 70, 136
Barlow, D. H., 240
Barnard, K. E., 109
Baron, L., 176
Barrera, M. E., 227
Bartky, J. A., 112
Bateson, G., 51
Battle, S., 39
Beck, D. F., 121
Bell, R. Q., 30
Belle, D., 197

Benjamin, A., 106
Benson, H. A., 280
Benson, M. C., 33
Berg, C. L., 14, 148, 160
Berkeley Planning Associates, 176
Bijou, S. W., 138
Black, K. B., 15, 36, 247
Blechman, E. A., 64, 138
Bloom, M., 232, 239
Blume, S., 189, 190
Booth, C. L., 109
Bond, J. T., 28
Bordin, E., 123
Bowlby, J., 26, 70, 181
Boyd, J., 109
Boyd, R. D., 87, 88, 106, 256
Bradley, R., 227
Brammer, L. M., 23, 122
Breakey, G. F., 84
Bremner, R. H., 18
Brethower, D. M., 239
Briar, K. H., 182, 183
Brickman, P., 65
Brinkerhoff, R. O., 239
Bristol, M. M., 29
Brodsky, A., 212, 213
Bronfenbrenner, U., 15, 28, 50, 51, 55, 70, 74
Brooks, M. R., 31, 32, 230

Bross, D. C., 217
Bry, B. H., 189, 190
Bryant, D. M., 37, 38, 39, 51, 69, 74-81
Buccizrelli, R. L., 38
Bueno, G., 138
Buhler-Wilkerson, K., 16, 21, 104
Burns, K. A., 190
Burns, W. J., 190
Burt, M. R., 197
Burton, R. V., 230
Butler, E., 193

Cabot, R. C., 21
Caldwell, B., 227
Cameron, R. J., 29
Campbell, J. D., 230
Campbell, M., 225
Cansler, D. P., 150
Caplan, G., 196
Carkhuff, R. R., 49, 95, 123, 153
Carrasco, C., 195
Cassell, J., 51
Catrone, C., 195
Cauthen, D. B., 33
Chamberlin, R. W., 37, 41, 70, 73
Chandler, M. J., 78
Chapman, J., 35
Chasnoff, I. J., 190
Clifford, R., 215
Clift, P. S., 39
Coates, D., 65
Cobb, M. M., 22, 148
Cohn, E., 65
Coelen, C. G., 33
Cohen, R. R., 46
Coletta, A. J., 222
Colletta, N. D., 196
Combs, A. W., 149, 159
Conover, M. B., 18
Cormier, L. S., 106, 121, 122, 123
Cormier, W. H., 106, 122, 123
Covey, L., 37, 194-195, 198
Cowen, E. L., 69
Cross, A., 35
Crouter, A. C., 75
Cunningham, C. E., 227
Cyster, R., 39

D'Zurilla, T. J., 64
Dangel, R. F., 139
Darlington, R., 30
Datta, L. E., 16
Davidson, H. W., 179
Davison, G. C., 64
Dawson, P., 25-26
Day, N., 190
Deal, A., 58
Dean, J., 109
Dell'Oliver, C., 225
Denson, D. B., 217
Dewey, J., 22
Dewey, J., 22
Dooling, E., 190
Dorn, F. J., 154
Doyle, N., 64
Dumas, J. E., 138
Duncan, D. C., 184, 186
Dunst, C. J., 47, 49, 58
Durlak, J., 95

Ecklund, K., 228
Edelwich, J., 212, 213
Egan, G., 101, 102, 106, 123, 129
Eitzman, D. V., 38
Ekstein, R., 109
Elstein, A. S., 66
Embry, L. H., 64, 138
Eyler, F. E., 38

Farber, S. S., 38
Feek, W., 245
Felner, R. D., 48
Fendt, K. H., 38
Ferguson, J. E., 95
Fiedler, D., 182, 183
Field, T. M., 37, 38
Fineman, S., 212
Fink, A. E., 18, 22, 23
Finkelhor, D., 176, 177
Finnegan, L. P., 190
Fischer, J., 232, 239
Fishbein, J. E., 66, 112
Fixsen, D. L., 30
Folkman, S., 228
Forehand, R. L., 137

Forgatch, M., 64, 139
Fortune, A. E., 158
Foster, S. L., 64
Fraley, Y. L., 175, 176
Freedman, J., 30, 34, 54, 87
Freudenberger, J., 212
Furuno, S., 100
Fusaro, B., 185

Gallagher, J. J., 29, 215
Gambrill, E., 102-103, 110, 112, 236,
    244, 257
Garbarino, J., 178
Gaudin, J. M., Jr., 176
Gelles, R. J., 181, 182, 186
Giles-Sims, J., 187
Glendinning, C., 27, 104
Goldfried, M. R., 64
Gordon, R. L., 129
Gordon, I. J., 30, 31, 236
Grantham-McGregor, S., 36, 252, 259
Gray, S. W., 28, 30, 31, 39, 153, 156, 230
Greenberg, R., 38
Greene, B. F., 138
Gregg, C. H., 196
Grosz, C. A., 217
Guinagh, B. J., 30, 31, 32, 236
Gutelius, M. F., 30, 31-32, 230

Hackney, H., 121
Haley, J., 64
Halpern, R., 15, 35-36, 37, 39, 45, 69,
    94, 194, 195, 198
Hannon, P., 21, 28
Hardy-Brown, K., 109, 156
Hargreaves, W., 232, 233
Hausman, B., 35, 69
Heinrich, J., 23-24
Heins, H. C., 95, 96
Hekimian, E., 176
Helfer, R. E., 180
Helgeson, D., 14, 148, 160
Henderson, C. R., Jr., 37, 70, 73
Herrenkohl, E. C., 175
Herrenkohl, R. C., 175
Hersen, M., 240
Herwig, J., 87, 88, 106, 149, 160, 169,
    222, 223, 256

Heston, L. L., 190
Hewett, K., 33
Heywood, J. S., 26
Hilberman, E., 182, 183
Hirst, K., 29
Hingson, R., 190
Hluchyj, T., 239
Hofeller, K. H., 182, 187
Hoff, P., 33
Holbrook, T., 16, 21, 104
Hollis, F., 21, 22, 121, 152-153
Holmes, T. H., 229
Hops, H., 64
Hosaka, C., 101
Hostler, S., 78
Hotaling, G. T., 177, 183
Howell, C. T., 38
Howrigan, G. A., 231
Hunt, J. M., 30
Hughes, D., 193, 194
Hupp, S. C., 244

Ignatoff, E., 38
Infant Health and Development Pro-
    gram, 77, 94, 214, 236
Intagliata, J., 38

Jackson, A. M., 28, 29, 176
Jackson, D. D., 51
Jacobs, F. H., 69, 245
Jahoda, M., 64
James, W., 22
Jason, L. A., 48
Jemail, J., 197
Jenkins, S., 98
Johnson, B. H., 47, 48, 49, 57, 58
Johnson, J. H., 193, 229
Johnson, K., 193
Jones, M. A., 121
Jones, M. C., 22, 148

Kadushin, A., 66, 109
Kagan, S. L., 36, 106
Kaiser, A. P., 244
Kalmuss, D. S., 183
Kaplan, B., 51
Karuza, J., 65
Kaslow, F. W., 189

Kaufmann, R. K., 47
Kayne, H., 190
Kelley, M. L., 64
Kempe, H., 32, 35, 46
Kent, M. E., 228
Kidder, L., 65
Kirsch, A. D., 31-32, 230
Klaus, R. A., 28
Kohlberg, L., 207
Kopp, C. E., 8, 35
Krauss, M. W., 229
Krugman, R. D., 217
Kubany, E. S., 100

Langholm, M., 26
Larner, M., 94
Larsen, A., 229
Larsen, D., 35-36, 232, 233
Larson, C., 28, 259
LaVange, L., 38
Lavee, Y., 229
Lazar, I., 30
Lazarus, R. S., 228
Leahy, K. M., 22, 148
Lenherr, M. R., 217
Levenstein, P., 31, 37, 209, 231
Levine, A., 16, 18, 20, 22, 104
Levine, M., 16, 18, 20, 22, 104
Levinson, H. L., 157
Leviton, A., 32-33
Lewis, I., 76, 80, 107
Linder, T., 244
Long, L., 129, 131
Long, T. J., 129
Lorion, R. P., 69
Love, J. M., 33, 87
Lutzker, J. R., 138
Lyons, C. T., 79

MacDonald, S., 31-32, 230
MacRae, D., 247
Madden, J., 231
Madden, J. S., 189
Mager, R. F., 102
Magyary, D., 109
Margolin, G., 55
Martin, G. H., 150
Matsuda, K., 101

McCartney, K., 37
McCormick, M., 194
McCubbin, H. I., 228, 229
McErlean, T., 31-32, 230
McGonigel, M. J., 47
McGuire, C. H., 66
McMahon, R. J., 137
McNeil, J. T., 28
Mello, N. K., 190
Miles, M. S., 66
Miller, B., 109
Miller, C. A., 24, 27-28
Minuchin, P., 52
Minuchin, S., 51
Missouri Department of Elementary
    and Secondary Education, 35, 69,
    81, 256
Mitchell, S. K., 109
Moritsugu, J. N., 48
Monteiro, L. A., 18-19, 104
Moore, K. A., 197
Moos, R. H., 228
Morelock, S., 190
Moroney, R., 18, 50, 196
Mountz, T., 189
Moynihan, D. P., 15
Muller, M., 32-33
Mulvey, L. A., 111
Munson, K., 185
Murray, H., 30

Nance, N. W., 95
Nathanson, M., 197
National Association of Social Work-
    ers, Inc., 206, 228
National Credentialing Program, 101,
    220
National Institute on Drug Abuse, 190
Nauta, M. J., 33
Nelson, M. D., 38
Neuwirth, S., 80
Newcomb, C., 31
Nezu, A., 64
Nguyen, T., 232, 233
Nightingale, F., 18-19
Norris-Shortle, C., 46
Nowakowski, J. R., 239
Nuckolls, K., 51

Nurcombe, B., 38

O'Hara, J., 231
O'Keefe, A., 30
Olds, D. L., 37, 70-73, 95, 197
Olson, D. H., 228, 229
Oppenheimer, E., 190

Pahl, J., 184, 187
Paradise, L. V., 129
Patterson, G. R., 64, 137, 139, 229
Pearl, A., 102
Pedersen, P. P., 154
Perlman, H. H., 66
Peterson, D., 64
Pfannenstiel, J. C., 81
Phillips, E. L., 30
Piaget, J., 70
Pickens, R. W., 190
Pierce, M., 182, 183
Pinker, R., 50
Pipe, P., 102
Polansky, N. A., 176
Polster, R. A., 139
Portner, J., 229
Poulton, G., 39
Powell, C., 36, 252
Powell, D. R., 36, 259
Powell, J. W., 228
Price, H. R., 69
Pugh, G., 29

Rabinowitz, V., 65
Rahe, R. H., 229
Ramey, C. T., 37, 38, 39, 51, 69, 74-81
Ramos-McKay, J., 69
Rauh, V. A., 38
Rausch, H., 123
Raven, J., 29
Reamer, F. G., 203, 206, 210, 218
Rees, S. J., 51
Renz, C., 185, 188
Reschly, B., 148
Resnick, M. B., 38
Rice, J. M., 138
Richmond, M. E., 19, 20, 46-48, 97
Riessman, F., 102
Roberts, D. E., 23, 24

Roberts, R. N., 35, 39-42, 59-61, 93-94,
    100, 108, 111
Robin, A. L., 64
Robinson, D. R., 176
Rogers, C., 123
Rogers, M. F., 190
Rosenbaum, P. L., 227
Rosenbaum, S., 193
Rosenberg, D. A., 217
Rosenfield-Schlichter, M. D., 138
Roy, M., 183
Royce, J., 30
Ruopp, R. R., 33
Ruttle, K., 30, 31, 230

Sadler, L. S., 195
Sameroff, A. J., 74, 78
Santelli, G., 225
Sarason, I. G., 229
Sarber, R. E., 138
Scarr, S., 37
Schaefer, E. S., 30, 31
Schectman, F., 159
Scheer, N. S., 184
Schmitt, B. D., 217
Schnoll, S. H., 190
Schweinhart, L. J., 30
Seay, T., 123
Seltzer, D. A., 81
Senay, E. C., 189
Shostrom, E. L., 122
Shulman, L. S., 66
Shure, M. B., 64
Sia, C. J., 84
Siegal, E., 35
Siegel, J. M., 229
Siegel-Causey, E., 225
Simeonsson, R. J., 223-224
Simons, J., 193
Slaughter, D. T., 231
Smith, B. J., 74
Smith, G., 29
Snipper, A., 30
Synder, D. K., 184
Solomon, B. B., 48-49, 99
Sparling, J. J., 37, 38, 51, 74-81, 107
Spieker, S., 109
Spivack, G., 64

Spratka, S. A., 66
Statistical Abstract of the United
    States, 174, 175
Steele, B. F., 175, 177
Stein, T. J., 102-103, 110, 112, 236, 244,
    257
Steinmetz, S., 181
Stoller, S., 38
Straus, M. A., 181, 183
Stringer, S., 37
Strube, M. J., 183
Stuber, M., 33
Suarez, T. M., 39, 69
Sugarman, D., 183
Sumner, G., 109
Summers, J. A., 225

Tatelbaum, R., 37, 70, 73
Tertinger, D. A., 138
Teti, D. M., 38
Thompson, S., 109
Toedter, L., 175
Trainor, C. M., 179
Trivette, C. M., 47, 49, 58
Trohanis, P. L., 78, 215
Truax, C. B., 95, 123
Turnbull, A. P., 225
Turnbull, H. R., 225
Twentyman, M. T., 176

U.S. House of Representatives, 175,
    190, 193, 194

Valand, M. C., 150
Vatz, C., 228

Wagner, M., 25-26, 104
Wagner, M., 25-26, 104
Wahler, R. G., 51, 138
Walker, L. C., 182, 183
Walters, R. H., 70
Wandersman, L. P., 39, 153, 156
Warren, D. I., 176
Wasik, B. H., 16, 37, 38, 39-42, 51, 59-
    61, 65-66, 74-81, 93-94, 111-112,
    127, 145, 228
Wayland, K., 185
Weikart, D. P., 28, 30
Weiss, H. B., 26, 35, 69, 81, 245
Weiss, R. L., 64
Weissbourd, B., 36, 55, 99
Weisser, R. J., Jr., 106, 122
Wells, K. B., 33
Witmer, L., 22
Whall, A. L., 54
White, B. L., 81
White, K. R., 247
Widmayer, S., 37, 38
Wilson, E. E., 18
Wolery, M., 245
Wolf, M. M., 30
Wolfe, B., 87, 88, 106, 149, 160, 169,
    222-223
Wood, M. E., 21, 22, 121, 152-153

Yanushefski, A. M., 175
Yarrow, M. R., 230
Yllo, K., 177

Zigler, E. F., 15, 30, 34, 36, 54, 87, 247
Zuckerman, B., 190

Subject Index

Abuse, *see* Child abuse of Family violence
Administrative agencies, 39, 42, 61
Administration for Children, Youth, and Families, 35
Administration on Developmental Disabilities, 35
Adolescent parenting, 193-199, 230; and knowledge of child development, 194-195; research, 193-196; resources for, 197
Advantages of home visiting, 13-15, 32, 45-46, 177
AIDS, 190-192, see also Substance abuse
Alcoholics Anonymous, 191-192
Alcoholism: visiting in families with, 188-193
Almshouses, 18
American Red Cross, 24
APA Ethical Principles of Psychologists, 206
Assessment in home visiting, 62, 219-248; importance of regular assessment, 232; used in research, 222-32, 235-238, 241
Associated Charities, 20

Barriers to home visit participation, 154
Baseline data collection, 242
Basic knowledge and skills, 104-108, *see also* Professional Training
Bayley Scales of Infant Development, 234
Behavior change principles, 136-139; and parent training, 137-139
Behavioral assessment techniques, 233-235
Behavioral theory, 51
Belgium: home visiting in, 28
Bureau of Maternal, Child Health, and Resources Development, 35
Burnout, 161, 212-15; prevention of, 212-215

Catchment areas: size of and scheduling, 160
Characteristics of home visitors, *see also* Credentials; related to process, 260
Child abuse and neglect, 14-15, 174-181; and substance abuse, 190; laws regarding, 179; reporting, 178-179, 202-203; research, 174-78; signs of, 178

Child Development Associate National Credentialing Program, 101, 220, 254-255; competency training, 255
Child neglect, see Child abuse and neglect
Child Survival/Fair Start Programs, 35
Child Welfare League of America, 23
Child welfare services, 24
Children: ages served, 60-61; as clients, 52-56; characteristics of children served, 59; needs during home visit, 164-165; other children present during a visit, 164; services, 56-58
Children's Act of 1948, 17, 26
Civil Works Administration, 23
Client Satisfaction Questionnaire, 232-233
Client, 53-56, 59-61; best interest of, 202; characteristics, 59-61; cooperation with program, 210; focus, 151-153; functioning, measures of, 228-231; mobility, 165-166; motivation, 211; needs, determining, 151, 222-224; satisfaction, 227, 231-232; self-report, 231; services, 40-42
Clinical impressions of home visitors, 226
Cocaine-addicted mothers, see Substance abuse
Cognitive reappraisal: as burnout prevention, 214
Cognitive theory, 51
Collaborative services, 32
Colorado Parent-Infant Project, 35
Communication: between clients and visitor, 169; skills, 123-134, 254; within teams, 217
Community colleges: and home visitor training, 256
Community issues, 257-259, 261; interagency functioning, 258; sensitivity to when hiring, 257; services available, 32
Competency training, see CDA, 255
Comprehensive Child Development Program, 34, 36

Conferences: American Academy of Pediatrics, 42; Family Support in the Home, 40; First White House Conference on Children, 23
Confidentiality, 208-209; in team discussions, 170, 208-209; of materials, 164; need to ensure, 170
Contagious diseases, 19
Coping skills, see also Problem Solving: measurement of, 228-229
Costs of home visiting, 247; Cost-benefit analyses, 247; Cost-effectiveness, 30
Credentials of home visitors, 91-98, 249, 254-55; age, 96-97; education, 93-95; ethnic background, 98; experience, 96; gender, 97-98
Crisis intervention, 122
Cultural differences: between visitor and family, 98-99; in childrearing, 179
Curriculum, 65-67, 76, 80, 86, 107

Data collection: baseline, 242; in home visiting, 219-248
Daycare, 37-38, 74-76, 79
Decision-making: and problem solving, 140, 144; based on assessment information, 243
Definition of home visiting, 13-14
Deinstitutionalization, 14, 29, 32
Delinquency, 19
Demographic information about families, 221-222
Denmark: home visiting in, 25-26, 28
Dependence: of client on home visitor, 153-154
Depression: maternal, 107, 204
Direct measures of behavior, 240
District nursing, 18-19
District visitor, 13, 17
Documentation, 219-248; amount required, 235; of home visits, 235-238
Dress: appropriateness of, 169
Drug use: in families, 15, 168, 188-193; reporting, 204

Early intervention programs, 45

Early Training Program, 28

Ecological theory, 20, 28, 50-51, 55; and practice, 256-259

Effectiveness of home visiting, *see* Program effectiveness

Egocentrism: of adolescent parents, 195

Empathy, 123-125

Employment procedures, 113-118; sample interview questions, 116-118

Empowerment, 48-50, *see also* Philosophy

England, home visiting, 26-29, 39; Children's Act of 1948, 17, 26; Warnock Report, 17, 26; Resource Worker Project, 27

Environmental conditions, 19

Escort: hiring for safety reasons, 167

Ethics, 201-212, 218; codes, 203-206; training, 207

Ethnicity: of data collectors, 231; of home visitors, 98

Europe: home visiting in, 16-19, 24-29, 104

Evaluation of program success, 92-93, 226-235

Expectations, of client, 149-150, 155-156

Extended families, visiting in, 198, 202

Family: characteristics, 253; family support movement, 36; focus, 36, 54-58; functioning, theories and measures of, 228-231; needs, determining, 222-224; services, 13-16, 19-22, 26-27, 57-59, 61-64; strengths, influencing outcomes, 254; systems theory, 51-52, 55, 165; violence, 181-188

Family Adaptability and Cohesion Evaluation Scales (FACES III), 229

Family Crisis Oriented Personal Evaluation Scale (F-COPES), 229

Family Environment Scale, 228

Families Facing the Future Program, 111

Family Information Preference Inventory, 225

Family Needs Survey, 223-224

Family-Oriented Home Visiting Program, 230

Federal Republic of Germany: home visiting in, 27

Fetal alcohol syndrome, 190-191

Financial support, 250

First visit, content of, 148-151

Flexibility, of scheduling, 160-163

Folkman-Lazarus Ways of Coping Checklist, 228

Frank Porter Graham Child Development Center, 11, 74-77, 78

Friendly visitor, 13

Friendship: between client and visitor, 155

Funding sources, 33-36, 40, 74, 77, 81, 83-84, 86

Goals, 249-251, *see also* Advantages: matched with measurement, 231; of client, 154; of home visiting, 91-92

Grandmothers: involved in home visits, 198

Great Depression, 23

Group homes, 30

Harvard Family Research Project, 69

Harvard University Preschool Project, 81

Hawaii Kupalani Project, 108, 110

Hawaii Healthy Start Project, 70, 84-86, 89, 107; *Hana Like Mother-Baby Book*, 86; *Hawaii Family Support Worker Baby Play Book*, 86

Head Start, home visiting in, 30, 33, 48, 54, 60, 70, 86-89, 93-94, 101, 132, 169, 255; Child and Family Resource Programs, 33-34; *Head Start Home Visitor Handbook*, 107; *Serving Handicapped Children in Home-Based Head Start*, 107

Health: of home visitor, 213-214

Health visitors, 19, 28, 35, 46

Helper characteristics, 123-125

Helper skills, 125-134; listening, 125, 128-129; observing, 125-128;

probing, 125, 133-134; prompting, 126, 133-134; questioning, 125, 129-133
Helper techniques, 134-135
Helping relationship, 49, 53-56, 121-122; components and skills, 121-122; promoting independence, 50; use of power, 49-50
High/Scope Foundation, 37
History: child-saving movement, 21; Elizabethan England, 16; Hull House, 21; immigration, 18, 19; nineteenth century, 16-19; of home visiting, 16-23; Progressive era, 21-22; public health nurse, 19, 21-22; Social Darwinism, 21; social worker, 13, 19-23, 54; visiting nurse, 19-23, 54; visiting teacher, 13, 19-20, 23, 54
Home environment: measurement of, 227-228
Home nursing, 18-19, 24
Home Observation for Measurement of the Environment, 77, 227, 228
Home Visit Report Form, 236, 283-287
Homemaker, 13, 22
Honesty, 204, 207-208
Household composition, 222
Houston Child Development Center, 69

Illness: exposure to, 168
In-service training, 255, *see also* Professional Training
Independence: of adolescent mothers from their mothers, 195; of client, 50, 153-154
Individualized Family Service Plan (IFSP), 225
Infant Health and Development Program, 9-11, 38, 70, 77-81, 89, 94, 106, 109, 159, 162, 214; documentation, 236-237; *Early Partners*, 80; evaluation, 80; intervention model, 77-80; *Partners for Learning*, 80
Infant mortality, 15, 19
Information needs, 223-224

Integration of home visiting components, 91-92, 249
Interpersonal skills: of home visitors, 123-125, 254
Interviewing, 113-118
Ireland: home visiting in, 28
Isolation, *see* Social isolation

Jamaica: home visiting in, 36

Kamehameha Schools, 35
Kansas Healthy Start Program, 35
Kennedy Institute for Handicapped Children, 32

Lay workers, 13-14, 94-95, 99-100, *see also* Paraprofessionals
Life Experiences Survey, 229
Low birthweight infants, 38, 77-80; and teen parents, 194

Maltreatment, *see* Child abuse
Management of home visits, 147-171
Marital conflict: and child abuse, 176
Materials: preparation and organization, 163-164
Measures, *see* Assessment
Medical training, 33
Mentor: home visitor as, 156
Midwife, 27-28
Missouri Parents as Teachers Program, 35, 70, 81-84, 89-90
Mobile Unit for Child Health project, 30-32
Modeling, 134-135
Morale of home visitors, *see* Burnout
Mother-Child Home Program (MCHP), 31, 37, 231
Motivation: of client, 154
Multi-problem families, 199
Multidisciplinary teams, *see* Team approach

NASW Code of Ethics, 206
National assessment of home visitors, 262
National Commission to Prevent Infant Mortality, 34

Needs assessments, 222-224

Needs: of clients and families, 222-224; of home visitor, 213

Netherlands: home visiting in, 28

Night visits, 162, 167

Norway: home visiting in, 26

Nurses: associations, 21; community health nurses, 22; credentials, 93-95, 100; history, 16, 19-23, 54, 104; public health nurses, 16, 19, 21, 230; training, 66, 255-257, *see also* Professional training; visiting nurses, 13, 18-21, 23-29, 37, 71, 75, 79, 89, 169

Nursing Child Assessment Satellite Training (NCAST), 85

Objectivity: of home visitor, 155

Office of Special Education and Rehabilitative Services, 35

Outdoor relief, 18

Paraprofessionals, 13-14, 85-86, 88-89, 93-95, 99-100, *see also* Lay Workers; training, 102, *see also* Professional Training

Parent-to-Parent Program, 37, 198

Parent-child interactions: measurement of, 229-231

Parent Education Program, 236

Parenting, 138; skills, improving, 14, 137-145, 198

Partners for Learning, 107

Peabody Picture Vocabulary Test, 234

Peer contact: home visitors' needs for, 214

Permission: from client to share information, 170

Personal possessions: safety on a visit, 168

Philosophy of home visiting, 18-19, 22, 48-50, 53, 65, 67, 104-105, 250-251

Physicians, 13, 33

Policy: based on program evaluation, 245-247

Poverty, 15, 18, 19, 30; and child abuse, 175

Power balance between client and visitor, 49-50, 156

Practical aspects of home visiting, 159-171

Pregnant women, 254

Premature infants, 15, *see also* Low birthweight infants; and teen parents, 194; and substance abuse, 189; home environment changes, 227

Prenatal/Early Infancy Project, 37, 69, 70-73, 89; evaluation, 73; intervention model, 70-73

Principles: of home visiting, 46-48, 61-64

Privacy: sensitivity to client's, 150, 162

Private home visiting, 57

Problem solving: and current philosophies, 67; and mental health, 64; and professional training, 65; as part of therapy, 64; family adjustment and, 64; in home visiting, 32, 51, 64-68, 139; measurement of, 231; parent training, 65-67; skills, 138

Problem Solving for Parents, 65-67

Problem solving model, 139-145; implications for home visitors, 145

Procedures: documentation of, 219-220, 235-238

Professional associations, 21, 262

Professional development, 99-101, 243

Professional issues, 212-218

Professional training, 19, 24, 66, 79, 90-92, 94-95; appropriate training for home visitors, 255; competency-based, 101, 255; components of effective training, 102-104; evaluating the need for, 252; experiential learning, 101-102; in-service, 255; lack of materials for, 255-256; peer teaching, 101-102; role playing, 101-102

Program documentation, 235-238

Program effectiveness: measured, 226-235
Program evaluation, 220, 244; as basis for policymaking, 252-253; planning for, 245-246
Program goals, 249-251
Program process, 249-260
Project 12 Ways, 138
Project CARE, 9-11, 37, 69, 74-77, 89-90, 236; evaluation, 77; implementation model, 74-76; *Learningames for the First Three Years*, 76; *Learningames for Threes and Fours*, 76
Psychoanalytic theory, 22
Psychological climate of family: measured, 228
Psychologists, 13, 66
Psychotherapy, 122
Public health nurse, 24; visiting teen mothers, 230
Public Law 99-457, 7, 17, 34-35, 47, 53, 57-58, 255; Individualized Family Service Plan, 34-35, 255; team approach mandated, 215
Public Welfare Amendment of 1962, 24
Purposes of home visits, 148, *see also* Philosophy

Rapport: establishing, 148, 150
Rating scales of parent-child interaction, 230
Rationale, 13-16, 45-46, 48, 148
Record of Family Contact (IHDP), 236
Record-keeping, *see* Documentation or Assessment
Reliability of assessments, 238-40
Research: current status, 259-260; findings, 36-38, 73, 77, 80-83, 86-87, 90; future directions, 260-262
Resistance: of client to program, 154
Resource Mothers Program, 96
Resources: allocation of, 252; client's access to, 154; knowledge of other, 173
Respect: for client, 123-125
Risk factors: for child abuse, 176-177

Role: of client, 149; of home visitors, 53-56, 58-59, 149, 213; of team members, 217; limits to home visitor's role, 209-210; shifts over time, 53, 58-59
Role playing, 135
Rural health missioners, 19

Safety: during home visits, 166-169; in households with abuse, 187; concerning drugs, 192
Salaries of home visitors, 250
Satisfaction, *see* Client satisfaction
Schedule of Recent Events, 229
Scheduling visits, 148, 151, 157, 159-161
School dropouts, 15, 19
Scotland: home visiting in, 27
Self-awareness: of client, 242
Self-determination, client's rights to, 152
Self-esteem: and child abuse, 175
Self-monitoring: of client, 242
Sequenced Inventory of Communicative Development, 234
Settlement House movement, 20-21
Sexual abuse, 174
Social isolation: and child abuse, 176
Social reforms, 19-23
Social Security Act of 1935, 24
Social support, 50-51, 57; and stress, 196-197; for adolescent parents, 196
Social Workers: credentials, 93-95, 100; history, 13, 16, 20-23, 104; school social worker, 20; visiting social worker, 19, 25, 27-28, 75, 79, 104, 121; training, 22, 66, 255-257, *see also* Professional training; ethical code, 206-207; and burn out, 212-214, 236
Spain: home visiting in, 27
Spouse abuse, 181-188; symptoms of, 184-85
Standardized assessments, 234
Stanford-Binet Intelligence Scales, 234
Stress: in families, 173-199; measurement of, 226, 229

Substance abuse: and violent behavior, 191; research, 189-91; visiting in families with, 188-193

Supervision, 90-92, 252; amount and type, 256-257; based on assessment information, 243; definition, 108-109; evaluation, 111; formats, 110; in the home, 244; roles of supervisor, 109-110

Support from colleagues: as burnout prevention, 214

Surgeon General, 8, 35

Surveys, 39-42; England, 39; United States, 39-42; services provided, 41; client characteristics, 60

Switzerland: home visiting in, 28

Systems theory, 51-52, 55, 63, 74, 78

Teachers, 14, 20; credentials, 93-95, 100; history, 13, 16, 19-20, 23, 54, 104; training, 66, 257, *see also* Professional Training; visiting teachers, 13, 19-20, 28-29, 75, 79, 83, 93, 104

Teaching style: measurement of, 230

Team approach, 215-217; advantages and disadvantages, 215-216; leadership, 216-217

Teen parents, *see* Adolescent parenting

Terminating home visiting, 157-159, 210-211; planning for, 157

Timing of home visits, 161

Training, *see* Professional Training

Transitions, 159

Travel: time required for visiting, 160

Trust: establishing, 150; with abused clients, 185

Turnover rate, 252

U.S. Children's Bureau, 23

Urban home visiting, 166-169

Urbanization, 18-19

Validity of assessments, 239-240

Values: of home visitors, 201; differences with client, 152-153

Verbal Stimulation Project, 30-31

Wasik Problem Solving Rating Scale, 228

Warnock Report, 17, 26

Wechsler Intelligence Scale for Children, 234

Widows' pension laws, 23

World Health Organization, 26

Ypsilanti Perry Preschool Project, 28, 30

About the Authors

BARBARA HANNA WASIK is a professor at the University of North Carolina at Chapel Hill where she teaches in the School of Education and serves as Director of Research Training at the Frank Porter Graham Child Development Center. She received her Ph.D. in clinical psychology from Florida State University in 1967 and was a postdoctoral research fellow at Duke University. She served as Associate Director of the Ford Foundation Education Improvement Program at Duke University. She is one of the directors of Project CARE, a longitudinal early education intervention program of the Frank Porter Graham Child Development Center that uses home visiting as part of its intervention program, and was codirector for curriculum in the national collaborative study on low-birthweight infants, the Infant Health and Development Program (IHDP). With Richard Roberts, she recently designed and conducted the first national survey on home visiting. The author of over 50 articles and book chapters, she is a fellow of the American Psychological Association, and has served as past-president of the North Carolina Psychological Association.

DONNA BRYANT is the Director of the Family and Child Care Research Program at the Frank Porter Graham Child Development Center at the University of North Carolina. During the mid-1970s she was a home visitor in an infant education program for the

Developmental Evaluation Center in Durham, North Carolina. This work led to other research projects with children, and eventually to a degree in psychology from the University of North Carolina. Since 1979, she has been affiliated with the Frank Porter Graham Center, previously serving as Associate Director for Longitudinal Studies and as Associate Director of Program Development and Implementation of the Infant Health and Development Program. In both Project CARE and IHDP, she was directly involved in training home visitors and in developing program documentation procedures. She has published in the field of early intervention and is currently working on programs for special-needs infants and toddlers in a mainstream child care center.

CLAUDIA LYONS received her Master of Science in Public Health from the University of North Carolina in 1974. She is currently completing a master's degree in social work from the University of North Carolina at Chapel Hill. She has had extensive home visiting experience, first as a VISTA volunteer in Montana in the late 1960s and later in directing a home visiting program for adolescent parents in Virginia. Most recently she has been associated with the IHDP, where she was directly involved in training home visitors and preparing their training materials.